# THE
# FUTURE
# SHAPE
# OF
# MINISTRY

## *A*
## *THEOLOGICAL*
## *PROJECTION*

### *Urban T. Holmes III*

T ... V YORK

*Second Printing*

All quotations from the Holy Scriptures,
except where otherwise noted, are from the
New English Bible, copyrighted 1961, 1970
by the Delegates of the Oxford University
Press and the Syndics of the Cambridge
University Press.

Copyright © 1971 by The Seabury Press, Incorporated
Library of Congress Catalog Card Number: 72–150697
Design by Carol Basen
ISBN: 0–8164–2025–4
Printed in the United States of America

# FOREWORD

The knowledgeable reader might wonder what warrants still another book on ministry. I would be less than candid if I did not admit that when such a project was suggested to me the same thought lingered in my mind. But as a teacher charged with equipping men for the practice of ministry, I have had a growing conviction that the more than ample literature in this field possessed certain gaps, which someone ought to attempt to fill. These might be considered three in number.

The first is the need for a historical perspective to complement the sociological and psychological analyses that abound. I am grateful for the works of William Clebsch and Charles Jaekle, John T. McNeill, and H. R. Niebuhr and D. D. Williams. But they do not provide the sort of reflection upon the past that I think we need: an attempt to enter the reality of each age as a clue to the prevailing shape of ministry.

Second, there is a great lack of theological work in the area of pastoral concerns today. Peter Homans, Charles Stinnette, Don Browning, Thomas Oden, and a few others are the exceptions; but much more is needed. I have sought here to speak out of a clear theological conviction and to develop my entire thesis in this light. In such a spirit I have attempted a much more imaginative or speculative approach than the social and behavioral sciences permit to students of ministry primarily committed to those fields.

Then, third, there is very little comprehensive study of ministry. Each work seeks to achieve depth in a particular area (e.g. pastoral care or counseling, social action, criticism of parish structures), but is isolated from studies in closely related fields. My hope is that this book will provide an all-important overview that will enable both clergymen and concerned laymen to develop a broad understanding as a context for pursuit of a particular facet of the whole.

In writing this study I am not angry or in despair. I am concerned, and yet possess a certain hope born of the conviction that we live in a most religious age. My commitment to the Church is necessarily colored by a lifetime in the Anglican Communion, and therefore I write as an Episcopalian. However, I think there is very little in these chapters of specific reference to practices in my own denomination that is not readily transferred to others. My experience in ecumenical gatherings is that our differences of function are largely superficial, as are the differences in problem areas.

Furthermore, it should be made clear from the start that in leveling some fairly general and heavy criticism at the Church today, I am including myself in its number; and yet I have no desire to ridicule or slight the sacrificial lives of countless pastors who have done so well in the face of many difficulties. Lack of dedication is not the crisis to which this book speaks. Rather, I write out of the conviction that the heroic witness of many Christians in all areas of ministry needs to be freed to have greater effect.

It will be immediately evident that theologically I am greatly indebted to such men as Karl Rahner, E. Schillebeeckx, Jürgen Moltmann, Wolfhart Pannenberg, and others who represent the two schools of the "theology of presence" and the "theology of hope." It is my conviction that they embody two sides of a theological coin that is consistent with this age and can lead to an effective encounter with Christ in our times. It follows that I am convinced of the relevance for this kind of study of the sociology of knowledge. For understanding in this fascinating field I am indebted to the works of Peter Berger, Thomas Luckmann, Max Scheler, Karl Mannheim, and Robert Merton, to mention a few. The sensitive reader may also become aware of my growing appreciation, as this book progressed, of the theological methodology of Bernard Lonergan.

I express my debt to them now, because I have attempted in the text to limit footnotes as much as possible. Only where the opinion of a specific individual is cited, exact statistics given, an unquestionably controversial point made, or some explanation demanded have I resorted to references which can be found at the end of the book. As it is, for some chapters these are necessarily large in number. I do not think, however, that they impede an easy reading of the text.

Obviously, any work of this kind involves drawing upon associations that occur over one's entire adult life. I think of the congregations whose faith and devotion I have shared: my home parish, the Chapel of the Cross, Chapel Hill, North Carolina; the good people in my first cure, St. Luke's and St. Paul's Churches in Salisbury, North Carolina; the literally thousands of students who passed through Louisiana State University in Baton Rouge and the faithful nucleus of faculty and their families at St. Alban's Chapel there; the delightful little community of St. Simon the Fisherman in Port Washington, Wisconsin, which I now serve on Sundays; and the students and their long-suffering families at Nashotah House.

My colleagues here have endured for a year now countless references to "my book," and a number—Roland Foster, O. C. Edwards, Thomas Talley, and Charles Goldsmith— have read portions of the manuscript and offered me invaluable advice. Others who have read and criticized chapters of the book in a very helpful manner are Loren Mead, Taylor Stevenson, Lawrence Walton and my father, Urban T. Holmes, Jr., who shares the dedication of this study. Russell Ford, Ernest Bel, James Tiller, and Robert Cooper, all priests enjoying creative ministries, have provided data for the study as have various officers of the Executive Council of the Episcopal Church, particularly Mrs. Robert N. Rodenmayer and the Rev. Richard G. Johns.

Any author knows the absolute necessity of the moral

support of his editor and family, and I have been blessed by the warm encouragement of Robert Gilday of the Seabury Press and my own Jane and our four children. I am also most grateful to David Olsen, a middler at Nashotah House, who typed the final manuscript.

So this is not really my book, though I am willing to bear the responsibility for the gaffs in return for the profits, tangible and intangible. It is the product of a continuing conversation, of the insatiable desire or need, or both, of myself and my associates to "talk Church," and to hope for something better than we have now. The invitation is now yours to join us in this dialogue; and so on to the task at hand.

Urban T. Holmes III
Nashotah House
The Feast of St. Matthew, 1970

# TABLE OF CONTENTS

*For my parents*
Margaret Allan Gemmell Holmes
and
Urban Tigner Holmes, Jr.

# PART I

## THE
## EVOLVING
## FUNCTION
## OF
## MINISTRY

## chapter 1

# CHANGING
# YET
# CHANGELESS

Ministry, the activity of the servant Church, necessarily involves office and function. Ask almost any Episcopalian, and for him the normative officer of ministry is the priest or presbyter.[1] Most laymen consider themselves the recipients of ministry, and consequently there is little sense of a lay apostolate. Despite announcements from chancel steps and in the parish bulletin in anticipation of the annual visitation of "our chief pastor," few churchmen consider the bishop much more than a distant administrative officer to whom one may complain when the local rector or the national office offends—though his presence certainly may lend a note of dignity to a prominent wedding, the consecration of a church, or the inauguration of the local mayor. As for deacons, they do not exist. It is always a small mystery why the rector does not let the new curate, just out of seminary, preside at the Eucharist; but then in a while he does, and "perhaps it was simply a matter of his learning how." The basic situation does not differ much in churches with another polity.

To put the same thing another way, in the minds of many churchmen the Church's ministry is gathered up in one office represented by the local pastor and his assistant(s). If we are beginning to recognize that there are pastoral dimensions different from the traditional congregation, such as chaplaincies in universities, hospitals, and even industry, these are still derivative of the image of the parish priest or pastor. In fact, it can be said that for many of us he is the Church. Preachers are fond of suggesting that people confuse a building with the Church, but I doubt that this has ever been true. We identify a man, the pastor, with the Church; but not necessarily in a creative way.

In a sense this is what many theologians have also been doing since the sixteenth century, attempting to define the Church in terms of ministerial office. Up until the last few years, Episcopalians have used the existence of the threefold ministry of bishops, priests, and deacons within our polity to guarantee for ourselves membership in the Church founded by Christ and to assure our Christian brethren of the truth of our teaching and the validity of our sacraments. This is the apologetic intention of the Preface to the Ordinal in the Book of Common Prayer, where we state that in preserving these three orders we are following what has been done from the time of the Apostles (page 529). Whether in fact we can claim quite such antiquity is open to question. The Council of Trent in 1563 argued the same point; but in the *Constitution on the Church,* Vatican II had the grace to qualify that claim.[2]

It now appears that there is less and less interest in the kind of argument which, in its most crude form, claims that we have an assurance of salvation *because* we are members of an institution possessing a ministry whose structure and character was given by Christ or the Apostles. It is a very bad theology that makes a doctrine of ministerial office the center of the "good news," and we can be thankful for a growing maturity in this regard. This is not simply to dismiss the question of office, but to turn to what is a related and yet more crucial question: the function of ministry.

We frequently hear today that clergy ought to behave like clergy and do what they are supposed to do. Yet I have the distinct impression that those who make these statements find it difficult to say just *what* they are "supposed to do." What is the function of ministry in the Church? That question cannot be answered until we see what the purpose of the

Church is. This is not to prejudge the question of whether the Church or ministry is prior, a point ably discussed recently by Robert Nelson, who concludes that there is no one answer.[3] It is to say that if the reader is concerned for this vital matter, which is so determinant of the future patterns of ministry, then he must begin and end his consideration of the subject by reflecting upon the Church's mission.

We as Christians believe that Christ embodies the will of God for man; he fulfills the Law, and is the means to achieve that will; he is our savior. The Church exists by divine intention to make possible man's encounter with Christ. Christ is the "sacrament of God," and the Church is the fundamental "sacrament of Christ" (the *Ursakrament*, German for the "primal sacrament"). A sacrament is of course that which partakes fully of the immediacy of human life and yet communicates a meaning that transcends human life. The ministry of the Church is then the function of offering this sacramental presence to man.

It follows that ministry derives its transcendent quality, that which exists outside the culture, from God and his creative purpose. If it becomes detached from this, it becomes demonic. It turns in on itself and becomes an instrument of the destructive force of man's self-will. On the other hand, the form and shape of ministry in every age is the result of man's self-consciousness and his social structures. Consequently, if it becomes detached from culture, it becomes docetic. It lacks the reality necessary to work with power among men. This is true of Christ's ministry, and it is true of ours.

Just as the sacramental function of the Church, which I have defined as the point of man's encounter with the transcendent reality of God, is a basic assumption of this study, so equally fundamental is the conviction that the very nature of the reality in which God acts in his Church is determined by man's own understanding of himself in his world. This reality is made up not just of objects in the world, but consists of these objects *and our consciousness* that is directed toward them. Consciousness is a function of my own individual experience, which in turn is a part of the common spatial and temporal perceptions of my culture. As cultures change, so does common consciousness, *and hence reality changes.* Reality is a "collective representation," as Owen Barfield has rightly described it.[4]

A few years ago Peter Berger and Thomas Luckmann published a book entitled *The Social Construction of Reality*.[5] The very title of this helpful exposition is a summary of the point I am trying to make. Each sociocultural entity constructs its own reality. If God is to be perceived in terms of the world we experience, if ministry is both transcendent and immanent, there is only this changing reality in which to work. There is no immutable kernel within the mutable. It is all one, and it is never the same. What you see when you look out on the world is *not* the same thing St. Paul, St. Augustine, St. Francis, or Martin Luther saw. When Captain Cook sailed among the Polynesian Islands, the Polynesians did not see a ship but a cloud. There was no "ship" in their "collective representation." Our perception is no less infallible, no less subject to "enlightenment" than theirs. Consequently, the *form* of God's appearing in Christ always changes with changing reality.

This is the sort of reflection, theological and phenomenological, that must lie at the heart of our projections of a future ministry for the Church. Yet since in a real sense all theology is historical theology and consequently rests finally in the theology of the Bible, if we are to speak of the future we must do so out of our past, beginning with the New Testament.

Therefore, in this first part I have set for us the task of understanding something of the function of ministry as it develops in the Church's life. In what I believe is not an altogether arbitrary fashion, it will be done in terms of three periods in which ministerial function seems to focus itself in

three different modes of operation, all of which are sacramental. During the first or ancient period (c. A.D. 30–325) it
is the sacramental person; during the second or medieval
period (325–1517) it is the sacramental rite; and in the third
or modern period (1517–1914) it is the sacramental word.
I shall leave our contemporary situation to Part II of this
study. In examining the history of the function of ministry,
my assumption is that structure is always secondary to intention and function, and that intention is the expression of a
dialogue between the eternal and transcendent reality of Christ
and man's existential condition.

## chapter 2

# THE
# SACRAMENTAL
# PERSON

Dom Gregory Dix, the distinguished
Anglican Benedictine scholar, stated
in a much discussed article, "The Ministry in the Early
Church," that the apostolate is the only ministerial institution that can be attributed to Jesus.[1] This minimal statement
itself is open to question. For what purpose would Jesus institute the apostolate?

The term "apostle" first occurs in the writings of Paul.
The basic meaning of the word in its verbal root is to *send out*
someone. The noun form, part of Greek nautical terminology,
came to mean *ambassador, delegate,* or *messenger.* Its use is
rather rare outside the New Testament, and there it has no
unified meaning.[2] Paul bestowed upon it the sense of his
authority as a messenger or ambassador for Jesus Christ. Particularly in writing the fractious Church at Corinth, he claims
his right to this title and the particular authority it bears. "Am
I not a free man? Am I not an apostle? Did I not see Jesus
our Lord? Are not you my own handiwork, in the Lord? If
others do not accept me as an apostle, you at least are bound to
do so, for you are yourselves the very seal of my apostolate,
in the Lord" (1 Cor. 9:1-2, cf. 15:9; 2 Cor. 11:5, 13). For
Paul an apostle is a member of the congregation who has been
called directly by God to preach Christ. The message he
preaches is verified by the life of Jesus. He is an example of
Christ to those he preaches to. "Agree together, my friends,
to follow my example. You have us for a model; watch those
whose way of life conforms to it." (Phil. 3:17, cf. 2 Thess.

3:7,9; 1 Cor. 4:16; 11:1; 1 Thess. 1:6). In his person men can perceive the age that is about to come. He is a prophet, an eschatological figure and teacher, as well as an apostle, to be supported by the congregation. He is also nonstipendiary (1 Cor. 9:15). It is worth noting that in Paul's view an apostle does not generally baptize (1 Cor. 1:17).

An apostle, of which Paul apparently considers himself to be the preeminent example despite protestations to the contrary, is principally an itinerant missionary. He is the embodiment in his person, as well as in his preaching and teaching, of the "good news" that in Christ man is created anew to that life for which God has called him before all time. In a sense, an apostle is the Christ, the word of God not only in what he says but what he is (1 Cor. 2:16; Col. 1:24).

Obviously Paul believed others were also apostles, but nowhere does he mention that the Twelve (meaning those whose calling is described in Matthew 10:1–16; Mark 6:7–11, 3:13–19; Luke 6:12–16, 9:1–5; and mentioned as chosen in John 6:70) are "apostles." Perhaps there is a hint of this equation in Galatians. If we are used to thinking of the two, the Twelve and the Apostles, as synonymous, this absence is a rather striking fact, particularly if we add the possibility that neither Matthew nor Mark knew of the Twelve Apostles. The word "apostle" appears once in Matthew 10:2, where there is some question about the reading (a Syriac version has the word for "disciples" instead). It occurs for certain once in Mark 6:30. In both instances, von Campenhausen suggests, it has no technical meaning at all, but simply describes the Twelve as "messengers." [3] In Mark 3:14 some versions will mention the Twelve as "apostles," but this is clearly a reading that has slipped in from Luke 6:13. The RSV gives it marginal notation.

In Luke-Acts, however, the technical term "apostle" for the Twelve figures prominently. In the Gospel of Luke the Twelve are identified as apostles five times, and in Acts twenty-six times. When Judas Iscariot leaves the number of the

Twelve, it is Luke in the Acts who describes how his place was taken by Matthias. Paul is clearly considered subordinate to the Twelve Apostles and must clear his policies with the Church in Jerusalem (Acts 9:26; 11:30; 12:25; 15:2, 6, 25; 18:22; 21: 15ff.). As with Paul, the function of an apostle is to be a missionary. "But you [the Twelve Apostles] will receive power when the Holy Spirit comes upon you; and you will bear witness for me in Jerusalem, and all over Judaea and Samaria, and away to the ends of the earth" (Acts 1:8). Why this sudden new emphasis, unknown to Paul, Matthew, or Mark? Luke wrote between A.D. 70 and 90, and is undoubtedly a second-generation Christian. Walter Schmithals, building on the work of scholars such as Hans Conselmann, makes the point that the identification of the Twelve reflects Luke's developed theological concern. For him Christianity is the true Judaism: there is an essential relationship between the old Israel, Jesus, and the new Israel that is to win the world. This theology of "salvation history" is rooted in the Jerusalem tradition of the Twelve Apostles.[4]

From Paul and then Luke two traditions of the apostolate flow side by side until they are joined in a very artificial way by Irenaeus in A.D. 170. They represent perhaps two schools of Greek Christianity. But it is extremely difficult to attribute either of them to a historical institution by Christ. Where the concept of the "apostle" that is found in both comes from is uncertain. Dix's theory of the Jewish *Schaliach*, which is apparently as old as Jerome (c. 342–420), is accepted by few scholars.[5] The *Schaliach* was an official sent from the authorities in Jerusalem, possessing legal authority to perform certain tasks among the Jews of the dispersion. He was not a missionary as an apostle was. Schmithals argues for a Gnostic source for the Christian apostolate,[6] Gnosticism being a highly mythological, dualistic oriental philosophy that strongly influenced elements of Judaism and early Christianity. It is well known in the second century, but some would question its existence in the first, and therefore would question Schmith-als' thesis.

If Jesus did not institute the apostolate, in what way did he provide for the future of the Church? We make the natural assumption, based upon our feeling that in an incarnational religion the Church has to have an institutional form, that this would require some kind of structured ministry. One possible reply might be that Jesus never intended to found such a Church. We must always keep in mind that the New Testament is written from a post-Resurrection viewpoint. The theology of the author (e.g. Paul or Luke) shapes his use of the material, even if he has before him the very words of Jesus. For example, the word for "church," *ekklesia*, appears in the Gospels only twice, both times in Matthew (16:18 and 18:17). This author, who wrote probably between A.D. 70 and 80, had a unique desire to show that Jesus granted the power to the people to participate in his authority; so Matthew's is a very "churchly" Gospel. Matthew 16:18 would appear to reflect a belief of the Palestinian Church (quite in opposition to Paul's theology) that it is founded upon Peter's teaching; or perhaps it was a polemic of the Jewish Christians outside Palestine against James' leadership of the Jerusalem Church.[7] Matthew 18:17 is apparently a rule from the same Palestinian Church.[8] The important thing to understand is that a Jewish Christian congregation attempted to establish their way of doing things just prior to A.D. 70 by attributing to their position the authority of Jesus, who probably had no reason to speak to this problem.

It would be a grave error for us to assume that the scholars who suggest that our Lord did not found the institutional Church do not take the Jesus of history seriously, have "lost their faith," or reject an ecclesial theology. In both Protestant and Catholic circles today the theology of revelation opens the possibility that the will of God for us does not have to be revealed in its entirety and explicitly in the history of Jesus

of Nazareth. This sort of biblicism is being avoided for the
sake of a more realistic and equally incarnational conviction
that our Lord stands as the crux of a totally revelatory history.[9]
Therefore it is possible to believe in the Church just as we
believe in the Trinity, realizing that in all honesty the human
Jesus may not have been conscious of either. Devotion to
Christ is not inconsistent with the belief that the Second
Person of the Trinity became man to the point that not only
was his theology consistent with his Jewish heritage, but that
he had no foreknowledge of his mission. He could indeed
have believed that the reign of God, which he preached, was
immanent. His cry of desolation from the Cross (Mark 15:34;
Matt. 27:46) could have been more than a dramatic device
of a pious Jew. It could have been a feeling of failure and
abandonment, since he was dying and the Kingdom was not
here. If this interpretation is correct, the fact that Jesus did
appoint the Twelve (which is probably a historically accurate
record) would have nothing to do with the establishment of
the institutional Church as we know it, but would be an
eschatological sign in anticipation of the fulfillment of Israel
in the Kingdom that was about to come, the Twelve not functioning as apostles (Matt. 19:28; Luke 22:30) but symbolizing the Twelve Tribes of Israel on the Day of the Lord.

A point that is often made in refutation of the claim that
Jesus believed himself to be about to bring in the Kingdom
is the well-attested institution of the Lord's Supper (Matt.
26:26–29; Mark 14.22–25; Luke 22:15–20; 1 Cor. 11:23–26).
Why create a means of remembering his death if you believe
that God the Father will momentarily intervene to bring all
to fulfillment? Does not the very existence of this cultic meal
imply the necessity for a form of ministry? Yet the question
persists of how much of this account reflects what our Lord
did, and how much is the interpretation of an emerging cultus
in the Greek Church. The accounts of the Lord's Supper
raise a number of problems. For example, there is no agreement as to the original nature of the Last Supper (a Passover

meal, as in the Synoptics? a Kiddush meal? a chaburah meal?)
and very little likelihood that we can ever answer the question.
Luke is clearly using a different source (and probably a more
primitive one) than Paul, Matthew, or Mark, and there is
evidence that much of his account, as well as all the others,
has been rhetorically shaped by cultic use. Perhaps Bornkamm
is right and the best we can conclude is that it recalls a meal,
not unlike other meals Jesus ate with his disciples, but special
in that on this occasion he is in particular expectation of the
coming of the Kingdom and of his parting from them.[10]

Massey Shepherd warns, however, against accepting too
readily the facile explanations of those who insist that Jesus
could not have founded the Church and, with it, an institutional ministry.[11] All of us have our theological bias, and much
within all our theories is highly speculative and consequently
subject to easy manipulation. The position I want to hold,
without going into a very profound issue that is beyond the
scope of this study, is that we should be careful about any
arguments concerning the nature of the Church and the function of the ministry derived from the historical Jesus. It is with
the Resurrection event that the whole question becomes alive.
For Paul and Peter as well as ourselves it is the central reality
of our Christian faith. Jesus is raised and glorified, he is the
"first fruits" of what we are and are not yet; and we are sent
to make known the mystery of his person throughout the
world until all be fulfilled in him.

It is with the impact of the Resurrection that the dis-
heartened disciples of Jesus become aware that not only does
our Lord live, but that we still live in the certain hope of the
Kingdom that shall come (note the words of the Lord's
Prayer). Yet we are left with an interim, out of which emerge
the themes of "sending" and "serving" that pervade the Gospels (Matt. 10:5, 10; 20:25–28; Mark 3:14; 6:7; 10:42–45;
Luke 9:2; 10:1; 22:24–27; John 4:38). The noun "apostle" is
rare in all the Gospels save Luke, but its verbal root, *apostel-
lein*, "to send out," abounds. The whole concept of the *func-*

*tion* of the Christian ministry can readily be built upon this word and that of the other verb, *diakomein,* "to serve."

It is generally accepted that after the Resurrection the realization that the Christian community must still wait for the Kingdom, the second coming of Jesus, meant for them only a short interval of time. Paul's thinking was completely caught up in this belief, at least at first. Look, for example, at his discussion of the fate of those who die before Christ comes back. He wrote to the Church at Thessalonica about A.D. 50: "first the Christian dead will rise, then we who are left alive shall join them, caught up in clouds to meet the Lord in the air" (1 Thess. 4:16–17). He is writing to an anxiety of that particular congregation, who have been led by him and others to believe that most of them will be alive at the Second Coming (cf. Luke 22:14–18; also Matt. 16:28; Mark 9:1; Luke 9:27). It would be understandable that he feels no compulsion to establish there or anywhere else a ministry that would enable them to endure as they are through the centuries.

Aside from the apostolate, ministry is therefore for Paul essentially functional, charismatic (given by the grace of God), and perhaps predominantly itinerant. (This is assuming that we may consider Romans, 1 and 2 Corinthians, Galatians, Philippians, Colossians, 1 and 2 Thessalonians, and Philemon all authentically Pauline.) Perhaps the most relevant passage is as follows: "Within our community God ·has appointed, in the first place apostles, in the second place prophets, thirdly teachers; then miracle-workers, then those who have gifts of healing, or ability to help others or power to guide them, or the gift of ecstatic utterance of various kinds. Are all apostles? all prophets? all teachers? Do all work miracles? Have all gifts of healing? Do all speak in tongues of ecstasy? Can all interpret them? [The answer to these questions is "No," though for Paul some persons possess more than one gift.] The higher gifts are those you should aim at" (1 Cor. 12:28–31). Here we do not have an authorized, ordained (i.e. a "laying on of hands" by men in a certain office) ministry; but one whose validity was tested by its right teaching (1 Timothy 4:1, for example, is perhaps a reflection upon the dangers of a divisive charismatic ministry). It is a ministry suitable to an eschatological community, in which the summons to join is pitched on the level of signs of God's purpose finally breaking into history (prophecy, miracles of nature and healing, and talking in tongues), explanation of its meaning (teaching and interpretation), and yet at the same time of care for the expectant community. The helpers are those who do charitable deeds, and perhaps are early harbingers of the office of deacon. Those with the power to guide, the administrators, are in the Greek *kyberneseis*, meaning "steersmen" or "pilots," hardly a bureaucratic term, but one suited to a pilgrim Church.

This hint that perhaps Paul realized the need for a ministry oriented to structural concerns of the community is elaborated in his appeal for the Corinthian Church "to give their due position" to Stephanas' family, who "were the first converts in Achaia" (1 Cor. 16:15, cf. 1 Thess. 5:12). Some have wondered whether we have here a protobishop; but probably it is a description of a function, not an office. Paul is concerned for the growth and unity of the community in Corinth; and John Knox is quite right in saying that it is inaccurate to speak of Paul as having no concern for the "institutional" ministry.[12] Yet it would be natural for him to appeal to the symbol of one old in the faith, if there was not yet a prescribed authority.

Our attention is caught again by Philippians 1:1, where Paul writes: "to all those of God's people, incorporate in Christ Jesus, who live at Philippi, including their bishops [*episkopois*, hence the word "episcopal"] and deacons [*diakonois*]." Perhaps now for the first time the reader feels himself entering into a familiar church life. But let us take a look at each term in turn. The Greek word *episkopos* literally means "overseer." In pagan Greek as well as in the Greek version of the Old Testament it is applied in a special way to God or the gods as those who care for the things of the world; and it is also applied in various ways to men. It can simply refer to a function, or it can describe an office in which the function of oversight of a technical or financial nature is performed. In the Qumran community we find something similar in the *mebagger* or "guardian," who possibly was quite distinct from the priest and together with him led the community.

In the New Testament the term is used similarly. Christ is called the *episkopos* of the Christian community (1 Peter 2:25). But more commonly it refers to a function, growing into on office, of men within the established congregation in a given place. The emphasis in Philippians is apparently upon the function of administrative oversight. The thought occurs as to whether here the *episkopoi* of Philippians (written toward A.D. 60) are not the *kyberneseis* of the Corinthians (written perhaps five years earlier), and that the change in vocabulary might reflect a dimming hope of an immediate second coming. In Acts 20:28 Paul is addressing the presbyters (of which we shall write shortly) of the Church in Ephesus, and describes them as *episkopoi* ("shepherds," NEB; "guardians," RSV), which is therefore obviously a functional description and not the name of an office. The only other two uses of the *episkopos* in the New Testament are in the Pastoral Epistles (written perhaps shortly after A.D. 100). In 1 Timothy 3:2 there seems little doubt that the author is speaking of an office, as well as a function, though probably synonymous with the office of presbyter. In Titus 1:7 it seems to me that W. H. Vanstone, in opposition to Austin Farrer, is quite correct, and the word *episkopos* either describes the function of *presbyteros* (1:5) or stands in apposition to it.[13]

There is another Greek word, *episkope*, which can mean either "visitation" (Luke 12:44, 1 Peter 2:12) or "position as an overseer." It has the latter meaning in a general sense in Acts 1:20, and is used in a specific sense in 1 Timothy 3:1.

Before leaving the question of the *episkopos* in the New Testament, mention must be made of the figure of James, the brother of the Lord, as the head of the Church in Jerusalem. In the Acts, reference is made to "James and the members" or "the elders" (12:17, 15:13, 21:18), and it is apparent that he is the presiding officer of the Church in the holy city. Paul speaks of him four times; once recounting how the risen Lord appeared to him (1 Cor. 15:7); and then, in Galatians, in writing of the controversy over the Jewish law, he calls him an "apostle," one of the three "pillars" (with Peter and John), and implies that he heads the Church in Jerusalem (Gal. 1:19; 2:9, 12). Eusebius (c. 263–340), who wrote a history of the Church, quotes Hegesippus, a second-century Christian (probably Jewish) as an authority for the "episcopate" of James. He also tells us that after James' death Simeon, a "cousin" of Jesus, succeeded to the "episcopate" and lived into the reign of Trajan (98–117).[14] As far as we can judge, this is not the prototype of the monoepiscopacy, though upon hindsight it might have served as something of a model. Rather it appears that, in the manner of the later Islamic caliphate, the brothers of Jesus, James and Simon, assumed the leadership of the Church in Jerusalem (cf. Matt. 13:55; Mark 6:3).[15] When in the second century a docetic Mariology began to take hold, the notion of the perpetual virginity required that they be made half-brothers (as with James) or cousins (as with Simeon), and eventually the Greek Church repressed the whole history.

If we then turn to the word *diakonos*, "deacon," and trace its use from Paul through the New Testament, we will discover something very much like the *episkopos*. We have noted the fundamental importance of the verb *diakonein*, meaning "to serve." In fact it is the New Testament word for the act of ministry. The noun for "ministry" is *diakonia*. One who "ministers" is a *diakonos*, originally meaning a "waiter" or "servant." In Mark 10:43 Jesus says, "Whoever wants to be great must be your servant [*diakonos*]." Paul describes the governing authorities as God's *diakonoi* for our good (Rom. 13:4). Does Paul ever use the word in more than a general sense? Hardy thinks that in Romans 16:1 it is "semi-technical." "I commend to you our sister Phoebe, a deacon [possibly "deaconess"] of the church at Cenchreae." He also suggested that in 1 Corinthians 16:15–16 the household of Stephanas might have been "deacons" to his "bishop." [16] It is hard to determine, and it seems probable to me that Paul uses the word purely functionally for one who helps with the practical affairs of the local congregation.

It is commonly thought that in the Acts 6:1–6, where Luke discusses the growing conflict between Greek and Jewish Christianity and the appointment of the Seven "to serve tables" in order that the Twelve Apostles might devote more time "to preaching the word of God," we have a description of the establishment of the office of deacon. Actually the title *diakonos* never appears in the Acts, although *diakonia* is mentioned (6:1,4), as is the verb *diakonein* (6:2). There is a "laying on of hands"(6:6), a traditional Jewish manner of conferring authority; but few scholars would insist without qualification that here the diaconate as we know it is established. We see these same Seven also preaching, after the manner of the Apostles (Acts 7:1–53; 8:4–8, 35–40); and Philip is spoken of as an "evangelist" (21:8). In hindsight this appointment might be considered a model for the office of deacon, but in the description itself there is no precise assignment of function to office.

In 1 Timothy 3:8–13 there appears to be the first and only passage in the New Testament where the title *diakonos* refers unambiguously to an office. We are not told there what a deacon does, but whatever it is he "must first undergo a scrutiny" (so it is the effect of his function, not the fact of ordination, upon which the emphasis is laid). Clearly women also fulfill this office (3:11). Yet the term itself still has a general meaning, for in 1 Timothy 4:6 it refers to "a good servant of Christ Jesus."

If we now take a quick glance over what we have covered in terms of ministerial function, we will see a largely itinerant ministry, headed by an apostle, who in himself is the prime ambassador of Christ, the prototype of the "sacramental person." Derived from him are numerous functions, initially most appropriate to a community in immediate anticipation of the Second Coming, but with a growing need to provide for the life of the Church during the interim. The two functions that seem to be important for the latter purpose are those of administrative responsibility (such as discipline, care of the indigent, and probably the organization of worship) and the "leg work." The more charismatic ministries continued alongside these, such as teaching, prophecy (Ephesians 3:5, probably written about A.D. 80–100, would seem to indicate its continued existence), and healing. Dom Gregory Dix insists that after the death of the original Apostles (he does not indicate whether he is speaking of the Pauline tradition or the Twelve or both), a "regional apostolate" continued independent of the function of the *episkopos* (e.g. Timothy at Ephesus, Titus at Crete).[17] There is no reason to believe that was not possible. The *Didache*, a Christian writing of A.D. 100–150 possibly from Syria or Alexandria, speaks of apostles visiting the churches, but it also tells of itinerant prophets and teachers (11:1 through 13:7), the former, however, being identified with the Apostle (11:5–6). Yet I think that Dix is far too concerned with proving that such apostles were the continuance of a dominical *office*, just as he with others feels an unnecessary need to suggest that the *episkopos* and *diakonos* are offices consciously adopted from the office of the "president" and his attendants at the *chaburah* (a fellowship meal in Judaism).[18]

The only office that emerges as an office in the apostolic Church is that of the presbyter (or elder), which was without doubt taken over from the Jewish community. Even when this is said, we must agree with Kilian McDonnell who reminds us that "The concept of office was not central to the thought of the Church in the first three centuries." [19] The term "presbyter" had several uses in first-century Judaism, both honorary and designating members of the Jerusalem Sanhedrin and the local disciplinary body of the synagogue. These groups were self-perpetuating and drawn from the wiser and more experienced men in the community (not just those older in years). They functioned in a tradition of elders dating from before the existence of the synagogue and Sanhedrin as the judicial and administrative leaders of the community (e.g. Susanna 5; Judith 8:10).

The Church appointed presbyters for the same purpose, but when the practice began is debatable. Those who would agree with Ernst Käsemann, a notable New Testament scholar, would want to make a clear distinction between Paul, the "individualist and free-booter," and early Catholicism. Whereas for Käsemann Paul indirectly prepared the way for an "ecclesiastically domesticated" Gospel, he himself was unconcerned about the organization that it involved.[20] It is true that the word *presbyteros* does not appear in the writings of Paul. Luke, however, reports that Paul and Barnabas appointed (the Greek word, *cheirotonein,* means "to elect by raising your hand," indicating how it was generally done, if not in this instance) presbyters in various congregations around Iconium (Acts 16:23). It is difficult to see why he would invent this to support his bias against Paul, and since much of the early Christian mission was initiated in the local synagogue, it seems natural for Paul to follow the usual organizational structure.

There are a number of other references in the New Testament to the office of presbyter. The author of 2 and 3 John describes himself as a presbyter. In 1 Peter the writer speaks to the presbyters (5:1) and admonishes the younger Christians to obey them (5:6). We have already mentioned the reference in Titus 1:5, in which they are spoken of as having the authority of oversight; and for this reason there can be little question that for this author at this time and in this place (A.D. 100?, Asia Minor?), the function of the *episkopos* is identical with the office of *presbyteros.* In 1 Timothy 5:17 the presbyters are described as leaders or rulers, who perform this role by preaching and teaching. This would be understandable in the tradition of Jewish elders, though I doubt that preaching or teaching was specifically their responsibility. The fact that presbyters preached, a function later reserved for the *episkopos*, reenforces the identity of the two offices at this time. Perhaps most interesting is the reference in James 5:14, in which presbyters perform a healing function. This is without precedent in Judaism, and is the first hint of any kind of any kind of sacramental or liturgical function given to the presbyter.

James 5:14 raises the very timely question of who was the individual charged with liturgical functions of the Church. We cannot here enter into a discussion of the earliest origins of Christian worship, but it is true to say that the assignment of specific liturgical responsibility does not seem to have been a crucial question to New Testament authors. Apparently Paul left most baptizing either to the presbyters or to any responsible Christian. We can imagine that when he or one of his fellow itinerant apostles was present in a congregation, he presided at the Eucharist-*agape* (the Eucharist was celebrated in the context of a fellowship meal, after the manner of the Lord's Supper). When they were not there perhaps one of the presbyters presided. It seems possible that the practice contributed to the designation of one of the presbyters as the principal officer of the congregation, upon whom the title of bishop (we are using this term for an office distinct from that of the presbyter) evolved, thus clarifying one dimension of the development of the monoepiscopacy (one man ruling as bishop).

The first concern for liturgical fnnction we have in the Church is in *I Clement*, written around A.D. 95 by one of the presbyterate in Rome to quell a disturbance in the Church at Corinth. Clement speaks of the offices of *episkopoi* and *diakonoi* (for which he gives scriptural precedent from the Greek version of Isaiah 60:17, which would indicate the offices are now developing divine authority). He mentions also presbyters (44:5; 54:2; 55:4, etc.), who are synonymous with *episkopoi*.[21] Apparently there has been trouble with schismatic gatherings for the eucharistic meal at Corinth, and Clement points out that everyone—bishop, deacon, and layman—has his prescribed ministry (*leitourgia*, meaning primarily "cultic service"). But, unfortunately, he does not tell us what they are. The *Didache*, which never mentions presbyters, has specific instructions about baptism and the eucharistic meal, tells the churches to elect bishops and deacons— "for their ministry to you is identical with prophets and teachers" (15:1)— but says nothing about their liturgical duties. It does say that prophets are to "speak in the spirit," that is, preach.

We are now passing from almost all New Testament witness to ministry and into the second century and the period of the Church Fathers. Whether or not contemporary German Protestant scholarship is correct about a sharp break between the free spirit of Pauline Christianity and *Frühkatholizismus*, "early Catholicism," the Church's self-understanding is undergoing a change. The institution and its life is more and more understood as the instrument of Christ's salvific activity in history. This understanding requires an order, so that Christ might be truly perceived; an allegiance to true teaching, so that no one may be deceived as to the real content of the Faith; and a proper observance of the cultic act, so that our unity in Christ might be manifest. It does not mean that the *kerygma*, the proclamation of the "good news," disappears; but it certainly is slowly being institutionalized. The changes require new emphases on the function of ministry. Discipline, teaching, and above all a ministerial witness to a visible unity become prominent. The officer of the liturgy does not seem to excite much polemic or even discussion, though Dix insists that the functions are well-defined by the end of the first century.[22]

It is important to call attention particularly to the fading of living prophecy, a function of ministry quite important to Paul and to the apostolic Church generally. Prophets were charismatic preachers through whom God's plan of salvation for the world and his will for every individual were made known. "The Lord God who inspires the prophets has sent his angel to show his servants what must shortly happen" (Rev. 22:6). "When a man prophesies, he is talking to men, and his words have power to build; they stimulate and they encourage." (1 Cor. 14:3). New Testament prophets were largely ecstatic and prognostic, and they lacked the social concern of the Old Testament worthies. The *Didache*, more than any other noncanonical writing, emphasizes the authority and importance of the prophets, but the centrality of this ministry soon disappears. For a pneumatic power, such as prophecy, is very hard to control; and in the doctrinal conflicts of the second and third centuries there was little room for the kind of freedom the prophets had exercised. Though Gerhard Friedrich probably says rightly that prophets existed in some circles up until A.D. 300,[23] it would have to be understood that with the diminished eschatological expectation of Christians there was less call for the ministerial functions (e.g. working miracles, speaking in tongues) that heralded the imminent end.

The future lay elsewhere, as an examination of the remarkable correspondence of Ignatius of Antioch, written prior to A.D. 117, testifies. Here we discover just what can happen in a short interval, when apparently the Arian Church is faced with schism from within and persecution from without. For at least in the city of Antioch by this date there is one bishop who has taken unto himself the principal functions of the presbyterate. All liturgical responsibilities, as well as everything else performed in the Church, can be done only by him or under his authority. Most important, the bishop is identified with God (Smyrnaeans 8:1; 9:1, Magnesians 3:1) and Jesus Christ ([Ignatius to] Ephesians 3:2; Trallians 2:1). "Where the bishop is present . . . there is the Catholic Church" (Smyrnaeans 8:2). The bishop is "master of the house" ([Ignatius to] Ephesians 6:1). There is no question but that he has become the sacramental person, providing in himself the encounter with God in Christ.

Massey Shepherd has an interesting theory of the evolution of the episcopal function exemplified in the Asian churches. He would say it began with a fiscal responsibility for gathering and distributing the offerings of the people (which we saw was implicit in the pagan notion of the *episkopos*) and moved to pastoral duties involved in giving aid. From there it calls for the liturgical presidency where the offerings (both in money and kind) were made. Finally it requires the supervision of the instruction and exhortation given by teachers and prophets (not prominently mentioned by Ignatius) at the common assembly, and consequently becomes an office fulfilled by one man.[24] Shepherd makes the further observation that nowhere in all the omnipotent responsibility of the bishop is teaching mentioned, and it is possible that this function is still retained by charismatic figures.[25] It may remain a function distinct from the threefold ministry during the second century. If this description of the development of the monoepiscopacy is accurate, it further reinforces the clear impression that ministerial function becomes more and more devoted to prevailing against heretical and schismatic teaching and discipline in the face of persecution.

Presbyters and deacons figure prominently in the letters of Ignatius. What the presbyters do is another question. He writes to the Trallians, "The presbyters are like God's council and an apostolic band. You cannot have a church without these. I am sure you agree with me in this" (3:1–2). Irenaeus (A.D. 170) describes them as authoritative teachers and rulers. An early third-century document, the *Teaching of the Apostles*, describes them as "counsellors" and "assessors." One gets the distinct impression that this is the beginning of two hundred years of empty honor for the presbyterate. It is no wonder that Dix suggests presbyters were unpaid for their work.[26] In fact, the *Apostolic Church Order*, probably an Egyptian document from about 300, foresees churches where there were bishops and deacons but no presbyters. But for the deacons, who now emerge clearly as the bishop's assistants (his "eyes"), it is a different matter. Although they are subservient to both bishop and presbyterate (Magnesians 2:1), they have liturgical functions and administer charity (Trallians 2:3); they preach and go out as missionaries (Philadelphians 10:1); and they are consulted as a body by laymen before anything can be done (Trallians 7:4). This is the beginning of what Hardy calls five hundred golden years for the diaconate.[27]

Willi Marxsen, another of the outstanding German New Testament scholars, has written a study of early Catholicism in the New Testament where, among other passages, he examines three verses in 2 Peter (1:19–21), probably the latest writing in the New Testament (dating from 125 to 150). In this selection the statement is made: "All this only confirms for us the message of the prophets, to which you will do well to attend, because it is like a lamp shining in a murky place. . . . (v. 19). Who, asks Marxsen, is "us"? His answer is the Church, for whom now prophetic teaching is taking on a catechetical shape. The ecstatic is deemphasized, and the acceptance of the correct interpretation of the Christ event as expressed in the teaching function of ministry is becoming important.[28]

There are teachers of the Church who stand outside the catechetical tradition in the second century. They are perhaps descendants of the Jewish Christian "rabbinate," which represents a dogmatic, philosophical, and speculative tradition. Matthew argued against them a generation before (Matt. 23:8). They were trained in a more sophisticated philosophical tradition than the simple catechist of a given Christian community.

An example of such teachers is Justin Martyr (d. ?165), an itinerant pagan philosopher who was converted to Christianity and established a famous school in Rome. Although we have no knowledge of his ever having been ordained to any office, he was a charismatic figure as influential as any man of his age. It was Justin who described baptism as that act in which "we [are] . . . washing the one who has been convinced," and the Eucharist as that assembly at which the "president," *proestos*, gives thanks. The feeling comes through that the function of ritualizing is more important than the office of the person who presides.

Charismatic teachers like Justin did not last long, and the catechists finally held the day. In Ignatius' letters there is no mention of Apostolic Succession. Fifty years later and after Justin the Christian world is different. Irenaeus, perhaps following the lead of Hegesippus, grounds his defense of the Faith in the authoritative succession of teaching handed down from the Apostles and found in certain notable episcopal sees established by them. He speaks of bishops as the successors to the Apostles (*Against Heresies* III, 3, 1). Their function is to bear witness to the teaching of the community that elected them, and it is to this that they are consecrated. The source of the teaching is then the congregation in that see, not the imagination or mental powers of the bishop.

It is obvious that Irenaeus' enthusiasm for this system of authoritative teaching is motivated by his desire to resist Gnosticism. It is also a further witness to the almost universal acceptance now of one bishop over one see. Even Rome, which had retained presbyterian government until the mid-second century, had come over to the monoepiscopacy.[29] The responsibility for the teaching function is now intimately related to the sacramental person of the community, though he may not actually perform it, as it shall remain to the present. It is noteworthy, however, that in Clement of Alexandria and Origen it is the authentic teaching that guarantees the legitimacy of the bishop and not the other way around.

A "test bore" of the function of ministry might now be made for the early third century, if we look at *The Apostolic Tradition*, attributed to Hippolytus, a Roman presbyter who became a schismatic bishop of Rome. It dates from about 215, and in one edition provides us with the ordination prayers of the Church of Rome at that time. Clearly by now each office had its specific function or "liturgy" within the Church. To what was each ordained? The bishop was to be a shepherd (an image identified with the sacramental person) to serve as high priest, to forgive sins, and to free men from demonic bondage (*Apostolic Tradition III*), all in accordance with the authority Christ gave the Apostles. It seems to me that the main thrust here is that the bishops, as apostles, were to have the authority of Christ; in fact, they were to be Christ to their local community. As Dix says, he is "the man" of his own Church. I have suggested my preference for the more descriptive term "sacramental person." This is the prime emphasis upon the nature of ministry in the Church from the time of Paul and his fellow itinerant evangelists; and it is to this that the functions of ministry are related. The preeminent ministry is that of those who, not only in word but in their very person, embody the Christ.

The presbyter is ordained to one function for a certainty in *The Apostolic Tradition III*. He is to rule, which Dix notes is not said of the bishop! [30] His is a collegiate office, for if he moves from one community to another he can be admitted only by consent of the other presbyters to their group. It may possibly be that he is also ordained to teach (the manuscript is corrupt here); if so, this would correspond with Irenaeus' description of the presbyterate as teaching and ruling. Of course, the possibility of a separation between the role of shepherd and administrator, and the subservience of the latter to the former, offers an illuminating precedent. No liturgical function is mentioned for the presbyter, though he undoubtedly had one, as we shall see. The continued correspondence between the Christian presbyter and his Jewish antecedent is, however, remarkable.

Hippolytus did not like deacons. It was from the diaconate that Callistus, his successful and, in his mind, heretical rival for the episcopate in Rome, came. One wonders if this rivalry influenced his recounting of the prayer of ordination for a deacon, which mentions only his liturgical function of presenting the offering to the bishop (*Apostolic Tradition* IX). Elsewhere in *The Apostolic Tradition*, however, he mentions that deacons should search out the sick that the bishop might visit them (*Apostolic Tradition* XXX). So the role of the deacon is to assist the bishop.

The function of the deacon soon came to involve more than being a sort of "errand boy." Deacons were the "civil servants" (in military parlance, the "warrant officers") of the local congregation. In Rome, for example, the deacon, Laurence, martyred in 258 under Valerian, was the treasurer of the Church. If we may get just a little ahead of ourselves, four hundred years later in Rome deacons ran storehouses, a hostel, and a bathhouse. The archdeacon (which means "bishop's deacon" or, since by them presbyters also had deacons, "chief deacon") was the bishop's legal officer. I might note at this point that there is very little precedent from this period for the present custom of taking a presbyter, calling him an "archdeacon," and putting him in charge of missions or education (functions that did not belong to deacons). Much more appropriate is the situation in the Diocese of Milwaukee where the chancellor (legal officer) is a perpetual deacon.

The spirit of the third-century ministry becomes clearer when we recall that a man was ordained to his specific office, without any intervening ordinations. For example Cyprian of Carthage was elected bishop of that city only two years after his conversion. There is no evidence he was ever ordained deacon or presbyter before being consecrated bishop, despite scholars such as Quastan who speak anachronistically as if he had been.[31]

This brings us to another issue. Dupuy points out that the term *sacerdos*, the Latin for "priest," is applied in the third century (particularly in the works of the Africans Tertullian and Cyprian) almost exclusively to bishops.[32] Undoubtedly the bishop's function as representative of the high priesthood of Christ demanded that this be so. Yet presbyters probably celebrated the Eucharist in the third century as well as in the second. Cyprian, despite his reservation of the title *sacerdos*, wrote his presbyters from exile to be sure to offer the liturgy for the confessors in prison, in the company of a deacon (*Letters* 5). As a matter of fact, deacons must have taken this responsibility unto themselves during the last great persecution of the Church (303–305), since the Councils of Elvira (306), Arles (315), and Nicaea (325) all found it necessary to forbid the practice. Cyprian also mentions presbyters or, in their absence, deacons absolving sins (*Letters* 12). Whether or not, as some scholars contend, presbyters in Alexandria ordained one of their number to be bishop of that city, in the presence of the corpse of his predecessor, we will leave for the study of others.

Reference to absolution calls to our attention the development, in the third century, of Penance. Up until this time there raged a controversy within the Church as to whether or not grave sins, notably adultery, murder, and idolatry or apostasy, could be forgiven after Baptism. Hebrews, for example, speaks of Baptism and then says, "When they have experienced the goodness of God's word and the spiritual energies of the age to come, and after all this have fallen away, it is impossible to bring them again to repentance" (6:4). But on the other hand, there began to develop a system whereby he who committed such grave sin could be restored to fellowship within the Church. *The Shepherd of Hermas*, a mid-second-century writing, mentions it (*Mandate* 4, 3, 1–6); and by the time we reach the third century it is an established public rite within the Church. It involved a confession of sins (whether open or not is debated), good works such as fasting, prayer, almsgiving, and public displays of contrition (e.g. sordid attire and a sorrowful countenance), and a period of excommunication. Readmission of the penitents called for the laying on of hands by the bishop or, in his absence, the presbyters or, in their absence, the deacons. It is doubtful that there was any private rite of penance prior to A.D. 400.

The important thing to see about Penance is its relationship to Baptism and the Eucharist. As with Baptism, it was an act of reconciliation to the Christian community—a fact very clearly declared by its public character—and a means of readmission to the Eucharist where the unity of the congregation with Christ was constituted. It was not so much a matter of an individual "getting right with God" as it was a restoration to the source of all health, the Body of Christ. Hence we can better understand the role of the bishop, the sacramental person within the community, as he becomes responsible for the discipline of the members of Christ. This relationship with each member symbolized his relationship to the whole congregation.

Mention must also be made of the so-called "minor orders," which become evident in the third century. Their importance for us will be greater in the next period under consideration. They number four or five. In order of precedence, the first is the subdeacon, who was a servant of the deacon. Hippolytus wrote, "Let each of the deacons with the subdeacons attend upon the bishop" (*Apostolic Tradition* XXX). The reference is in regard to the ministry to the sick. The second is the acolyte, which means not a sweet little boy in a red cassock but "one who follows." Apparently acolytes started out as messengers and attendants for the bishop, under the deacons and subdeacons. Tixeront tells us that Cornelius (a bishop of Rome, d. 253) wrote to Fabius of Antioch that there were forty-two acolytes in Rome, six in each of seven regions serving under a subdeacon.[33] The third minor order was the exorcist, an office given over in the third century to the dismissal of demons which previously had simply been a charismatic gift of "Christian men" (Justin Martyr, *II Apology*, 6). The same Cornelius mentions them, and there is other testimony as well from around 300. Their function related particularly to the catechumenate, and when it dies out they cease to fulfill a practical purpose (about the fifth and sixth century). The fourth is the lector or reader, which Tixeront believes is the oldest. Tertullian speaks of readers in *The Prescription of Heretics* (xli, 8) written about 200, and there are epitaphs of lectors that predate this. When reading was a skill not all possessed, it is quite obvious that specialists were required. Interestingly enough, if a young person in the fourth century wished to enter the clergy, he began by becoming a reader. In the West there was also a fifth minor order, the porter, who was what we call now a sacristan. Romanus, a companion in martyrdom with Laurence, was a porter. It can be readily seen from these descriptions that although the original idea did not so intend, the functions of these four or five offices quickly became largely liturgical. It might also be noted that in one theological tradition in the West the subdeacon is not in minor orders but the first step in major orders, a result of the merging of the episcopate and presbyterate. The desire to maintain the sacred number "seven" consequently requires an additional minor order.

In summary, if we are going to understand the pattern of ministerial function in the ancient Church, we must remember that with all its inhumanity the world at this time was extremely personal. The rich man knew the poor man who slept at the gate of his house. People lived on top of one another in crowded streets and multistoried apartment houses. War was no farther away than a short sword, and justice was meted out by the emperor's intimates. Therefore, it is no surprise that the successor of the Apostles, the representative of Christ himself, sat in practically every eucharistic assembly and knew his people by name as any good shepherd. It is hard to describe the sacramental person as a ministerial function. As a respected and loved leader of the community, willing to suffer torture, exile, or death for the Kingdom he believed imminent, he embodied the expectancy of the transcendent with the immanence of the personal. He more "was" than "did";

but certainly all functions derived their authority from his person, which was a living thing in the small community of the ancient Church.

Although it is extremely difficult to make precise definitions or to achieve any order of the ministerial functions that we have noted emerging in the life of the Church's first three hundred years, I would call your attention to eight. One, which I have not discussed as yet, is obviously present, namely (1) cultic preaching. It must be distinguished from (2) evangelism, or missionary preaching, simply because they were and are two different things. (3) Teaching, both catechetical and philosophical, became more and more important, while its partner, (4) prophecy, waned to reemerge another time. (5) The ritual life of the Church was central, natural, and little debated. (6) Discipline was more an immediate concern and grew in importance. From the time of the Acts of the Apostles (7) the care of the poor, the orphans and widows, the aged, and the infirm was carefully maintained. It is interesting that (8) administration seems to have been something relegated to those who would do it, the presbyters.

No doubt as we examine this list there is a sense of familiarity about it all, but let us not assume too many easy equivalents. Just as we would be lost in the liturgy (which lasted three hours), bored by the homilies, and perplexed by the curious world view of the early fourth-century Christian, we will find that no ready "blueprint for contemporary ministry" can be unearthed by recounting what was done over sixteen hundred years ago. Beware of the "archeological school" of pastoral theology. Yet there is in the sacramental person and the derivative functions of ministry a quality of transcendence vital to the encounter of Christ in his Church. Therefore, the vitality of the Church's mission in future centuries can very well be measured by its creative incorporation of what is eternal in the early centuries of the Christian era.

## chapter 3

# THE
# SACRAMENTAL
# RITE

The Council of Nicaea (325) has traditionally represented a convenient breaking point in what was without question a gradual transition in the character of the Church, a movement that altered the function of the Christian ministry from what we have so briefly described to something that lasted with minor alterations for more than a thousand years and that is far more familiar to our twentieth-century perspective. I treat it here as one period. It is in fact three: the Heroic (500–1100), the Renaissance (1100–1300), and the Late (1300–1500). In each period there was a definite development of Christian thinking; but at the risk of a gross generalization I will contend that ministerial function grew out of a universal cultural foundation.

The pre-Nicene Church consisted of a great number of local congregations, each headed by its own bishop, which in themselves were microcosms of the Church Catholic. Only on such occasions as the ordination of a new bishop, or the arrival of a distinguished theologian taking refuge from enemies within his own community (Origen, for example, going from Alexandria to Caesarea), or when the remoter congregations harbored fellow Christians fleeing a local persecution (or, as in the case of Ignatius, on the way to a martyr's death), would the average churchman be vividly aware of the Church beyond his local situation. It was a private, self-sufficient Christian life. Certainly orthodoxy was a more and more common concern, and provincial synods, called for its safeguarding, were well known as we move further into the third century. But national liturgical commissions were unknown and freedom of rite prevailed. Even the canon of the New Testament differed in some ways from place to place. There was a feeling of being a colony of heaven in an alien world, a sense of being called apart, a disciplined elite acting on the orders of the Word.

Theologically, despite some loss of an immediate anticipation of the end, it was a "pilgrim church." But now the Church owned buildings and even had some wealth. At the end of the third century, for example, a Christian basilica was located on rising ground in full view of the imperial palace in Nicomedia, then the eastern capital of the Empire. The beginnings of the monastic life—a puritanical movement that clearly strove to recapture a "lost rigor" and singleness of purpose— reach well into the third century. But the movement has to be understood as the ultimate compulsion in a Church living a precarious existence with periodic active persecution and immersed in an esoteric, idealistic, intellectual climate (the ascetical theology of the Desert Fathers is a Christian expression of a prevailing pagan notion of spirituality). A "secular theology" would be impossible in such a world.

Furthermore, the ancient Church was part of an urban society.[1] Therefore, the kind of cross-fertilization of ideas that we identify with such living existed, and the average Christian was deeply involved in the intellectual issues of his Church. The language of the Church, both literally and figuratively, was his own.

In the post-Nicene Church the first of two issues arose, which together with the decline of Roman civilization in the face of the barbarian invasions, would change the whole context of the Christian mission. Constantine, Roman emperor from 306 to 337, around the year 312 declared Christianity a permitted religion and then took an active role in its affairs. The question then and for centuries to come was who would control whom, the Church control the State or the other way around? Prior to the eighteenth century, the separation of religion and politics was beyond the ken of anyone. The State now comes to support the Church, and the latter has an investment in the good order of the Empire. Inevitably, bishops acquire power and property; real estate and privilege are magnified many times over. Those who today resent clergy discounts, "fixed" traffic tickets, and buses to parochial schools can blame it all on Constantine.[2] More important, it was the beginning in the West of the two worlds of civil and canon law, which would do so much to shape the face of medieval Christianity in the next thousand years. For the present it created the problem of whether or not the Church was to transform the world or be conformed to the world. As the episcopate became more and more a part of the government, it appeared the latter would be the case.

Of course, if one is a member of the Church that is the religion of the entire civilized world, one cannot help but develop a deep sense of one's membership not just in a local congregation but in a universal Church that corresponds to a universal empire. The first great ecumenical council was called and presided over by Constantine at Nicaea, and it was only the beginning. Christians from all over the Mediterranean world now made pilgrimages to Jerusalem. There is a growing urge for more visible expression of unity within the Church, not only theologically but in other ways. The canon of the New Testament is more or less evolved toward the end of the fourth century. There is also an obvious pressure for all to accept the prevailing faith and to abandon paganism. Inevitably, this became less and less difficult to do.

Worldliness, hypocrisy, and tepid devotion produce their inevitable reaction; and early ventures in the monastic life now become the forerunners of a wave of anchorites and cenobites who filled the deserts of Egypt and then moved west. Though without doubt the religious life (as monasticism is known) was a God-sent instrument to the mission of the Church in later centuries, as we shall see, its initial impetus was largely a *lay* desire to achieve a sanctity believed possible only when one abandoned a material world full of "unspiritual people," such as now infected the Church. It had a puritanical, self-centered motivation, not unlike that characterizing the "dropouts" of our own affluent society. As such it was the source of a revival of prophecy that would call for the reform of the Church again and again in the centuries to come.

As far as the West is concerned (and the thrust of the first part of this book must be a continued narrowing of the area of our study), the curious relationship established between imperial Rome and the Church by Constantine's recognition of Christianity lasted only about a hundred years. The city of Rome fell to the invading Visigoths in 410, and the last Roman emperor of the West was deposed in 476. This is the second great issue of the post-Nicene Church: the assimilation of a largely Germanic people into the Church, a people given to tribal structures and a primitive world view. Some of these tribes were Christian, but usually of an Arian variety (believing that Jesus was a semidivine, created being). Others were pagan, more overtly committed to a superstitious and magical religion they brought with them into their Christian faith. All carried with them a strong sense of the numinous, born of their life amid the deep forests, high mountains, and angry seas of northern Europe, of which their gods Woden, Thor, and Freyr (known to us only in the days of the week and in the custom of the Christmas tree) were personifications. Conversion of such people was usually brought about by the baptism of the tribal chief, whose example was obeyed by all his followers. This was a far cry from the careful preparation of the catechumens in the early Church, exemplified say by the *Catechetical Lectures* of Cyril of Jerusalem (c. 315–386); and it was clearly expressive of a mechanistic doctrine of baptism.

In our reflection upon the conditions under which ministry functioned in this changing world, we must add to the new movements and foreign pressures the heightened struggle of the Church to define its faith in the face of continued and

growing divergence of teaching. One general council after another was called (Nicaea, 325; I Constantinople, 381; Ephesus, 431; Chalcedon, 451; etc.), not to mention many local and
provincial gatherings. They all required the presence and support of the episcopate, which now more clearly than before
was the source of a teaching in the Church that seemed intended more to assure commitment to the definitions of the
councils than to give personal knowledge of Christ.

It was in the face of this preoccupation of the bishop
with all the new demands, plus the rapidly increasing number
of Christians, that in the fourth century the "parish priest"
began to appear. If the bishop had remained the accustomed
president of the local Eucharist, the number of the episcopate
would have had to be greatly increased. Whether it was a matter of too few qualified men or the fear of distributing power
too widely, the Church chose another course. The presbyterate, out of which the sacramental person of the bishop
emerged as the focal office of the local congregation, now re-
gained that central position, but with the difference that it
never captured the role of the sacramental person assumed by
the episcopate. *Instead, it functioned as a sacramental instrument, which is a fundamental distinction to keep in mind.* The
presbyter more and more was the normative celebrant at the
Sunday assembly, save at the bishop's own church. He baptized without the presence of the bishop, which created the
confusion in the theology of Confirmation that we possess to
this day. Later, as public penance died out and the Celtic practice of private penance was adopted, he also heard the confessions of the faithful.

Along with this assumption of the stress role, achievement
of the priesthood became a matter of an ecclesiastical *cursus
honorem.* A man "worked up through the ranks" of the minor
orders and the diaconate to priestly ordination.

The right to preach, identified more closely with the person of the bishop, was not as readily conferred upon the presbyter as the sacramental functions. The fourth-century sermon

was a prolix and florid piece of oratory, based upon Hellenistic rhetoric, called the "Greek homily." We have examples dating from the second century (*II Clement* and the *Homily on the Passion* by Melito of Sardis), but its richest illustrations come from the fourth century. Rather long and rambling, it was mainly a compendium of advice and admonition to its Christian hearers. It would require a skilled orator, which was perhaps one reason why it was reserved to the more educated bishops. Its greatest practitioner was John Chrysostom (347–407).

Augustine of Hippo (354–430), whose bishop was criticized for allowing him to preach in his presence while Augustine was yet a presbyter, introduced into the West a much simpler and straightforward sermon style, the so-called "Latin sermon," which unfortunately was not equaled for a thousand years. After him, with some notable exceptions like Leo I (d. 461), Caesarius of Arles (c. 470–542), and Gregory I (c. 540–604), bishops preached with much less effect and presbyters hardly at all. This is despite the fact that in the sixth century priests were now urged to preach. The impression we get is that few men were really capable of composing a good sermon.

For in truth the quality and breadth of education greatly declined in the early Middle Ages, and this drastically affected the function of ministry. The decline can easily be exaggerated, but it is true that the general demand for learning diminished. The rhetors' schools of Rome disappeared in the fifth century. It was to such heathen schools that Christians had always sent their children, and in their own catechetical instruction had never tried to replace them. When the rhetors' schools died, and education retreated to the bishops' schools and the monasteries, there was no general effort to make up the loss. The monasteries themselves were begun in an anti-intellectual spirit, and Decarreaus says, "The schools of the Eastern monasteries were only rarely pedagogical or intellectual centres."[3] In the West, after Benedict (c. 480–550) founded his order, monks were required to read the Scriptures, and this necessitated a measure of education. Therefore, a modicum of learning prevailed, more or less as a sideline at first. Then in some places great centers of learning did develop in the monasteries, particularly in eighth-century Britain. In all circumstances the education was strongly biblical, and only as we approach the Medieval Renaissance does the preservation of the Latin and Greek classics become a concern for the monks.

We spoke of the emergence of the "parish priest," which leads to what is meant by "parish." The English word is from the Greek *paroikia*, from which the Latin is *parecia*. It means first a "neighborhood" or "collection of dwellings," and then in the Greek Old Testament and in the New Testament it can be translated "sojourn" or "temporary dwelling" (1 Peter 1:17, RSV: "exile"). It came to be applied in the early Church to each Christian community, particularly as *ekklesia* meant more the universal Church. Eusebius quoted Irenaeus and Apollonius in this sense.[4] But it needs to be understood that for a long time "parish" was synonymous with what we now understand as "diocese," itself a secular and political term employed by the Roman emperor Diocletian (284–305) for the fifteen major divisions of the Empire.[5] Although as early as the fourth century the word "parish" is used in our modern sense, in two ninth-century councils (Celebyth and Clovesho) it was clearly the equivalent of a diocese, as it was in some twelfth-century glossaries.[6] Therefore, it is no contradiction to discover that into the eighth century "parish priests" in France lived with their bishop and rode circuit out to the rural churches on Sunday.

These particular rural churches would be the baptismal churches, outside the cities, which reached prominence in the sixth century. There services were held regularly, a font was to be found, and from the sixth century the archpresbyter was authorized by the bishop to baptize. During the seventh to ninth centuries, as the result of German law, the local church owned by the lord of the *villa* grew to be the more normative center of worship (called the *Eigenkirchen*). Here appoint-

ment of the parish priest was under lay control; and the benefice system arose, which is the lease of a church (with or without the cure of souls) for rent. The Church fought the *Eigenkirchen,* but Roman synods in 826 and 835 recognized them.
The "parochial banns" tied the people to their local church,
and at the Council of Nantes (658) it was decreed that people must attend Sunday Mass in their own parish church. The
establishment of parish boundaries came from the practical
need to regulate the tithe, which was first established at the
Council of Macon (585) and approved by civil law probably
from Pepin (714–768), for whom it was a way of getting
church reform without returning church lands sequestered
under the *Eigenkirchen.* Lay control of churches grew in the
towns as well, but there also arose there collegiate churches,
where apart from the cathedral itself a community of priests
lived under a rule (e.g. that of Chrodegang of Metz, d. 766,
and of Aachen), and came to be called "canons" (meaning
"rule").

The *Eigenkirchen* declined in the ninth century during
the investiture struggle, and by the mid-twelfth century the
system was replaced with that of patronage. In this system the
parish priest, in holding the benefice permanently, had to be
approved by the local bishop; but if it was a nonpermanent
appointment, there was still no recourse to the bishop. What
can be seen from this brief history of the parish is what Colin
Williams calls to our attention in reminding us that the parish
as we know it is only a thousand years old.[7] Prior to the juridical structuring of the institution, the local churches tended
more to symbolize the "pilgrim Church," which the very word
"parish" implies: the temporary nature of man's earthly residence. The parish priest was the *instrument* through which
the success of the journey to heaven was assured. Even with
the ordering of the local church, the Medieval Church never
lost to the social and political structure the vertical sense of its
parish life. As Clebsch and Jaekle state, the "ladder of humility," which was the principal tool of pastoral care symbolizing

the ascent from earth to heaven, had its bottom rung at the local altar.[8] It was to be left to a later era—the contemporary even more than the modern—to lose all sense of the original meaning of "parish" and to make of the structure the end itself.

So it is evident that in its temporality, the evolving parish was not a legal, independent corporation as today. Since its realty and income were the possession of either the bishop or a wealthy layman, it is not surprising that the struggle for the control of the appointment of priests and the life of the local community went on literally for centuries. The end of the Roman Empire had not only seen the decline of the city, but also the towns, and during the Heroic Period of the Middle Ages, civilization retreated to the villa-now-becoming-manor. With its fields and serfs, this became a self-sufficient unit and the integral entity of the feudal system. This is what led to the benefice system, where the endowments and tithes of the church within the unit were under the control of the lord of the villa/manor. Such monies provided the heart of the entire economy. Only when the holder of a benefice was also a bishop did the Church possess an unencumbered hold on the life of that parish; and even then such a bishop was himself more often than not appointed by the ruler of the jurisdiction in which his diocese lay, and was subject to him for calls upon his time and loyalty.

We cannot go into the complicated problems of Church and State that are implicit in this arrangement. The episcopate was very much caught up in the power struggle, and consequently devoted most of its time to administration and secular pursuits. It is no wonder that in the old French epic *The Song of Roland* (written at the end of the eleventh century about Charlemagne, c. 742–814) the only ecclesiastic mentioned is Archbishop Turpin, "who is too zestfully occupied with warfare to concern himself with mercy and charity." [9] But we must be careful lest we judge him by the standards of another age. Furthermore, it would be grossly unfair to assume that all bishops were like the legendary Archbishop Turpin, though it is clear that with the obscuring more and more of the bishop's ministerial role, the Church lost a needed point of identification.

A glance at ecclesiastical life in the time of Charlemagne, who was the outstanding figure of western Europe between 604 and 1047, can give us an idea of what the function of ministry was. For over four hundred years the lower clergy (priests and those in minor orders) were drawn largely from the serfs (peasants tied to the land of a noble). Not infrequently they were *compelled* to seek ordination, for there was a shortage of secular clergy ("secular" meaning "in the world," as opposed to "regular," meaning monks or canons, those who lived by a "rule," a *regula*).[10] They studied under another parish priest, and their education was poor. They often could not read the Latin they used at Mass. Frequently the local noble would use the income of the parish church for his own purposes, and they would have to "moonlight," perhaps in illegal ways, to stay alive. Their principal entertainment was the drinking party, a leftover from recent pagan days. Although they now lived in their parish, their main task, when they were not doing other things, was to celebrate the sacraments: baptism, the mass, and penance. One thing that could be said for them is that they were very much a part of the people whom they served, and the consolation of religion was close to the hearts of the people.

If the function of such a ministry in 800 was minimal, we can thank God that no longer, as seventy-five years earlier, was there reason to be concerned as to the validity of the sacraments of unbaptized clergy. Furthermore, among a people whose religion was largely magical and for whom the subtleties of Alexandria, Antioch, Constantinople, and Rome would be sheer jibberish, the near-ignorant parish priest nonetheless provided a referent of meaning. He performed rituals consistent with the people's self-consciousness and was effective in communicating a redemptive dimension to their lives. This was the age of "bleeding hosts" and "talking ambries," expressive of a sense of the numinous that we cannot despise. When Paschasius Radbertus (c. 790–859), a monk of Corbie in France, wrote the first treatise on the Real Presence and declared that the bread and wine did indeed change into the spatially present Body and Blood of Christ, he taught a *modification* (in the direction of Augustine of Hippo) of the popular piety of his day. His theory culminated in the scholastic definition of Transubstantiation, declared *de fide* at the Fourth Lateran Council (1215), which was still an effort to overcome the prevailing crass literalism. Be it ninth century or thirteenth century, for the average Christian right up until the Reformation the primary function of ministry was the miraculous daily repetition by the parish priest of Christ's bloody sacrifice. It was beside the point that the worshiper understood not one word said, and it was thoroughly consistent with his understanding of Christ's presence that he *dared* make his communion no more than the one time a year required.

If I may pause for moment, I wish to urge the reader not to place some moral judgment upon the man of the Middle Ages because he was by our standards so ignorant as to believe in magic, portents, and the like. He did the best he could with what was available to him, and maintained through it all a deep faith in God. For example, the word "monster," which we associate with childhood fantasies, comes from the Latin *monstrare*, "to demonstrate," as such unnatural creatures were believed to show us something of God's future. We admire the thinking of men like Augustine of Hippo, Thomas Aquinas, and Martin Luther. Any reading of their works will reveal beliefs in magic phenomena that were simply conditioned by the inability to explain observable occurrences like electricity, decay, etc., for which man had to wait centuries for an accurate understanding.

I have already mentioned several times the assumption of Penance by the priest in the Middle Ages. This did not happen suddenly. Rather as the practice of public penance before the bishop began to die out as a regular custom, a custom of private penance after the manner of the Celtic Church of the fifth and sixth centuries was imparted by Irish missionaries. This consisted of the confessions of sins, reconciliation, and the imposition of a penalty, called a tariff penance, in proportion to the gravity of the offense. The penalties were exacted from a book called a "penitential," of which a goodly number survive to this day. The great stress in these rules was upon sensual and violent sins, which we might expect in a culture still not deeply influenced by the gentle ways of education.

The whole system began with an ancient medical model (i.e. sin was thought of as a disease) and through the centuries became quite mechanical, highly juridical, and required no great pastoral sense on the part of the priest. The Carolingian Church was of two minds about the disappearance of public penance and the development of the penitentials and private penance, and the Roman pontificals (liturgical books for the use of bishops) carried provision for public penance until the fifteenth century. But despite efforts to the contrary, the private practice that we know today prevailed, and the Lateran Council in 1215 made confession to the parish priest an annual obligation.

The upper clergy at the time of Charlemagne were generally drawn from the nobility or were commoners who by some good fortune received the education to assume the responsibilities of a bishop or a deacon. Among these, under the leadership of the learned deacon Alcuin (c. 735–804), Charlemagne attempted to improve the educational level of his empire, reform the liturgy, and enhance the spirituality of the people.[11] One noteworthy result was a compilation of homilies to be used as source material by clergy for the exposition of the Sunday propers to their people. There was a widespread desire that some explanation of Scripture be included in the liturgy. These homilies were only the first to be published, but the impression persists that, unfortunately, they found infrequent use.

Perhaps it occurs to the reader that mention of bishops and deacons as consisting of the "upper clergy" is inconsistent in the second degree with the Ordinal of the Book of Common Prayer (page 535), which speaks of the diaconate as "this inferior Office." Such was not the case in the Carolingian Church or the Anglo-Saxon Church. To condense what is in fact a very complicated evolution of custom and law, it is necessary to keep in mind that from the sixth century on if a man was educated (i.e. could read or write) and had not already received the tonsure, he came under canon law.[12] Unlike its civil counterpart, canon law was based on the Theodosian Code of 438, in which the duties of the imperial civil servants are outlined in detail, rather than the Germanic common law. Church administration adopted these officials and their functions. One such early and important officer was the notary, who attested deeds or writings, and could be in minor, or deacon's, orders. Theodore of Tarsus (c. 602–690) brought his own notary with him to Canterbury. Later there appears the rector, who is the appointed ruler of the land of a local church. He might be a layman, often a deacon or subdeacon, and only later a priest.[13] In the tenth century the title "dean" comes into use, meaning in the Theodosian Code a messenger between the local officials and the supreme authority. Abbots of monasteries (who, incidentally, were sometimes deacons and not priests), when they began to travel in the king's court, appointed deans for the local community; so did the bishop in his cathedral. But since the bishop was, like the abbot, often at court, the cathedral dean began to assume the wealth and importance that we now identify with him. All of these could be deacons, because this was the order charged with administrative responsibility in regard to church business and not a sacramental function.

An interesting phenomenon in the Western Church developed because of the size of the dioceses, which were much larger than in the East. The problem was the bishop's management of his duties. The first solution, adopted from the Eastern Church, was the use of the chorepiscopus, a country bishop without a particular see who served in a restricted manner under the diocesan bishop. Chorepiscopi are reminiscent of our suffragan bishops. They were very common in the eighth century in Germany, and largely fulfilled a lesser sacramental role. But the chorepiscopi became ambitious in the ninth century, and their use rapidly waned until, in the twelfth century, they disappeared. This presented the diocesan bishop with no great difficulty, however, because his problem was administrative rather than sacramental (he was not concerned, as the modern Episcopalian is, about confirmation); and his solution was to assign one or more "chief deacons" or archdeacons to supervise an area. Their task was to assure obedience by rural clergy to the canons, and consequently they were legal officers. The rural dean was a version of the archdeacon, who remained in residence in his district. He was a twelfth-century English development.

The archdeacon's visitation offers a further insight into the function of the parish priest, as we see in the instructions of Hincmar (c. 806–882), Archbishop of Reims, to his archdeacon. He tells him to make sure that the priests administer baptism and penance, train young clerks (meaning someone in minor orders) for the priesthood, provide for the altar, expound the Lord's Prayer and creed every Sunday, maintain the property, and keep a list of the poor to be fed.[14]

This sounds in some ways little different from the description of the function of the parish priest in the thirteenth century, four hundred years later; only the archdeacon was more victimized by a more developed system, usually better educated, and certainly under the ideal of stricter discipline. In England the living of a parish would be given, usually for a financial return, to an absent rector, who less than 25 percent of the time was himself a priest. Out of his income from the parish he would hire a priest to provide the sacraments for the people. After the late twelfth century the hired person might be a vicar, which meant a priest with lifelong tenure and a guaranteed, if very small, income. The vicar in turn might hire a chaplain for an outlying chapel at an even smaller remuneration, and the chaplain might or might not have more than an annual employment. Some priests were paid less than an unskilled worker in their day.[15] Out of his income the priest, vicar, or chaplain, or perhaps someone hired on for only a year, would, until the late thirteenth century, have to keep up the church. In addition he would possibly pay his deacon and certainly his clerk (no one seems to know what the deacon did, but the parish clerk was a combination sacristan, acolyte, secretary, etc.), and perhaps support his wife or concubine and their children. Celibacy of course was demanded of the clergy from the fourth century, but it was not always observed through the Middle Ages by the secular clergy. It was no wonder that the average parish priest farmed right along with most of his people.

Undoubtedly the parish priest in this period provided the Christian with what he longed for most, the support of the sacraments in the routine and the critical events of his life. But we are faced at the same time with a subtle difficulty that has cursed the Church since Constantine. The parish priest does not come off as a very convincing "Christ figure." He was too conventional to be the local sacramental person, and therefore he did little to contribute substantially to the visible presence of the personal incarnate Lord. He did "holy things," but it was difficult to think of him as *the* "holy man." Despite papal efforts at reform, he was not that set off from the laity. His education was not much different. He was tonsured and was expected to dress in a more somber manner than his people. Yet he worked and played alongside them. The respect of the people was based not on who he was but on his power to say Mass and pronounce absolution. This had its strong points, as I have previously suggested and as anyone who knows the value of "worker priests" will admit. But where did people acquire the sense of the transcendent person?

In speaking of the medieval episcopate, we have to think more and more of the prince-bishop. As the title indicates, he had long since abdicated much pretence at ministerial function beyond administration and discipline, and had certainly ceased to embody the sacramental person in anything but a dogmatic sense. Moorman described the thirteenth-century bishop, in whose diocese there would be from two to three thousand secular priests.[16] If he made a visitation, which was not too frequent, it was more like moving among his priests as a circuit judge than as a shepherd of the flock. Sacramental acts were peripheral to the main purpose, and his great retinue would guarantee him freedom from personal contact with the mass of people. It is worth noting, however, that in apparent deference to the earlier concept of the bishop, the Western Church did not translate bishops until the eleventh century.

Of course in the teaching of the medieval Church the true sacramental person was the Vicar of Christ, the Pope. I hope that it is immediately apparent, however, that outside of dogmatic definitions, this teaching violates any concept of the personal presence of Christ in the community.

Perhaps the working solution in the Middle Ages for this ministerial need, which is so central to the servant Church, was found where we have only briefly looked so far, in the monastic orders and later in the friars. In the West, much of the function of ministry from Benedict on was carried out by the religious, be they clerks, deacons, priests, or bishops. Their devotion to education, which broadened through the centuries, we have already mentioned. Equally important was their evangelical zeal. When the Church was confronted by the pagan Germanic tribes, it was men such as Augustine of Canterbury (d. 604), Willibrord (c. 658–739), Boniface (c. 680–754), and Anskar (801–865) who went out as missionaries of Christ. Every one of them was a Benedictine monk.

Aside from their catechetical and evangelical function, the religious offered a continuing prophetic witness. Prophecy, which is that call to God's will addressed to the Christian community, was puritanical, reforming, and discriminating. In this spirit the Abbey of Cluny was established in 909 to rejuvenate a depressed Christian spirituality, and it had great impact. Yet, as Russell says, "The curse of the Church is that nothing fails like success";[17] and as it succumbed to its worldly fame it was followed by the disciplined and demanding Carthusians and Cistercians at the end of the eleventh century. When they in turn had begun to enjoy the respect of the world, the mendicant orders around 1200 took up the prophetic cry against corruption and heresy. During the four hundred years embraced in these three movements there was no lack of prophecy.

But above all the contribution of the religious life was found in the holiness of person witnessed in men such as Bernard of Clairvaux (1091–1153), Dominic (1170–1221), and Francis of Assisi (1181/2–1226), and surely as well in other less-known figures. Perhaps here was the successor of the pre-Nicene bishop. For what the medieval pope and his prince-bishops may have represented in dogma, these men represented in fact. Yet monks and friars, contrary to popular notions, did not generally serve parish churches, and tragically their contact with the rank and file of the Church may not have been wide or deep.

I have alluded to the church reforms of the Medieval Renaissance. From, say, 1048 to 1303[18] there was a great awakening economically, politically, educationally, and spiritually in Western Europe. At the center of all this was what Russell calls the papal "revolution" and Southern the papal "restoration," [19] which began with perhaps the greatest of all the medieval popes, Hildebrand, or Gregory VII (c. 1021–1085). The history of the Middle Ages can be divided into periods "before" and "after" this commanding figure, whose understanding of the papacy set the Church irrevocably on

the road to Trent and Vatican I. His reforms were, on the
face of it, constitutional. He sought to establish the power
of Rome against Europe's secular rulers. He was concerned
about a disciplined cadre of clergy committed to the papacy,
so he set about to make the division clear between them and
the laity. This was rooted in the earnest desire to separate
sacred things from venality. Also expressed in his concern,
however, was the need to protect church properties from the
problems of inheritance rights, and consequently he sought
to enforce clerical celibacy in the face of stiff resistance. He
also introduced a more juridical view of ordination, which has
unfortunately obscured a more ancient Catholic tradition.
Perhaps most far-reaching for our purposes was the evolution
of the bishops' schools into our first universities. These institutions, however, were primarily given over to the study of the
"liberal arts": the *trivium* of grammar, rhetoric, and dialectic;
and the *quadrivium* of arithmetic, astronomy, music, and ge-
ometry. Canon law was a popular postgraduate study for those
seeking court positions; but theology was a very arduous postgraduate course, offered in the thirteenth century only at
Oxford, Cambridge, and Paris, and taken only by men devoting themselves to study and teaching in the universities.

If we understand the top-level nature of this "revolution," it might be easier to perceive why the new spirit in the
Church of the high Middle Ages influenced the everyday
function of ministry only slowly. Church control of its episcopal offices had small effect on parish life. What did it matter who chose your superior if his purposes remained the
same? It was going to take more than papal enthusiasm to
change the life of the poor priest, as long as there was no
popular protest among his people about his function. By the
thirteenth century in England, although there were university
graduates among the ordained priests, there were only from
one out of twenty to one out of four in a given diocese, and
there was no guarantee they would serve in parishes.[20] However, the ideal of an educated clergy was acknowledged; in the

early thirteenth century, Jacques de Vitrey makes some sneering comments about ignorant priests.

Gradually there were improvements. A sermon in a parish of the early thirteenth century was a rarity, yet in the latter part of that century sermons were more common. This came about because the friars, whose delightful, picturesque, and often ribald and dramatic preaching captured the imagination of the people, were imitated by the parish priests. For the first time pulpits began to appear in churches, as did seats for the worshipers. We can imagine that the clutter of furniture impeded the customary use of the parish church for community social gatherings, which included dancing and games within the nave of the church. But it was for a good cause. Preaching crosses were erected outside that were reminiscent of the preaching of the Crusades over the past two hundred years. Listening to sermons became a pious duty carrying with it certain indulgences. It could also be fun with popular preachers, who developed the particular form of the late medieval sermon that in some ways is the precursor of modern preaching.

Of course there was now a superb intellectual tradition, growing out of the scholastic movement and culminating in Thomas Aquinas (c. 1225–1274), that was a part of the "revolution." It only affected, however, the Church life of the theologically elite. Much more important for the general worshiper during the Late Medieval period would be the horror of the Black Death, the constant wars between nations struggling for identity, and the uncertainty begotten of an immigration, after six or seven centuries, from the country to the towns to take up the life of tradesmen and artisans. Despite some notable evidences to the contrary, these influences seem to have deepened the patterns of ministry established over the centuries since the conversion of the Germanic tribes. Clebsch and Jaekle point out the emphasis now upon sacramental grace, in pastoral care,[21] which I do not mean to disparage by saying that it was more what we would consider "magical grace." For example the reification of Christ present in the sacred species is emphasized in the rise of the service of the Benediction of the Blessed Sacrament in the early fourteenth century, a development that was utterly foreign to the ancient culture of *personal participation* in Christ. Frequent communion is unknown, and communion in one kind the rule.

Perhaps most symptomatic of the spiritual needs of the people was the development of the chantry. Originally "chantry" meant any service performed by a private chaplain, but by the thirteenth century it evolved into the provision for having a mass said daily for the repose of the soul of an individual or a family in perpetuity. To do this one had to endow a priest, whose sole task would be to celebrate once a day for this purpose in the presence of his clerk or page.[22] Visitors today to European churches get only a small sense of the importance of this custom by viewing the many chantries with the tombs of the donors. The extravagance of employing a priest was not necessary, and more generally they made use of any available altar.

The medieval ministry of caring was codified in the seven corporal acts of mercy, with seven corresponding spiritual acts of mercy. The corporal acts were to feed the poor, give drink to the thirsty, clothe the naked, shelter the homeless, visit the sick, ransom the captive, and bury the dead. These were taken quite seriously. It was the task of the parish to feed its poor from its income, often made difficult by the greed of the owner. The sacramental ministrations of the Church were brought to the sick and dying, which was a source of great comfort. Beyond this the religious houses from the time of the early Middle Ages provided hospitals (Latin: "places to receive strangers") for sufferers of all kinds. The most common form of hospital, the alms house for the aged, began to decline in the fifteenth century. However, monastic hospitals were still being established in the seventeenth and eighteenth centuries in Roman Catholic countries, and many

a notable instiution in Europe today can trace its origins
to these homes of refuge.

The pre-Nicene Christian developed his sense of identity
in terms of participation in a community, of which the doctrine of the Church as the mystical body of Christ is the
theological expression. The eucharistic assembly was the fore-
taste of the messianic banquet, Baptism a public witness to
that calling into freedom of ·a chosen people of which the
Exodus was a prototype, and Penance a readmission into the
company of God's elect. To be a Christian was to have been
changed already from mortality to immortality, and to be in
the process of deification. It was possible to believe all this if
for you the real life was already a mystery in which participation was the goal, and if you had no sense of your individual
identity apart from your corporate existence in a dynamic
new and future order. The ministry was a function of this
outlook.

Medieval man was heir to a different world view. Read
everything Thomas Aquinas wrote, and you will find no doctrine of the mystical body of Christ. It has been replaced by
Christendom, which briefly is the belief in a providential visible Christian society of which the pope and king are the
divinely endowed rulers. The natural world, from the earth
and its rocks to man and his society, is a translucent mirror
of a transcendent unchanging supernature. The real always
lies behind the apparent, and man's destiny and the Church's
task is to bring man to that reality, only known in this world
in a Golden Age that had once been. Everything good works
to the beatific vision of the awesome God that lies beyond
nature, but man is beset from the time of his conception by
the demonic, which pervades the world lying in wait for his
soul. The emphasis was upon man's sin and Christ's redemptive sacrifice, not upon the Greek notion of deification. The
relationship between man and God was juridical, not participatory,[23] and consequently the doctrine of grace leaned to-

ward the mechanical. Sickness, adversity, poverty were the punishment of sin. The Eucharist was the propitiation of the wrathful judge, Baptism the release of the claim of hell, and Penance the weapon against the demonic powers. Medieval man was earthly and practical. He was no "latter day Manichean," save for the heretical Cathari; but neither did he believe "the proper study of mankind is man."

Medieval culture was dominated by the evolving dialogue between the Church and State and between Germanic and Roman civilization. It is easy to caricature its "barbarities" in comparison to the ancient world and to exaggerate its ignorance and cruelty while ignoring the same thing in other eras less tempered by sincere spirituality, including our own. The "collective representation" of medieval man did not offer necessarily the most perfect instrument for Christian belief, as Christian romantics since Sir Walter Scott have suggested; but neither was it a tragic interlude between Plotinus and Descartes. We must, however, take care to define the medieval self-image, as compared to the ancient, modern, and contemporary ones.

When we do this I am struck by two divergent thoughts. The first is a regret at the loss, through the fortunes of history, of the opportunity for a continued and immediate participation in a focal figure I call the sacramental person. But then my second thought is that, this opportunity being lost, the Middle Ages embraced what would be the next most creative dimension of ministry, the sacramental rite. Modern anthropology tells us of the necessary and constitutive role of ritual in the life of any people. The fact that the medieval Church was able to retain in some sense all the functions of ministry results from the fact that a transcendent yet incarnate Christology was embodied in its rites.

The medieval theology of ministry was a clear explication of this cultural development. First of all, there was a growing belief that the priesthood was the highest order of ministry and that the episcopate was only a special function of the same. This was first suggested by Jerome (c. 340?–420), the Ambrosiaster (a fourth-century anonymous commentary on the Pauline epistles), and Pelagius (fifth century). It was a reaction to the assumption of the normal sacerdotal functions by the presbyters, which functions were more and more the touchstone of ministry. The medieval Church consequently divided the priest and bishop as to function only on the basis of canon law. The distinction was made by saying that they both possessed the same *order*, but that they had a different *office* or *power* (and later, *jurisdiction*). There are too many suggestions of presbyterial ordination of both bishop and priest prior to this time even to say absolutely that only the bishop had the power to confer orders. It was not until the Council of Florence (1438–45) that bishops were explicitly declared to be the ordinary ministers of orders.[24] As Hardy says, by the twelfth century the union of priest and bishop in one order was the accepted theology of holy orders.[25]

The mention of *order* brings up a second point of medieval theology. The early Church undoubtedly thought of the authority to exercise ministry as invested in an individual through the Church. The local congregation acclaimed a man bishop, and the ordination by other bishops manifested his relationship to the universal Church, and the Apostles "sealed" the election. Dix says that by the time of Augustine, however, we begin to get the idea that *order* is something possessed by virtue of the ordination of the individual who exercises it.[26] This is the result of the breakdown of the sense of community and the emerging notion of the priest as one who is sent by God through the agency of the bishop to the given congregation. From this teaching of Augustine developed the doctrine of *character* (in Latin *character* meant the instrument with which you brand or mark something), though he did not use the term and spoke of the rite as having this quality rather than the office itself. From the twelfth century, and in Thomas Aquinas, *character* is used to mean more and more the power of office conveyed in ordination in the sphere of worship, an indelible mark as in Baptism and Confirmation.[27] The Council of Trent declared this teaching *de fide;*[28] and interestingly enough the doctrine appears in many Anglican theological manuals as self-evident, despite the fact that it is not a universal teaching and is of questionable current value. The concept would appear to answer the natural question of medieval man: how is it possible for my neighbor to perform this miracle which I cannot? The reply is that he has special character, which is "something" given to him by the bishop at ordination; and, according to popular piety (though not Thomas Aquinas or Trent), he will have this forever. This is a very effective way to avoid the ambiguity of the Donatist heresy, which taught that only the sacraments of a morally pure priest were valid. It also obviously lends itself to the kind of reform sought by Gregory VII in setting the clergy apart. It would seem to me, however, that a doctrine of the ontology of the mystical Body would make such an ontological doctrine of ministry superfluous.[29]

But this is a question really aside from our principal concern. Judged by our standards, the Middle Ages were a brutal and ignorant time. Teaching and preaching, which to us in their more stimulating forms depend upon a literate audience, were extraordinarily simple in one sense and usually quite limited. Yet there were notable exceptions in the fourteenth and fifteenth centuries, as well as occasionally earlier. There was prophecy, and it was often heard, because there was a reality to the assumed commitment of its hearers. The Church's care was frequently a humanizing force when compared to the barbarism it confronted. Administration was almost totally removed from the local scene (unless we include custodial functions under this heading), and together with penitential discipline assumed a juridical form sought by unsophisticated subjects. As I have said, all these must be seen in the context of the predominant ministerial function of the sacramental rite.

If a healthy society is to be measured by the congruence

of its rituals with its sense of identity, and it is probably as good a measure as any, then the medieval world was strong and vital. If we judge its rites theologically, however, I think we would have to say that the Christ met in the medieval Church was not entirely the Christ of the Gospels nor the Christ whom you or I might know today. But this raises the perpetual hermeneutical problem of how we can assure ourselves that the Lord we know in any age is more than the projection of our own fears and our sense of need born of those fears. If we ridicule the image of the tortured Savior upon the fifteenth-century crucifix, who is to say that our popular songs depicting him as Palestine's most famous "yippie" are any more consistent with the historical Jesus and the cosmic Christ?

## chapter 4

# THE
# SACRAMENTAL
# WORD

There is some justification in suggesting that elements of the Gregorian reform of the eleventh century came to fruition almost five hundred years later in the sixteenth. As we have seen, Hildebrand and his successors sought to center ministerial function in a disciplined, educated clergy, clearly distinguished from the laity. They succeeded only sporadically and gradually. The revival of learning, the flowering of scholasticism, and the new sophistication of the arts dating from the eleventh century and marked by the Crusades and their side benefits, followed by the Renaissance beginning in southern Italy, delineate a period often poorly appreciated in our times. Yet nothing in this period contributed to the disciplined reshaping of Church life quite as much as the climate of widespread humanism, the rise of the middle class, and the development and expansion of the European nations that ushered in the modern period (1517 to 1914). It was a troubled time, for as man's understanding of reality changed, perhaps as it had not done since the end of the classical period, it was inevitable that the past would be interpreted to the present in different ways and at varying tempos.

The name of Marshall McLuhan is almost a household word today, but to many his rather extravagant style has clouded the profundity of his theories. *The Gutenberg Galaxy*, an early and less known work by McLuhan, offers as the key to the entire transformation of reality in the sixteenth century the invention of movable type (in 1454). Such technology,

McLuhan suggests, changed Western civilization from an oral to a visual culture and made possible a whole new system of communal interdependence based upon the modern market, the price system, literacy, and industry.[1] The calculated testing of nature, which gave further impetus to the rise of modern science in the sixteenth century, and the systematic exploration of politics by the Machiavellian mind, which provided a sophisticated appreciation of power, are characteristic of the spirit of the age.

McLuhan makes the point that a division now emerged between the "heart" and the "head"[2] and a rift appeared between the good and the beautiful, which is at the root of the Protestant ethic.[3] A middle class devoted largely to trade and craftsmanship found a great meaning in values such as work, education, family, and duty; it had little patience with what seems unproductive: beauty for its own sake. Medieval man did not demand of culture a practical use; modern man did. It does not take much perception to see the impact of such a mind-set upon the Western and later particularly American ideal of the successful man.

It has often been debated whether Martin Luther (1483–1546) was the first modern man or the last medieval man. This is perhaps symbolic of the ambiguity of the period from 1517 to 1648; fulfilling on the one hand many of the ambitions of the Medieval Renaissance, it marked on the other the end of the former culture and the beginning of another that is very different. There is little doubt that Luther's passionate search for a conviction of individual salvation, which was finally met in his study of Romans, springs from Ockham (c. 1300–1349) and a late medieval German piety. At the same time individualism and the humanist movement, which facilitated much of Luther's movement and of which the best known representative is Erasmus (1466–1536), was greatly aided by the printed book. Luther himself was not a committed humanist, for he was suspicious of classical learning and the powers of human reason. His disciple, Philipp Melanchthon

(1497–1560), however, was most certainly one of the humanists; and John Calvin (1509–1564), particularly in his devotion to the rhetorical tradition, may be counted among their number.[4] The humanist tradition was then a radical break from the medieval world view and, as we shall see, made a profound impression upon aspects of ministerial function.

The opening of the New World and the rise of nationalism—which McLuhan claims "depends upon or derives from the 'fixed point of view' that arrives with print, perspective, and visual qualification"[5]—made possible the many breaks within Western Christendom that characterize the Reformation. In this sense our suggestion that the Gregorian reform, with its desire for the supremacy of the Papacy over the temporal world, was fulfilled in the sixteenth century is obviously not true. However, it is important to see that the notion of Christendom prevailed, that in some Reformers such as Calvin the role of the Church as the final temporal as well as spiritual arbiter was affirmed (if not always actualized), and that in the Lutheran doctrine of the "two kingdoms" the independence of the Church from the control of the State was at least protected. Where royal supremacy prevailed, as in England and France, we must acknowledge a complete surrender of the Gregorian ideal. Yet between the heritage of medievalism and the new ideal of the Renaissance and Reformation there is a synthesis which established a milieu that bred a particular type of cleric.

He was a man destined for one thing, to carry most of the burden of ministry upon his own shoulders, for it needs to be kept in mind—and here I conclude my reflection on the transition from the medieval period to the modern—that the role of laymen in ministerial function was undoubtedly potentially greater before 1517 than after 1648. In between these dates, the Reformation itself was not able to maintain the lay leadership that marked its earlier decades, nor did it bequeath to later generations the lay responsibility for ministry affirmed in its theology. Christopher Brooke makes the point that "it was the tragedy of the medieval Church that it never found a way to develop, encourage and educate the [lay] enthusiasm it could inspire." [6] In the modern period, despite the affirmation of "the priesthood of all believers" and the occasional vital role of the layman, such as in Pietism and the Methodist movement, the enthusiasm was lacking and there was a growing spirit of professionalism in terms of both Catholic and Protestant scholasticism that left the layman in a more and more passive role. The valiant effort to harness lay witness in the contemporary period is a clear testimony to this phenomenon.

The Protestant Reformation itself (which I date from 1517 to 1648), personified in Luther, Calvin, and Zwingli (1484–1531), developed out of the educated classes. Luther was a university lecturer at Erfurt, Calvin was trained in the law, and Zwingli possessed a Master of Liberal Arts degree from the University of Basel. Even Conrad Grebel (c. 1498–1526), the spiritual father of the evangelical radicals, came out of a humanist background. It is not difficult, therefore, to see that a number of forces, which we have briefly summarized, focused in these men to develop a theology that not only centered about the Holy Scriptures (now widely available in the vernacular) as, or revealing, the Word of God, but also led naturally to an understanding of ministry as first of all an agency for the proclamation of that Word. For Luther the continuity of the Church was not found in the structure of the ministerial priesthood, but in the priesthood of all believers expressed in the proclamation of the Word.

Lutheran polity is completely consistent with this theology. For it has always taught that a man is ordained to the pastorate to fill a cure; that is, in response to the call of the congregation to minister the Sacraments and preach the Word to them. He is ordained to perform a function, not to an order. This would appear to be in direct contradiction to the Catholic tradition: *agere sequitur esse*. It should be noted, however, that there is this element in both Roman Catholic and Anglican canon law. A Roman Catholic bishop is not to ordain a man unless he "judges him necessary or useful for the churches of his diocese" (this being, of course, a secular priest),[7] and the canon law of the Episcopal Church requires evidence of appointment to some cure for a deacon to be ordained priest (Title III, Canon 11, Sec. 9). Clearly at least a juridical relationship is understood to exist between the presbyterate and doing something for someone, rather than just "being." That "doing" is the same as in the Lutheran tradition: preaching the Word and ministering the Sacraments.[8]

The Reformation was initially an act of prophecy, the speaking forth against the obvious moral abuses of the day and the apparent theological support for them. From this stemmed an emphasis upon the preaching and teaching functions for the local pastor. In the Lutheran Church there was a rapid cooling of prophetic passion as a result of the excesses of the Peasants' War (1524–1526), and an attempt to organize the country parishes as efficiently as possible through a system of visitation by a group of theologians and lawyers whereby oratorical passion would be tempered by sound teaching and clear discipline. In the visitation instructions, emphasis was placed upon pure doctrine as opposed to Roman Catholicism on the one hand and evangelical radicalism on the other, and upon living a moral life. Luther's two Catechisms were the standard, and together with the German Bible and the postils (short sermons upon texts which he hoped would be memorized and delivered orally), formed the principal ministerial aids for the Lutheran clergy. Of course, there was a great shortage of pastors at first, and consequently only the worst were removed, and a number of poorly educated individuals were ordained as emergency clergy. But Luther urged the German princes to provide solid theological education for men seeking ordination, and by the time of his death great improvement could be noted.

This same emphasis upon an educated clergy, whose primary function was to preach and teach, can be found in

Calvin. When he returned to Geneva in 1541 he had developed the organization of the Church around four orders: elders (later known as ruling elders), teachers, pastors (later known as teaching elders), and deacons. The task of the pastor, of which there were six in the three parishes of Geneva, was primarily to preach, instruct, admonish, and administer the Sacraments.[9] Calvin had every intention that the Holy Communion be available weekly in the city, but this quickly lost out to the overarching importance of the proclamation of the Word. Preaching not only went on at three services on Sundays, but also was the rule on three mornings a week.

When Calvin first came to Geneva in 1537 he had published his *Instruction in Faith*, which was intended for lay readers and served the same function as Luther's Catechisms: to be a standard for teachings. His ultimate goal was to create a college in which pastors could be theologically trained in a much more thorough manner. He did not achieve this until 1559. It is interesting that with Calvin the order of teachers or "doctors" itself seems to have been more like the faculty of a school of theology and a board of examining chaplains combined. It was to guard the purity of doctrine and to secure a succession of well-equipped ministers, who would then do the actual instruction of the people. By 1559 when his college was started, however, it was combined with the order of pastors.

When the contemporary American Protestant reflects upon the Reformation Church, it is important that he remember two things. There is no notion in either Lutheranism or Calvinism of a separation of Church and State (Luther's doctrine of the "two kingdoms" is nothing like our contemporary notion), nor are they congregationalists. Administration, including care of the buildings and clergy salaries, is in the hands of the State, which was consistent with the fact that in Germany the religion of the prince determined the religion of all in his principality, and in Geneva the Church was the State. Discipline, which actively pursued a moral and doctrinal conformity consistent with the seriousness of the age, was under a supraparochial consistory or church court in both Lutheranism and Calvinism. (Calvin consciously attempted to revive the penitential system of the early Church.) This method did not always prevail in succeeding generations, though the presbyteries in Scotland maintained a firm hand over members of the Church well into the eighteenth century. As congregationalism crept into Calvinism, discipline became a local concern there as did administrative functions. Nonetheless Calvin's understanding of the Church in relation to the State clearly bespoke a sense of Christendom that had prevailed since the fourth century and had a profound effect upon the shape and expectancy of ministerial function.

For example, prophecy, where it appeared in the more radical groups, tended to follow the example of the very early Church, rather than the Old Testament prophets. It was not so much social as ecstatic and millenarian. The State is identified with the total worldly establishment including the institutional Church, which is despised. The prophetic goal is apocalyptic, not revolutionary. On the other hand not only did the State care for the clergy and their churches, but the pastors themselves functioned as registers for the State as concern for accurate records of births (in the form of baptismal records), marriages, and deaths grew in the modern nation. Where men died for their faith, it was not in the name of religious pluralism in the face of tyranny, but as a casualty in a religious war.

The corporal acts of mercy, which was the closest the members of the established churches came to social action, persisted as functions of the Church largely until the nineteenth century, when the State began in earnest to assume the responsibility that led to our present welfare state. As noted in the previous chapter, in Roman Catholic countries it remained the function of the religious. Protestants had to handle it differently. Calvin had intended that his deacons would be of two kinds: those who looked after the money and those who cared for the sick and needy. In succeeding generations looking after the sick and needy became more the function of the local session. In Lutheranism and Anglicanism it seems to have been left up to private voluntary church organizations and the compassion of wealthy Christians. It would be possible to say that Protestants as a whole in the modern period probably evidenced less pressing concern for those who were suffering than did the Church at any previous time. However, lest I be unfair, it should be said that vestries both in England and Virginia engaged in considerable relief of the poor. In Virginia parish budgets exceeded those of the counties, and the major part was invested in this cause.

The English Reformation, which moved from a crass doctrine of royal supremacy under Henry VIII (1491–1547) to a more subtle form of the same under Elizabeth I (1533–1603), was ostensibly politically motivated. However, it would be foolish to suggest that it was only incidentally influenced by movements on the Continent. Lollardy, a name given to those who came after John Wycliffe (c. 1329–1384) and were given a theology very much akin to reformed teaching, survived into the sixteenth century in England, and English traders returned from German ports to their native land with Lutheran notions. Robert Barnes, prior of the Cambridge Augustinians, was an example of an early follower of Luther, and was involved with most of the leaders of the English Reformation in the 1520s. However, Henry VIII himself never succumbed to Continental theology, and once Elizabeth I came to the throne after the polarities of her half-brother Edward VI (1537–1553) and half-sister Mary (1516–1558), an "extremely conservative Protestantism" prevailed.[10]

As elsewhere at this time, and as has always been an issue, the clergy of sixteenth-century England were much criticized for being ignorant, grasping, and drunken. It must be said on their behalf that they weathered the changing winds of ecclesiastical fortune with remarkable equanimity. When the Prayer Book of 1549 was promulgated there was some rebellion in Cornwall, and there was some unhappiness, contrariwise, when Mary followed Edward VI and all priests who had married were deprived of their benefice unless they agreed to live apart (amounting in York to about 10 percent of the clergy and in Essex to 25 percent).[11] There is no evidence that great numbers of clergy were ardent Protestants, but the rapid changes in high places did create a shortage of curates. This is despite the fact that the dissolution of the monasteries under Henry VIII and then the chantries under Edward VI must have left some priests with little to do. When in 1559 Elizabeth I came to the throne there were 9,000 or so parish clergy in England, and they almost all conformed once again with little disturbance. The English Reformation was an affair of state, and apparently while Thomas More, John Fisher, Anne Askew, Thomas Cranmer, Nicholas Ridley, and others died for their particular understanding of the faith, most parish priests went on doing whatever was expected of them by whoever was in power.

The sixteenth century was, among other things we have noted, a time of considerable economic change. The flood of precious metals into Europe from the New World, the change in England from farming to the use of enclosures for raising sheep, and the loss of certain gifts to clergy in the Reformation, all revised the economic base of the parish priest in England. However, his financial status seems to have improved from Henry VIII to Elizabeth I. Besides his regular income from tithes, he also was able to farm; and he often maintained an ale-house beside the parsonage for profit and the refreshment of visitors. His house was generally better than those of farm laborers, and it is significant that at the end of the Elizabethan period a study was customarily appended to it.

The study is indicative of the fact that one thing particularly expected now was a clear exposition of the Word according to the prevailing theology of the priest. *The Bishops' Book* (1537) and *The King's Book* (1543) were published for the guidance of those with cure of souls, and then in the reign of Edward VI the *Book of Homilies* (akin to Luther's postils) and the *Paraphrases of Erasmus* (a kind of commentary on the Gospels) were ordered for every parish church. The Marian Injunctions (1554) demanded that the bishops issue homilies for the instruction of the people in each parish. Elizabeth was concerned more for the unification of England than anything else. During her reign the clergy were expected to conform to the authorized liturgical norm as an act of political loyalty. Yet she published the Thirty-Nine Articles; and she permitted only licensed priests to preach and otherwise authorized clergy only to read the homilies. This was, according to one nineteenth-century observer, because "The clergy in Queen Elizabeth's time [were] very ignorant (and no wonder, their stipends in most places being exceeding small) and moreover the state [had] a jealous eye upon them, as if they were not very well affected to the Reformation." [12]

Mention of the preaching license makes this as good a place as any to call attention to the concept of faculties in canon law—the granting of permission by competent authority to, say, priests to perform certain functions not automatically given by ordination—which in the Roman Catholic Church today pertains to such things as preaching, the hearing of confessions, and the solemnizing of marriages.[13] Whereas the idea may appear strange to some, it has merit (as we shall discuss in a later chapter) as well as a long history. First, it should be remembered that preaching had always been the bishop's special prerogative. The Fourth Lateran Council (1214) insisted that every bishop sustain a sufficient number of preachers in his diocese, the obvious implication being that no one thought ordination automatically gave the right to preach. Whereas the problem in the thirteenth century was in getting men to preach, in the polemical sixteenth century the opposite difficulty obtained. As regards confession, the Council of Trent extended the jurisdiction of the bishop over who could hear the confessions of seculars (people not in religious orders) in his diocese to regular priests, which was an extension of his authority of sometime standing over his own diocesan clergy. Third, the development of canon law (in systematic form from the eleventh and twelfth centuries) and the assumption of ecclesiastical jurisdiction over marriage is relatively contemporaneous. The faculties concerning marriage undoubtedly evolved in order to protect the pastor's revenue for such acts and also to prevent the petty bickering over who was going to preside at the liturgy (which is not unknown in Anglican churches today between rector and curate).

To return to the sixteenth century Church in England: for reasons that should now be apparent, the education of the clergy was an overriding concern as it was on the Continent. Success in accomplishing this goal was less than spectacular. In 1603, at the death of Elizabeth I, 22 percent of the clergy had college degrees.[14] The cathedral clergy were generally well educated, but otherwise ignorance abounded. This was not helped by the fact that appointment to a benefice was by the State, and it preferred men who were not so educated as to become troublesome. Furthermore, the Crown so plundered Church revenues that there were few stipends capable of supporting an educated man. We should not even assume too much about those who did have university degrees, for Oxford and Cambridge at that time had not achieved the distinction they now hold.

It is interesting to raise the question as to the correlation of education with income. In 1628 in England a priest could make as little as five pounds a year. Between 1600 and 1638, a concerted effort was made to improve the financial status of the clergy of Scotland (something not done in England until two hundred years later). The minimum goal for a pastor was 500 merks, or five to six times as much as the English equivalent. At the same time a comparable rise in the educational standards of the Scottish clergy is to be noted.[15] The reader might well ask what the lesson is in this paradigm.

The main thrust of this chapter is to show how the priest or pastor of the modern period assumes a ministerial function that focuses in the Word. The implications become clearer as we look at ministerial function in the seventeenth century, the period of transition from the Reformation to scholastic Protestantism. The effective clergyman, according to the spirit of the times, is the learned man. Actually there is no great difference in this among Anglicans, Protestants, and Roman Catholics. Pierre Janelle has made the interesting point that all ecclesiastical education of this time has its roots in the humanist movement and, in particular, in the work of the Brothers of the Common Life (founded in 1494). John Sturn, a Protestant educational pioneer, was educated by them at Liège. Ignatius Loyola, founder of the Jesuits, who were the leaders in Roman Catholic education, was inspired by them.[16] The Council of Trent lent the authority of the Roman Church to this movement by requiring that a seminary be established in every cathedral and bishop's church. The general pattern was a school of twelve years, devoting itself first to grammar and the fine arts, followed by a study of all the theological disciplines with particular emphasis upon those leading to the practice of the priestly office.

Not only did the Tridentine reform, which was part of the Counterreformation, seek better training of priests; it also emphasized preaching, pastoral visits, the holding of conferences, and the hearing of confessions. The teaching of the Jesuits and the Capuchins, a stricter version of the Franciscans founded in 1529 and dedicated to preaching and evangelism, is an indication of this common concern that swept Christendom, unfortunately with a highly polemical concern. One interesting technique developed in the late sixteenth century, which was picked up in the Catholic revival in nineteenth- and twentieth-century Anglicanism, was the "mission." This was a one- to three-week intensive appeal to the masses by a visiting cleric, with a stress on preaching, teaching, and hearing confessions. It became particularly prevalent in seventeenth-century France.

During this time preaching in general became a popular

pastime in the Gallican Church. In many areas the "comical buffoonery," which had been fashionable for four or five hundred years, remained; but among the greatest preachers (Bourdaloue, Bossuet, Fénelon, etc.) it was an accomplished art, not without its need for courage, for these men were willing to attack the excesses of Louis XIV (1638–1715). Father Houdry, who published twenty-three volumes of seventeenth-century French sacred oratory, used only 25 percent of his collected materials.[17] France was not the only country on the Continent that exhibited great preaching, for the preaching service (apart from the Mass) was an accepted practice in many Roman Catholic countries.

The style of these preachers was occasionally affected, and given to a superficial gloss of erudition. In the English Church, where such notables as John Donne and Jeremy Taylor justly gained a great reputation in the pulpit, this sermonic style took the form of the "witty" sermon, the point of which was to wring from the text every possible meaning. It was intended to impress its hearers and undoubtedly did those who came looking for this kind of oratory. The sermons of the Puritan fathers tended to be far more serious, highly biblical, and prophetic. Consequently, they appealed more to the middle class, who took themselves very seriously.

It is important to understand that it was an age that believed explicitly in the *order of life*. Everything has its place, and the good life is that which conforms to this harmony. In politics we had the "sun king" in France, Louis XIV, and the Stuarts tried unsuccessfully to convince their English subjects of the divine right of kings. In learning Descartes found the essence of man in his abstract cognitive powers, divorced him from his irrational passions, and set the philosophical tone for three hundred years. Newton's theories developed at the end of the seventeenth century were thoroughly consistent with the prevailing world view, and built upon the "spacious firmament" already revealed by Copernicus (1473–1543). With a sense of order goes a sense of discipline and a repugnance at uncontrolled behavior. The purpose therefore of preaching and teaching, and particularly the training of the clergy, comes to be formation in Christ, who is both personal savior and the *logos*—the eternal source of truth in all life. The disciplined life accorded with the universal order.

The *Spiritual Exercises* of Ignatius Loyola had the purpose of producing disciplined servants of Jesus, who in their lives embodied the truth they taught. This is *not* to say that Ignatius or his Jesuits were rigid or lacking in flexibility or compassion. The purpose of seminary training was not only to produce educated clergy, but men formed in Christian discipleship. To this end the French seminary was even stricter than the Tridentine model, requiring a longer curriculum and admitting only men destined for the priesthood. It should be noted, however, that not all priests in France were trained in seminaries, and many country pastors were the product of local presbyterial schools. The ideal priest of that age was described as "grave, temperate, of exemplary behavior and good sense, wedded to order and uniformity." [18]

It was not until after the Oxford Movement (beginning in 1833) that this ideal became explicitly dominant outside the Continent and Roman Catholicism in schools of theological learning. In Anglicanism in the last one hundred and twenty-five years it has been part of the seminary model in many quarters.[19] The priest is considered one whose personal discipline and decorum is a source of teaching and preaching. This is not to say that prior to this time the Church of England or continental Protestantism was unconcerned about these matters. In its instructions to its missionaries, the Society for the Propagation of the Gospel specifically demanded of its clergy that they stay out of taverns, which judging by the frequent repetition of this standard was a constant problem generation after generation. Lutheran discipline of the clergy seems at this time to have been more concerned with orthodoxy than anything else. In the duchy of Braunschweig in 1690 it was the custom for pastors, after passing their university examinations, to spend a year at the cloister church where they were observed and criticized in preaching, teaching, and pastoral care.[20] The modern notion in theological education of the "pastoral year" or "intern year" is hardly new!

The priest or pastor emerges in this description as an educated, disciplined man, destined to preach and teach an ordered, approved theology to a people literate and interested in ideas. It sounds like a ministry to the court or the middle classes, and one wonders about the simple folk. Of course we must realize that we are talking often about the *ideal* priest, and even in that most churchly century, the seventeenth, this ideal was not always accomplished. Also, although there is no doubt that the emphasis in ministerial function was upon preaching (particularly to strengthen the weak in faith, to convict people of their sins, and to condemn heresy) and teaching—not to mention the discipline of those who refuse to repent of their sins—there is mention in the contemporary books of pastoral care, such as Richard Baxter's *The Reformed Pastor*, of calling upon the sick.[21] Sometimes this would take the whole morning each day, for the numbers were large, people were scattered, and lingering illness was common. Routine house calls, as George Herbert tells us, were also very important.[22] Although it is clear that the purpose of calling on the sick or generally in the homes was to preach another sermon, the impression is gained that there was often a close, if somewhat dependent, relationship between the pastor and his people.

Raymond Cunningham has outlined the rationale of the home visit of the nineteenth-century Protestant pastor.[23] It differs in no way from the seventeenth, but radically from the twentieth-century notion. The pastor is, according to the textbooks of the day, to visit his people regularly, including all the members of the family, *if* it does not interfere with his sermon preparation. "A house-going minister makes a church-going people." [24] His explicit purpose is to speak about the spiritual state of everyone in the house, and he is *not* to engage in a social visit. In some calls actual sermons were expected and delivered in the home. Often these visits would be made by appointment. It is worth reflecting on the fact that although many pastors in the twentieth century will plead fervently for regular house calls, a strange mystique has emerged about the "surprise call"; often religion is formally broached only if the parishioner brings it up (which they rarely do); and we have no hard data to prove that calling increases attendance.

It is important in looking to the seventeenth-century pastor to perceive the mood of his times and to understand the nature of his ministerial function in its light. It is hard for us in a different time not to criticize too harshly Herbert's admonition to the country parson: "[He] is generally sad, because he knows nothing but the cross of Christ, his mind being defixed on it with those nails wherewith his Master was." [25] It was not a time to "celebrate life," because the sole hope of a rather grim life was a heaven beyond the grave. Given the prevailing set of mind, there was great profundity in the pastoral advice. The lovely Jeremy Taylor in his classic *Rule and Exercises of Holy Dying* wrote in the dedication of the work:

My Lord, it is a great art to die well, and to be learnt by men in health, by them that can discourse and consider, by those whose understanding and acts of reason are not abated with fears or pains: and as the greatest part of Death is passed by the preceding years of our life, so also in those years are the greatest preparations to it; and he that prepares not for Death before his last sickness, is like him that begins to study Philosophy when he is going to dispute publicly in the Faculty.[26]

The truth of this statement is something that we are just now beginning to recover in pastoral care. There is a grandeur to the words of these men, betraying a great insight appropriate for their times. Richard Baxter's hymns must have comforted many:

> Christ leads me through no darker rooms
> Than he went through before;
> And he that to God's kingdom comes
> Must enter by this door.

They were not without their gentle joy:

> Let us, with gladsome mind,
>   Praise the Lord, for he is kind;
> For his mercies aye endure,
>   Ever faithful, ever sure.

Those are the words of the young John Milton. But this is the best of the age, and one wonders how deeply such sentiments of obviously learned men permeated the life and ministry of the country parson.

Mention of the term "parson" offers a moment to reflect upon the role of the sacramental person in the modern period. It would appear that the use of the term "parson," which Blackstone's *Commentaries* in 1765 describes as the most dignified term a parish priest may possess (even more dignified than "rector"),[27] is related to this all-important concept. The word "parson" is derived from the Middle English (and Old French) *persone*, and first appears in an Old English sermon of about 1250. It is from medieval Latin *persona*, all of which lies behind our modern English word "person." [28] Its technical meaning was "a holder of a parochial benefice in full possession of its rights and duties." [29] By the seventeenth century it had the general meaning of a parish priest, but still carried with it the sense that he was *the person* of the parish, the embodiment of the whole man in Christ. Bishop Stillingfleet of Worcester in a pastoral charge in 1691 stated that although the term "parson" may be one of reproach to some, it has a dignity that dates from the reign of Henry II (1154–1189). It obviously was (and still is?) used in jest, perhaps because all too many who carried the title made a lie of what it proclaimed.

For there is ample evidence that the post-Reformation parson rarely lived up to the embodiment of the sacramental person. Not only was it because of the worldliness of the clergy, which stood in direct contradiction to the piety of the age. More, there was a clear distinction between the higher clergy—who were destined from the start to be bishops, court priests and pastors, cathedral and cloister church pastors, and the occupants of the better benefices—and the lower clergy of the poorer benefices, the vicars, and the curates. The latter tended to come not from the middle classes, but from the simple folk. In fact, a middle-class clergy was really a nineteenth-century development—about the time, strange to say, when the middle class and the Church enter into a mutual decline. Consequently, without a natural status in the community and generally lacking in the kind of education common among the higher clergy, the seventeenth-century country parson was capable of fulfilling the role of the sacramental person, as did the bishop of the early Church, only in the case of truly heroic saintliness.

What now should begin to be clear in the brief survey of this period is that ministry focused upon Word had its greatest effect among those who were literate and shared the conceptualization that lay behind such an emphasis. As Cyril Richardson is reported to have said, instead of praying the Lord's Prayer they gave a long discourse on it. This is not to say that there were no forms of verbal communication that appealed to the less literate, but such tended to get away from a sense of rational decorum sought by the modern scholastics if they were to be effective. Therefore among the lower classes, as well as among others who found little consolation in rational discourse or rhetorical flourish, the question emerged: how was the Church to minister to them?

Among Roman Catholics a partial answer was the deepening of the individual spiritual and devotional life. The Counterreformation produced not only the earthly saintliness of Theresa of Avila (1515–1582) and John of the Cross (1542–1591) in Spain, but in France Francis de Sales (1567–1622) began an era of piety that was marked by his own gentle and tender personality, which sometimes erupted into a saccharine spirituality that many today would find rather cloying. Devotion to the Blessed Sacrament grew (the Benedictine Nuns of the Blessed Sacrament were approved in 1661); Jean Eudes (1601–1680) promoted devotions to the Sacred Heart of Jesus as a counterattack upon Quietism and the Jansenists; and there was a revival in retreats and pilgrimages. Apparently there was a vitality to the Church's ministry as it presented opportunities for extraliturgical devotion.

A French Roman Catholic reformer and spiritual writer, Pierre de Bérulle (1575–1629), together with Francis de Sales, formed a great influence upon Vincent de Paul (c. 1580–1660), who in turn was a pioneer in France in ministry to the poor and country people. His work for educating priests to minister in this field was taken up by Jean-Jacques Olier (1608–1657), the founder of the seminary at Saint-Sulpice. Olier, who was also influenced by Jean Eudes, was in turn a popular figure among the followers of Philipp Sener (1635–1705), the founder of the pietist movement among Lutherans. Our point in tracing this line is to emphasize the *coherence* of the general turning in some parts of Christendom from a stress upon the intellectual grasp of the Christian message to a religion of feeling. Ronald Knox suggests that there was a relationship between the Pietists and the Quietists (those who generally condemn all human effort—Fénelon tended in this direction), as well as the Jansenists (a Roman Catholic form of Calvinism).[30] For our purposes it is important to remember that the Pietists emphasized, as did French piety, identification with the humanity of Jesus, reinforced through group prayer and Bible reading. It would be my observation that whenever ministerial function becomes excessively rational and emotionally arid, or commits itself to work amid the power structures of society or is identified with them—both of which happened with a vengeance in the seventeenth century—a re-action of this kind sets in. Its ministerial form is either of the spiritual direction of individuals in acts of rather emotional devotion or of the gathering of esoteric groups. Something of the feeling of this movement can be sensed in these very familiar lines from the great pietist hymn writer, Paulus Gerhardt (1607–1676).

> Commit thou all that grieves thee
> And fills thy heart with care
> To him whose faithful mercy
> The skies above declare.

The most amazing disciple of Spener was his godson, Count Nikolaus von Zinzendorf (1700–1760). Teaching a "religion of the heart," he evangelized much of the Continent, England, and America, and counted in his "Order of the Mustard Seed" Catholics and Protestants (not to mention the Archbishop of Canterbury). His Moravian Brethren spread widely, settling among other places in the piedmont of North Carolina, where a community still exists in Winston-Salem and the name of Count Zinzendorf compliments several com-mercial establishments. The importance of this movement for us is its influence upon the Wesleys and the Methodist move-ment. Combined with a Puritan ethic and an Anglican sense of order, Moravian piety helped form that particular brand of enthusiasm that was the only Protestant ministry in England and America to attempt seriously to minister to the lower classes.

John Wesley (1703–1791) did not in fact change the pre-vailing pattern of ministerial function. He simply took it out of the parochial context and with the assistance of lay preachers ministered to those who were untouched by the English

Church. George Whitefield (1714–1770), the greater preacher of the two, shared this concern for the neglected English lower classes. However, theologically they differed radically, and consequently without Wesley's organizational genius Whitefield's impact was confined to the latter half of the eighteenth and early nineteenth centuries (although perhaps Whitefield, through his influence on the Evangelical Movement in the Church of England, lived on in the Tractarian Movement and its curious wedding of a Calvinism and Catholicism),[31] whereas Wesley created a style of Christian life among the upwardly mobile Anglo-Saxon folk that lives among us today.

The secret of their appeal, other than its emphasis upon the emotions and the power of the group process, is hard to understand. Without access to churches because of the irregularity of their manner, Wesley, Whitefield, and their followers drew thousands to hear them preach in the open air. It was said of Whitefield (I hope apocryphally) that at his first sermon he drove fifteen people mad. His secret died with him. Any reading of such sermons finds most of us today only bored. Certainly the societies that first gathered to complement and then dissent from the parish church provided an emotional outlet and source of participation and involvement that had been woefully lacking to its members prior to this time.

I shall pick up again the remarkable function of preaching in the tradition of Wesley and Whitefield—which is really, in fact, evangelizing rather than a churchly discourse (to which we give the name "preaching")—particularly as it moves into the nineteenth century and America. However, first we need to set this phenomenon in the context of conventional, established Christianity of the eighteenth century.

On the Continent the impact of the Enlightenment, the self-styled name for an optimistic rationalism that held all ecclesiastical orthodoxy in highest suspicion, left the Protestant and Catholic churches pretty well shattered in spirit. Lutheran scholasticism, based on a biblical fundamentalism, collapsed. The preaching was very bad, and that had been the mainstay of ministry. A Lutheran pastor's wife describes her husband's efforts:

They were sermons weighty according to the season, either with practical advice or wrathful expositions of duty. There was one every year when the threshing time was at hand on the text: "Arise and thresh," explaining with patient exactitude the best methods for doing it. There was the annual harvest sermon on Matthew xiii, part of verse 26, *tares*, after yet another year of the congregation's indifference to chemical manure . . . and there was the Advent season, when the annual slaughter of pigs drew near, on Isaiah lxv, part of the fourth verse, *swine's flesh*. This sermon filled the church.[32]

The Roman Catholic Church in eighteenth-century France was little better off. There was the radical division still between the higher and lower clergy. Of twenty-five million Frenchmen there were 130,000 clergy (approximately one out of every 200), which would require over a million clergy in the United States today to equal it! While there were among the higher clergy those like Cardinal de Rohan, who attempted to seduce Marie Antoinette, most of the bishops "were neither scandalous nor edifying but simply more influenced by the attraction of this world's pleasures than by the prospects of eternal happiness in the next." [33] They lived well and enjoyed the current philosophies. The lower clergy, who if beneficed could make about 700 francs a year or if a curate only about 300, were not as well off. They were poorly educated, despised the learning of their city brothers, and yet held a position of respect in their communities. They kept the registers, read the king's edicts, supervised the school (education was entirely up to the Church), and visited the sick. It is noteworthy that when in the French Revolution the Church turned over its charitable institutions to the State, there were 2,200 hospitals and 14,000 nursing sisters! Generally it can be said that where the priest was an integral part of the French peasant's historic community he functioned well on a minimum of talent, education, and creativity. There was a sort of earthy piety about him. But where there was a break from soil and a new sophistication, the ministry of the Church was woefully lacking.

The English Church was equally distinguished by a clear division between the higher and lower clergy, even when they studied at the same universities. The son of the English yeoman who worked his way through Oxford or Cambridge knew his place well. Those destined for the higher clergy left the university for immediate preferment, and were frequently ordained deacon and priest the same day. They found it possible often to be appointed to several benefices, despite laws against it, and to avoid residence at all of them. (In 1809 there were 7,358 nonresidents of the total of 11,194 benefices in England. In 1835 there were 5,330 curates, of which 4,224 were employed by nonresidents.) [34] The lower clergy (from the ranks of whom those with benefices hired the curates to serve their parishes) often waited years as deacons to be ordained priest. They could look forward to a curate's salary averaging 30 to 40 pounds (it increased somewhat toward the end of the eighteenth century), or possibly they might be lucky enough to get a small living at about 70 pounds a year.

The main thrust of ministry was the sermon, which even after the challenge of Methodism remained unemotional and arid. The Georgian church adopted enclosed pews, in which it was possible to sleep or converse irrespective of what went on in the pulpit. They lasted until the mid-nineteenth century. The poor were relegated to benches at the back of the church. From the seventeenth century the Holy Communion was celebrated perhaps monthly, or just four times a year. In London it could, however, be found weekly. The children were generally faithfully baptized, mothers "churched," and the children catechized (something which was strongly emphasized in the Hanoverian Church). Often the parson also taught school, and at the end of the eighteenth century the "Sunday School" was devised to teach apprentices (who had to work during the weekdays) to read and write and do simple ciphering, as well as some religion.

In the visitation of sick parishioners, the diaries of Cole, Woodforde and Skinner testify to the conscientious discharge of this branch of the pastoral office. All three clergy were diligent in ministering both to the material and spiritual wants of the poor, reading prayers and carrying foods, whilst upon one occasion, Cole, being a high churchman, pronounced a formal Absolution over a parishioner.[35]

It was a time for the foundation of hospitals throughout England. Sykes lists no less than twelve in London alone that were established between 1719 and 1765.[36]

So there is no doubt that the Church in England in the eighteenth century was dull and unimaginative. There was a great abuse of the priestly office in plural holdings, the poor were patronized or ignored, and churchmanship was more and more synonymous with citizenship. But there was still some vitality to its ministry as well. The "fox hunting parson" existed. Perhaps it is no excuse to say there was nothing else to do in some lonely cures. But the important thing to perceive is that the ministry of the Church of England continued to appeal to the middle class, its morality and prejudices.

In America, from the settlements at Jamestown and Plymouth until the Revolutionary War, the Church—be it Anglican, Presbyterian, or Congregationalist—possessed the same staid, intellectual, middle-class tone. Harriet Beecher Stowe describes the Puritan divine of the eighteenth century, wearing a "full-bottomed, powdered wig, full, flowing coat, with ample cuffs, [and] silver knee-and-show-buckles." [37] Sermons could last well beyond two hours, though usually they were thirty minutes to one hour in length. The minister might spend eight to ten hours a day in his study in preparation of these documents.

In the late 1730s the American Church had been jolted with the so-called "Great Awakening," led by the preaching of Jonathan Edwards (1703–1758) and highlighted with the visit to this country of George Whitefield. It was a Calvinist movement through and through, characterized by vivid reminders of the horrors of hell that awaited the damned. In 1797 another movement of a similar nature, known as the Great Revival, began on the American frontier (principally in Kentucky), as an overt attempt to bring a ministry of the Word to those untouched by established religion. (There was, it should be noted, an Eastern parallel to this movement.) There was a great concern that the Christian religion was dying in post-Revolutionary America. Deism was popular, the Church no longer occupied leadership in society, and the frontier itself promoted a rather rough, irreligious existence. In response to this there arose itinerant evangelists, first of a Presbyterian stripe, who developed a preaching effective not so much because of content as style. It produced in some of its havens a form of hysteria—catatoniclike seizure, groaning or screaming, weeping—which was attributed to the power of the Holy Spirit. These preaching events were great social occasions as well as opportunities for conversion, and after the first flush of enthusiasm they were by 1830 institutionalized into the "camp meeting" familiar to rural America.

The Great Revival moved theologically from Calvinism and was a ministerial function ideally suited to the Methodist circuit rider. It marked the shift in missionary momentum from the Presbyterian-Congregational-Episcopal axis to the Methodist-Baptist-Disciples axis. The clergy of the latter groups, trained in "frontier colleges" rather than in Eastern universities, were often only part-time preachers. Methodist circuit riders made in the early years $64 a year, and consequently often farmed on the side. Their ministerial functions were limited by long hours on horseback to studying, preaching, prayer meetings, weddings, and funerals. Revivalism began in an anti-intellectual spirit, pitched to an emotional response, with a desire to produce a sense of *personal* salvation and morality (with "sins of the flesh" chiefly forbidden). In its successively more sophisticated and contrived forms under Charles Finney (1792–1875), Dwight Moody (1837–1899), Billy Sunday (1862–1935), and Billy Graham (1918–    ), this thrust has never really been lost. Infected with an ever more bland pietism and emotional appeals to a conservative political philosophy which it identifies with Christianity, revivalism today seems to me an anachronism.

The revivalist movement was in part a reaction to a sterile intellectualism, which raises for us the question of the nature of theological education in the established Church of this period. In Protestantism, as we have seen, it was centered from the Reformation in the universities, though without doubt many men simply read for orders. The Roman Catholic seminary suffered a severe decline in Europe during the eighteenth century, and many men were prepared in a less systematic way. In America, Harvard, William and Mary, Yale, and Princeton were all founded with the training of clergy foremost in mind. The content of this training, both here and abroad, was appropriate to men whose primary task was to preach learned sermons: Latin, Greek, Hebrew, logic, sacred divinity, moral philosophy, Church history in Anglican schools, etc. Upon finishing their university studies they simply stood a more or less formal examination for ordination.

Coming into the nineteenth century a change took place in the pattern of American theological education. The forces of secularism were beginning to control the universities more and more (in 1782 there were two professing Christians among all the students at Princeton),[38] and church authorities were more and more convinced that they must assume direct charge of the education of their men; for there was a great need for clergy. In 1791 the first Roman Catholic seminary was founded in Baltimore. The Episcopal Church in 1808 provided for a year's theological education, and in 1817 opened the General Theological Seminary in New York. When a professorship in theology failed to meet any need at William and Mary, its incumbent moved to Alexandria, Virginia, and in 1823 the

Virginia Theological Seminary began in earnest. In 1826 the Episcopal Church expanded the curriculum to three years at its three seminaries (a frontier seminary, Bexley Hall, had been opened in Ohio in 1824).

Why three years? Perhaps it was after the model of the Roman Catholic major seminary (which was, in fact, four years, but then the diaconate could be counted as the fourth), or after the model of professional education in medicine or law. I am inclined to think that if we could enter into the minds of the Church fathers at this period, we would see that it made perfect sense to them to hit upon the idea of three years as a literal following of our Lord's three years training of the Apostles. It is certainly not unthinkable that at this time the New Testament could be used for such forms of guidance.[38-a]

It was not until 1841 that a B.A. from a college was required for admittance at the General Theological Seminary, and several seminaries (e.g. Virginia and Nashotah) provided for many years a preparatory department for students who could not come with a college degree. The B.D. had no standardization in the nineteenth century. Only the Episcopal Church, along with the Presbyterian, Congregationalist, and Lutheran, had a real tradition of theological education during this time. It is interesting that in 1924 of 131 institutions in the United States called "seminaries," sixty considered themselves carrying on post-college education, and only five restricted admissions to college graduates.[39]

Clearly our conception of a defined curriculum of four years of college and three of theology as preparation for ordination was never universal or even widely accepted during the modern period. In England during the nineteenth century there was a greater emphasis upon a clergyman's being a university graduate—a notable improvement took place from 1830 to 1860—and the theological college began to emerge. Not always intended only for candidates for Holy Orders, institutions were founded such as St. Bee's (1814), the Church

Missionary Society's Institute (1825), St. David's, Lampeter (1827), King's College (1831), University College (1828), and others in succeeding years. The course of study was eighteen months. At first they were conceived as being in lieu of a university education. Edward Pusey suggested that the curriculum required for a B.A. be shortened and that the diocesan seminary be required after a university education in order that a man receive more direct training in the work of the ministry. As it was, when the universities became less and less explicitly Anglican, these theological colleges did in fact become complements to university training.

A word must be said here, just in passing, about the education of the laity in American Protestantism. The principal supplement to the pulpit was the Sunday School, particularly in the latter half of the nineteenth century. It is the enthusiasm for this form of ministry that has given rise to the Sunday option in many American Protestant churches of going *either* to preaching or Sunday School. In 1824 the American Sunday School Union was founded. After the War Between the States, Dwight Moody established the International Sunday School Association, with which was associated the Uniform Lesson Plan, the Moody Bible Institute, and the Chautauqua Institute. It is difficult to visualize today the central role this movement had in American culture—to the point that in 1910 Congress adjourned to watch the parade of the Adult Bible Class Federation.

Mention has already been made of the Church Missionary Society and its Institute, which directs us to the subject of missionary work in the modern period. Throughout the period from 1517 to 1914 Roman Catholic missions to non-Christians were vigorous, courageous, and often quite subtle. The Society for the Propagation of the Faith was founded in 1622, a seminary of the *Société des Missions Etrangéres* in Paris in 1663, and overseas bishoprics created in great numbers (in a stunning contrast to the procrastination of the Church of England in America). The Jesuits led in foreign missions until the order was suppressed (1773, restored in 1814), and then the secular clergy took over. Yet there was little to show for their work by the end of the eighteenth century.

Among Protestants there was very little missionary activity until the Pietists. Stephen Neill points out that in fact Protestant scholastics argued that missionary activity was neither obligatory or desirable on the part of the Christian.[40] As we have seen, the Pietist movement fed what became a great religious awakening at the end of the eighteenth century and that manifested itself in a remarkable missionary movement we cannot begin to recount here. "The early missionaries were primarily preachers" [41] and though they certainly carried with them some of the onus of colonialism, there can be no doubt that their preaching, which became teaching and simple caring, made such an impact upon the poor, ignorant, and oppressed in many corners of the world that by the end of the modern period the religion of Europe had become a religion of the world.

It is difficult to say what inspires one Christian to abandon home and loved ones to preach the Gospel in far-off lands and what leads another to stay in his own backyard. Certainly there is a question of emotional involvement, as witness the Pietist and the later Evangelical thrust to missionary activity. Perhaps there is also the tendency in members of established churches to identify their theological position, if not their God, with the nation. Certainly there was an element of this in the eighteenth-century English Church. Dissent on the other hand requires an emotional commitment that also breeds a missionary spirit. It creates as well a different way of handling other ministerial functions, both when it is persecuted and where it becomes part of an ecclesiastically pluralistic society.

Theoretical Congregationalism (as opposed to Anglicanism and Presbyterianism) was, despite certain connections with the Anabaptists, an English phenomenon. The pilgrims who landed at Plymouth were Congregationalists, as were

Oliver Cromwell (1599–1658) and his immediate followers. *All ministerial function* was theoretically invested in the independent congregation. When Anglicans, Presbyterians, and even to some extent Roman Catholics came to America they often became practical congregationalists. For example, in the Episcopal Church the vestry system—designed to care for the financial concerns of the parish, just as does the local pastor in the Roman Catholic Church and the session in the Presbyterian—acquired a power that haunts theories of the Church to this day. Such congregationalism has not tended, however, to promote the image of the clergyman as a sacramental person in the local setting, as was the case in the early period; it has rather tended to create a sense of the pastor as its servant, *vox pulpiti vox populi*—sometimes even the "scapegoat" of the congregation (in a literal biblical sense).

Congregationalism was one solution to the problem of a Church controlled by civil expediency. For those unwilling to take this path, the alternative could be a grim one. In the French Revolution, the devastating effect of which upon the European mind we in America little appreciate, efforts were made to force the Church into subservience to the State. Countless priests died and many more were forced into exile. In 1792 the responsibility for the registers of births (baptisms), marriages, and deaths was transferred from the control of the religious to municipal authorities. Adrien Dansette's comment about this is significant:

This was an extremely important move because it marked the break between the world and the Church and also marked the introduction of the secular State, definitely discarding the old conception of the Christian monarchy which had given a religious character to all great events of life.[42]

The myth of Christendom, formulated with Constantine in the fourth century, was dead; only there are those who fail to realize its implications even today.

In England nothing like the massacre of the clergy happened. What did occur was first the Evangelical Movement,
which, while Calvinist in theology and initially rather pietistic,
produced clerical members who were about the only "alive"
priests in the Church. It educated the masses, engineered the
abolition of the slave trade, and awakened England to a missionary zeal. Some of those raised as Evangelicals were leaders
in the Oxford Movement, which really began with the *Tracts
for the Times* in 1833. *Tract I* protested the Irish Church Bill
before Parliament, which sought to reduce the number of
episcopal sees in Ireland for financial reasons. It declared that
God made bishops, not parliament; and that Apostolic Succession was the source of their authority, not royal writ. Consequently, it took sides against a calloused Erastianism.

Thus began the Tractarian Movement, which coupled
with its Evangelical predecessor changed the entire nature of
the English clergy. It was a movement of intellectuals, and the
Word still held sway. Yet its leaders were also men of profound personal piety, informed by a deep if uncritical learning,
inspired by the Romantic reaction to the Enlightenment, who
believed that the integrity of the Church could only be retained if it recovered a sacramental ministry by priests disciplined to the sacred nature of their office. Ultimately their
commitment succeeded to a great measure through recalling
the Anglican priest (and even others) to their vital liturgical
function. Their initial leader, John Henry Newman (1801–
1890), may well emerge in history as the most enduring theological mind of that century.

From 1830 to 1860 a remarkable spirit seized the English Church, probably motivated mostly by public opinion.
Through the work of the Ecclesiastical Commission, made im-
perative by the problems of growing religious pluralism (although Brilioth makes the point that it was not until the
church constitution in 1919 that the Church of England offi-
cially recognized this fact),[43] collapsing churches, and starving
clergy, the manner of supporting the Church was drastically

revised. The number of nonresidents was finally greatly reduced (there were 3,078 curates of nonresidents in 1838 and only 955 in 1864),[44] although that reform did make it difficult for curates to find jobs. Plural holdings were severely limited, and two services were required on Sunday in each parish church. The cathedrals came alive; for example the nave of St. Paul's in London had never been used, except on state occasions, until choral evensong was instituted on Sundays. The number of clergy in secular work dropped radically, although the salary of a curate (about 70 pounds) was still low—roughly equivalent to that of a coachman. Despite the great ritual controversies that were to rock the Church, there is no doubt that a renewed piety and sense of vocation prevailed, even if the changes in ministerial function were only superficial. There was a sense in which the clergyman was now viewed as someone set apart, "different," perhaps as never before in the history of the Church—a not unmixed blessing resulting from a middle-class Protestant ethic touched by a romantic pseudo-medieval mysticism. "In 1830 it was a matter for comment if a clergyman could be distinguished from a layman in ordinary life, in 1860 it was a matter for comment if he could not be so distinguished." [45]

The problem was that all of this came at the end of the "modern" era. As the Oxford Movement and the subsequent Catholic Revival in Anglicanism sought to awaken our ministry to a reality that had passed three or four hundred years before (to make what Dietrich Bonhoeffer calls the *salto mortale*, the "death-leap" back into the middle ages),[46] the very reality that bred its leaders was slipping out from under them. Once again, as in sixteenth-century, German scholarship, this time under the aegis of men such as Friedrich Schleiermacher (1768–1834) and Ferdinand Baur (1792–1860), would force upon English theology the cold winds of change. Rome suppressed its prophets and called Vatican I (1869–70). Anyone who is even slightly aware of the change in the spirit of Vatican II knows that far more than ninety years separates those two august councils. They did not meet in the same world.

The task of this chapter is to speak to the reality of the modern period (1517–1914) and to describe the form of ministry that functioned within it. We refer to its demise here only in passing, leaving for the introduction to Part II the emergence of the contemporary world view. However, since not a few churchmen today find it difficult to understand the radical shift in the world view that has occurred over the past hundred years, we need to hold in mind this much. What Sören Kierkegaard (1813–1855) demanded in his *Attack on Christendom* in 1854, history was already effecting; Dansette pointed out one effect of the French Revolution, which characterized the beginning of a continuing instability for France and her church ever since; Germany and Italy did not arise as modern states until the nineteenth century, and their relations with the Church have never achieved complete equilibrium. Furthermore, the European mind, after the convulsive events in France and the sweeping implications of the philosophy of Immanuel Kant (1724–1804) and his successors, set about to restructure its assumptive base completely.

Martin Marty, in describing what he calls the "modern schism," by which he means the relocation of religion from the world in which man lives and thinks to a private world in which he really only feels, points to the forces that brought about the radical change in Christian thinking on the Continent.[47] Industrialism, urbanization, and nationalism, joined with all that the names Compte, Marx, Darwin, and Freud symbolize, simply brought to an end—an end less well perceived in England and almost unnoticed in America—the reality upon which the modern churchman based a ministry of the Word.

Raymond Cunningham, in his very perceptive article "From Preacher of the Word to Physician of the Soul," to which we have previously referred, clearly illustrates how even at the end of the nineteenth century preaching could be considered the *raison d'etre* of the Protestant pastor, whereas today it is counseling.[48] If Roman priests were poor preachers it was not because they did not accept the same thesis. Their emphasis was teaching, as witness the vast parochial school system growing out of the nineteenth century. The other ministerial functions went on: a growing, ideologically confused evangelism; a discipline less and less able to be enforced; pastoral care with an ear to the homiletical opportunity; administration evolving into an increasing congregational pattern; and a prophetic spirit quickly suppressed at the beginning of this period and struggling to be heard at the end. Last of all, the liturgical ministry was badly battered by Roman Catholic pietism and some indiscriminate adoption of its worst elements by nineteenth-century Anglicanism. Throughout the whole period God the Father remained the remote tyrant and the Christ grew into the "pale Galilean" or "sweet Jesus," neither of which was like any human condition that we know. This we would attribute to the perhaps inevitable lack of the sacramental person who could bestow upon the concept of the personal God an integrity, a participation in life at all levels, and a humanity that would act as a corrective to our intellectualism, sentimentality, and cynicism.

## chapter 5

# THE
# FIRST
# NINETEEN
# CENTURIES

The purpose of Part I has been to explore the historical implications of the theological presupposition that the function of ministry is to make explicit, in a given culture, the Church as the primal sacrament of Christ (the *Ursakrament*).[1] Within the limitations of the impossible task we set ourselves, a certain agenda has developed: (1) the nature of ministerial function is apparent; (2) the form of the "incarnation" of its ultimate transcendence in a given culture has become manifest; and (3) a number of assumptions about the shape and development of a ministry in the world have been refined or even challenged.

To speak of Christ's incarnation and to refer to the Church as the primal sacrament is to assume the nature of God's ways with man. It is an assumption rooted in the belief that, as found in the contemporary thought of Wolfhart Pannenberg (a leading German theologian) and his associates, God's revelation is that of his indirect self-disclosure in history. Furthermore, I believe that it is in the *history of persons* and their lives within the chosen community Israel and in the broader community of mankind that we meet God as personal. Ultimately its supreme expression is in the *person* of Christ, his life, death, and resurrection. Here we perceive the promise of the fulfillment of our personhood. As Christ's ministry was that of his person, so the ministry of the *Ursakrament*, the Church, is of the person. We have seen, therefore, that the essence of Christian ministry is that individual who embodies in his person the Church's vocation. This is what I have called the "sacramental person," and I have said that ministerial function derives itself from this source.

There is no doubt that the Church has in one way or another attempted to focus its ministry in the sacramental person. Without any attempt to absolutize the early Church— which should be avoided at all costs, for it can be extremely stultifying—it would seem that since the third century the Church has been less than successful in that objective. Some of the problems in ministry that we have recognized in successive centuries seem to be rooted in this depersonalization of ministry and the adoption of more and more mechanical models.

We have identified eight ministerial functions which, with varying degrees of emphasis, have been present at all times in the life of the Church in one form or another. There is a universal quality to these functions, and if they are lacking, the Church's ministry is deficient. These are preaching, teaching, prophecy, caring, evangelizing, ritualizing, administration, and discipline. I shall make no attempt to rank them as to their importance, even though at given points in history a choice has obviously been made.

These eight functions do not correspond, I am aware, to Samuel Blizzard's oft-cited six categories of preacher, priest, pastor, teacher, organizer, and administrator. In part, this is because our approach has been historical, and Blizzard's is apparently analytical. Organization is only a contemporary function of the clergyman, and I shall have a few comments to make about how valuable a role it is in the next section. Furthermore, Blizzard forgets discipline, although it may be included under the role of the pastor. I would insist that preaching is a churchly, if not always liturgical, discourse, of the nature of paranesis (the proclamation of ethical admonition), or instructive address (after the order of the Greek homily). Evangelism is not churchly, it is more kerygmatic, and does not have to be verbal (e.g., living among a people to set a Christian example for the purpose of conversion is evangelism). Prophecy does not necessarily have to be verbal either, but is always future oriented, whether in terms of judgment or apocalypse. Preaching has been a carefully guarded prerogative in the history of the Church, even more than sacerdotal functions. Evangelism has been as much or more a lay function than not. Prophecy is always charismatic.

Three discrete cultural epochs are discernible within the history of Christian ministry. The ministry of the ancient Church (30–325) we would characterize as expressed within a generally persecuted community, living in a homogeneous, ordered civilization. A high priority is set on oral literacy, promoted by a reasonably cosmopolitan life within the Roman municipalities. It is the time in which the sacramental person is the focus of ministerial function. The transcendent dynamic of ministry expresses itself primarily in an eschatological sense. The sacramental person was a man who lived on the edge of the dawn, the servant of a Lord whose invitation to the Messianic banquet was in his hand.

The medieval Church (313–1517) passed through many periods of storm and stress, peaking in the reforms of Gregory VII. Despite the very crucial changes for which that great pope called, and in the face of the obvious cultural differences that prevailed between, say, the Carolingian Empire, the Scholastic movement, and the War of the Roses we would insist that the heterogeneous populace, the stratified feudal society, the fragmented sociopolitical climate, the ideal of Christendom, and the injection of a sort of popular Platonism that joined itself to the animistic feeling of the Germanic mind, produced a world view that made the sacramental rite the particular context for Christian service in those twelve hundred years. The understanding of transcendence expressed itself supremely for these times in the sense of the supernatural, both demonic and angelic. For the medieval mind the

Mass was the most translucent window into a reality for which the entire world possessed varying degrees of opacity.

For the modern Church (1517–1914) technology made possible the awakening of Western man to his own cognitive abilities. Order was reconstituted, not just about the Roman Law, but around the powers of reason and the written word. Nationalism created cultural homogeneity, and education became a goal to be treasured. The middle class devoted itself to work, duty, and family for their own sake. In such a world the sacramental word became the incarnate expression of Christ's ministry, even when its appeal was to the heart and not just the mind. Such a ministerial function had behind it the transcendent *logos*, that divine order that pervaded all creatures at the will of God the Father.

By looking back through all these centuries a certain perspective develops that enables us to make some judgments about the nature of ministerial function that an immediate involvement in the crisis of the moment often does not allow.

First, ministerial function is related only loosely to any ontological theories of ministerial order. There is a narrowing first of routine ritualizing and then later preaching in the presbyterate, but all other functions tend to be quite fluid. With the advent of the modern period there is a further tendency to focus all active ministerial functions in the presbyterate,[2] leaving to the episcopate (where it exists) only the questions of higher policy in administration and the incidental ritual functions. The diaconate disappears after the twelfth and thirteenth centuries, despite all efforts to revive it, as a significant realm of ministerial function. The trifold order of deacon, priest, and bishop is maintained in Anglicanism as a sacramental guarantee of the dominical nature of the Church and its ministry, but this dogmatic question seems to have little relevance to the pastoral one. Furthermore, in Roman Catholicism the nature of the trifold arrangement is never clear; for the episcopate may well be the priesthood in its fullness, which would then require the subdiaconate as the lowest order.[3] Certainly ordination to each order successively, as one "climbs the hierarchical ladder," has no substantial theological basis and is not of universal historical practice.

Kilian MacDonnell says that "the formation of the doctrine of ministry was the result of a theological reflection on the pastoral needs." [4] This is a historical fact, but not always the approach of the systematic theologian. The development of an ontology of ministry is, as we have already suggested, in response to a way of thinking about the priest's role in the Eucharist at a time when such reflection is divorced from any doctrine of the Church as the mystical Body. Joseph Fichter insists that it missed the very simple point that we are what we do, not the other way around.[5] Any doctrine of the ministry must therefore ultimately fall back on function. But contrary to Fichter, I would agree with MacDonnell that for an order to exist it must have a distinct function, and therefore the presbyterate developed that which it calls its own throughout history: ministering the Sacraments and preaching the Word.[6]

Second, once the Church becomes deeply involved in the power structures of the society (313 on), there is a growing desire to set the clergy apart from the rest of mankind in dress, work, education, family, and morality. It appears to be a need of the Church that holds dear the concept of Christendom. The ideal of the priest who wears distinctive garb, does no secular labor, can read and write, is celibate, and does not enter taverns seems to be almost an overreaction to a Church that has become intimately involved in the taxes, wars, intrigues, and affections of the natural man and his state. There is a great ambiguity here in the life of the Church, whose motivation is complex, but it appears related to the wish to assure itself that despite its worldliness its leaders among the people are otherworldly. There were practical and disciplinary reasons as well as moral ones. Its effect, among other things, was to mark off the ministry as the Church, as opposed to the laity, whose status grew progressively more passive. This occurs particularly as ministerial function is ontologized and the Church is highly developed and hypostasized. The interesting thing is that the Church best succeeds in bringing this goal to pass in the nineteenth and early twentieth century, when in fact it had ceased to have a significant role in the daily routine of society.

Third, until the emergence of a middle-class ministry in the nineteenth century, there is a clear distinction between a lower and a higher clergy in most places. Salaries of the lower clergy seem to have been widely equivalent to those of semi-skilled laborers or the lower civil servants. The situation did not change when the middle-class clergy arose, but they were apparently able to supplement their income from independent means other than secondary employment (such as farming, making ale, etc.). There is also a clear correlation between salary and education, though not necessarily between education, salary, and effectiveness (though no one has ever succeeded in discovering any way to measure this beyond the *very* deceptive matter of numbers). A universal standard of education of the clergy was never more than an ideal prior to the contemporary period, although the higher clergy were always well educated in the modern period and frequently so before that. However, education in the first fifteen hundred years was the general learning of a man trained to read, write, and think. Since then there is an increasing desire for "professional education in ministry," but we are never quite clear as to what that is beyond a grasp of various confessions. One of the problems of current talk of distinctive education in a sacred profession is that we have very little history of this apart from the higher education of any learned man. As Fichter says, "A clear function distinction between secular and sacred seems to be of relatively recent origin." [7]

Fourth, the personal dimensions of ministerial function (one to one or one to a family) were almost entirely a caring by comforting, often in terms of a dole, and a disciplining, frequently in terms of a call to repentance. The present state of a man's life was generally covered by a homiletical summons to his duty in his station in life. If the pastor fed the hungry, clothed the naked, ministered to the sick—which was done with remarkable-consistency—it was generally in the context that this world's present sufferings were a preparation for a better home beyond the grave. Prophecy usually took on this apocalyptic dimension and lacked the social concern of the Old Testament worthies (for whom the only life was that within the community of Israel here in this world). When it adopted a moral tone it was directed more toward personal sins, drunkenness, murder, adultery, apostasy, than social sins. The biblical idea of the corporate person and of social sin was quickly lost to Hellenistic individualism. It is important to note that prophecy was always directed to the Christian community even when it was spoken to the State; for the concept of Christendom was that Church and State worked hand-in-glove to bring about God's will.

Fifth, ministry is never organized in a programmatic way; in other words, the local congregation does not sit down and say, "What should we be doing?" Unlike contemporary efforts to encourage "parish planning," it was assumed that we knew what we should be doing. Ministerial function was in response to the command of Christ, the natural expectation of the people, and in reaction to obvious need. When after the dissolution of the western Roman Empire the schools of the rhetors closed, the Church provided the education needed and continued to so do until the State reassumed the obligation in the nineteenth century. Education was never divorced into two absolute categories: religious and secular. The same was true for hospitals and orphanages. Only at the end of the modern period, as the ministry of the Church became isolated from the mainstream of man's sociopolitical life, do we find the conscious planning of "programs for parishes." Such isolation was unknown in the eighteen hundred years under consideration in this section; for the Church was never subject, particularly while it was being persecuted, to the devastating dismissal of being irrelevant.

Although it has taken us a hundred years to become clearly aware of the direction of history, it is quite apparent that today this is precisely what is happening to the Church. It is therefore our task now to analyze what is the response of ministry to the climate that creates the conviction that we live in a post-Christian age. As shall be seen, part of the problem of such a response has been too little appreciation of the flexibility and multiple form of ministry in the past, which has limited our understanding of the many ways in which Christ can make himself known in his Church.

# PART II

## THE
## CONTEMPORARY
## FUNCTION
## OF MINISTRY

## chapter 6

# THE
# FOURTH
# CHRISTIAN
# EPOCH

Ernst Bloch, the eminent Marxist philosopher, has written, "Today no man, not even the most pious, believes in God in the same way in which the most lukewarm and skeptical believed in him two hundred years ago." [1] Probably Bloch underestimates the ability of a few to remain impervious to the reality of the times, but speaking generally there is no doubt of the truth of his statement. Where once the Roman Catholic Church could proclaim that "error has no rights," at Vatican II it sought to protect the freedom of private conscience. Where in the eighteenth century a Christian might confidently look to his Bible for answers in the realm of biology and history, Langdon Gilkey quite rightly points out that since the nineteenth century "theological truths no longer contained the sort of knowledge which entails particular factual propositions." [2] Few people today would swallow whole the systems of Henri Saint-Simon, Charles Darwin, or even Sigmund Freud; but no intelligent person, even though a devout Christian, can live today as if positivism, the theory of evolution, and psychoanalysis have not changed the whole context of reality.

This is not to exclude other forces of the past hundred years, for these three men and their schools only symbolize an incredible change in the quantity, shape, and dynamic of learning. It has been commonly said that the extent of man's factual accumulation doubled from 1900 to 1950, and doubled again in the following twenty years. In 1850 it took just as long to get from Rome to Istanbul as it did fifteen hundred years before. Now we can travel to the moon in a shorter time. The most terrible battle of the War of 1812, where two thousand Englishmen died (and thirteen Americans), was fought at New Orleans more than two weeks after the war ended because communication was no faster than it had been for thousands of years. Yet what American over forty is unaware of where he was *at the very moment* the bombs were dropping on Pearl Harbor? Prior to World War II the average physician had about four drugs available to him—aspirin, belladonna or atropine, quinine, and the opium derivatives (principally morphine)—and today there are hundreds. No wonder life expectancy in the United States jumped from 48 years for males and 51 for females in 1900–02 to 66.8 for males and 73.4 for females in 1962.[3] This contributes to the nightmare of the population explosion, and all its ecological implications, where the population is now doubling in 35 years, compared to doubling in 70, 200, and 1,000 years before.[4]

It is often argued that these external factors really do not change man and the meaning of "truth" for him, because the individual has been the same through the centuries. Given the fact that since the human cranial capacity has evolved from 500 cc. to 1500 cc., but now appears to have remained relatively stable in size for thousands of years; and acknowledging the possibility that some of the fascinating speculations of some of the ethnologists might just be true; and granting the truth that beneath the technology the barbarity of Auschwitz seems no less tempered than the Roman arena; I still want to reinforce that theory of reality to which we pointed in Chapter 1 and insist that even man's persistent proclivity for evil is a function of his situation. Without doubt this claim itself of the historical nature of "original sin" and of man's natural dependence upon his "field" or "system" is expressive of this contemporary period. For there are few students of humanity today who, quite unlike their grandfathers, do not in some way acknowledge that man, though he must needs be responsible, is none the less a function of his environment. John Donne said it 350 years ago, "no man is an island," but it has taken us until now to discover something of its radical meaning.

Our claim is that the twentieth century is, at the least, as crucial a time for readjustment of man's perception of his world, *his sense of what is real*, as was the first, the fourth, and the sixteenth (with an acknowledgment of the twelfth). The implication that follows from this claim is that ministry must change its pattern today to fulfill its God-given vocation in this new world, as it did three times previously. I hasten to add that it *has* changed in accordance with the principle of an effective incarnation of the transcendent for our times.

But first I want to examine in further detail the nature of the shift from the modern period to the contemporary, for this forms a fundamental context for the rest of this study. Many scholars are telling us how 1970 is different from 1850. I cannot begin to exhaust their findings, but these four points will be indicative of what is being said.

First, there is no allegiance in our society to an inherent, universal principle of coherence. This concept, upon which metaphysics is based (the metaphysics of "process theology" derived from Alfred North Whitehead [1861–1947], which is founded upon the certainty of change, is an exception), goes in the face of man's present sense of his contingency, relativity, and temporality. I do not want to appear to deny the possibility of all metaphysics except those based on Whitehead. Bernard Lonergan certainly offers a convincing argument for the possibility and, indeed, absolute necessity for metaphysics. But his system, while *appearing* to affirm the pre-contemporary approach, does in fact place metaphysics within the structure of knowing (that is, within subjectivity) and the moving historical horizon. In this regard, he is much more akin to the process theologians than the classical metaphysicians. Langdon Gilkey, who discusses at length these three characteristics of modern man (and one more, as we shall see), defines "contingency" as the sense that the causes of our existence are neither necessary, rational, or purposive; "relativity" as the sense that everything is subject to change; and "temporality" as the sense that all things come to an end.[5] Some years before Gilkey, Hans von Balthasar described how man's perception of his world has moved from the cosmological, where everything including himself had its foreordained place and it was simply a matter of knowing what that was, to where he sees everything now from the viewpoint of his own subjectivity.[6] He calls this the "anthropological shift." In this light, we cannot underestimate the force on contemporary man of Ludwig Feuerbach's (1804–1872) argument that theology is in fact anthropology, man's projection of his own subjectivity. It marks a turning point in Christianity's entire apologetic to which von Balthasar is speaking. (In a real sense ministry or pastoral theology is a department of apologetics, and so this remains a very important question for this study.)

He who does not believe in the ultimate coherence of life, such as his counterpart in the modern period conceived, is not only he who is sceptical of metaphysics, but is also he for whom appeals for moral behavior on the basis of natural law are unconvincing. If Joseph Fletcher and the "new morality" are not altogether persuasive—its anthropology fails to take into account man's social dimension and the depth of his personality—documents such as *Humanae vitae* operate in categories that are incomprehensible to contemporary man. It is one of the ironies of the pastor's role today that often his parishioners demand of him a moral certainty which his very personal morality forbids him to assume as he perceives the reality of which he and his people are a part.

A number of analysts of our time have attempted a description of contemporary man, for whom life is no longer the working out of his providential role in a coherent world of God's making. Herbert Marcuse does so in criticizing the one-dimensional man, who has surrendered his idealism, imagination, creativity, and spontaneity to the horror of commercially dictated taste and the obscenity of mass production.

Today's novel feature is the flattening out of the antagonism between culture and social reality through the obliteration of the oppositional, alien, and transcendent elements in the higher culture by virtue of which it constituted *dimension* of reality. This liquidation of *two-dimensional* culture takes place not through the denial and rejection of "cultural values," but through their wholesale incorporation into the established order, through their reproduction and display on a massive scale.[7]

What he is talking about is the rise of kitsch, the popularity of *Playboy*, and the "Madison Avenue Freud," which the cultural critic may recognize as common to the great American "silent majority."

Philip Rieff is less critical and more descriptive in his discussion of "psychological man," who in the light of his own awareness of his inner dynamics as a member of the post-Freudian age chooses to live somewhere between his inherited repressions and his neighbor. Recognizing that there are no absolutes that require of him a denial of his instinctual life, yet acknowledging that lack of inhibition is self-defeating, "psychological man" suffers from neither moral passion nor social commitment.

Freud taught lessons which Americans, prepared by their own national experience, learn easily: survive, resign yourself to living within your moral means, suffer no gratuitous failures in a futile search for ethical heights that no longer exist—if they ever did . . . With no place to go for lessons in the conduct of contemporary life, every man must learn, as Freud teaches, to make himself at home in his own grim and gay little Vienna . . . The grimness is relieved by the gaiety of being free from the historic Western compulsion of seeking large and general meanings for small and highly particular lives . . . With Freud, individualism took a great and perhaps final step: toward the mature and calm feeling which comes from having nothing to hide . . . To be truly free and yet social means to cultivate detachment as opposed to alienation . . . Freed from all suspicions of divinity psychological man can continue to work efficiently in all kinds of institutions, but without permitting his feelings to be entrapped by institutional service.[8]

Perhaps the thought arises, "What, then should churchmen do? The answers return clearly: "become, avowedly, therapists, administrating a therapeutic institution." [9] As Rieff says, this would require a new form of seminary training.[10]

Obviously Marcuse is one of those people "seeking large and general meanings," whom Rieff severely criticizes; but they both describe contemporary man as one who has clearly abdicated any sense of universal meaning and transcendent direction to life. It is interesting that Moltmann lays the blame for this present frame of mind upon Platonism and Cartesianism and its doctrine of man as one who *has—has* a body, *has* a spouse, *has* a job—rather than one who *is* his body, is his marriage, is his vocation.[11] But there is also a break from the Cartesian theory of knowledge in contemporary man, and this is my second point. Peter Homans, in his discussion of three contemporary interpreters of Freud—Marcuse, Bakan, and Rieff—says that the last-mentioned leaves the master in a sharp subject-object dichotomy.[12] In this regard Rieff's "psychological man" may not be a comprehensive description of contemporary man. For there is an indication of an awakening in our culture to a participatory, or what Michael Polanyi calls personal knowledge, which contrary to Descartes demonstrates the artificiality of the subject-object dichotomy.

All knowledge consists in a *from-to* [*from* the inner core of my being *to* the focal centre of attention] relation . . . Unlike the traditional ideal of wholly explicit, self-guaranteeing truth, from-to knowledge cannot be instantaneous; it is a stretch, not only of attention, but of effort, effort must be lived, and living takes time. Knowledge, therefore, is embedded both in the living process . . . and in the uniquely human form of living process: in history. Yet, be it noted, the emphasis on the personal participation of the knower, and on knowing as a form of living process, does not entail, in Polanyi's theory, a retreat to an irrational subjectivity. . . . It is, indeed, quite true, as Polanyi and others have convincingly argued, that pure objectivity, pure exteriority, is impotent to account for the existence of conscious life, or, indeed, of any life at all.[13]

Thomas S. Kuhn in *The Structure in Scientific Revolutions* has shown convincingly the role of the scientist in the paradigmatic nature of knowledge in "normal science," and shares Polanyi's commitment to tacit knowledge and intuition.[14]

Neither Polanyi nor Kuhn is suggesting that their theories of knowledge are unsystematic, much less irrational. But as they both call for an awareness of the person in all his complexity as part of the knowing process, they cannot avoid the role of the body and the emotions in the act of knowing as well as the mind. This is a clear break from the theories of knowledge that undergirded the intellectual life of the modern period and the principal thrust of the Church's ministry.

For example, there has been a recovery in the contemporary period of the function of language. Thanks to linguistic analysis and research into the unconscious meaning of words, we know now that they are not precise rational signs, pointing to some objective reality. We know that their meaning is related to the particular use of those words by the individual and his community, including the unconscious history of both, encompassing passion as well as cognition. We are conscious of the symbolic value of words, that they are means of participating in the power and meaning of that for which they stand, and of their analogic value over their digital significance.[15] The German school of the New Hermeneutic, following the later Heidegger, goes so far as to tell us that words have the power to call man into being as we encounter their meaning.

Martin Buber opened to Christian thought the whole question of the interpersonal in the life of man as a means of his coming to be and to know himself. There are many offshoots of this kind of thinking, some of which Buber would never recognize as related to his own thought, but which have at least a tenuous connection with this theory of knowledge. Michael Novak has described the somewhat romantic embrace of community, sex, and nature by the more radical youth as a way of knowing.[16] The whole sensitivity movement, with its desire to free people to share feelings, is an effort to find new approaches to knowing. Nonverbal exercises, of which the epitome may be the group-oriented mutual caressing of one another's naked bodies, may appear sick to some and terrifying to others (and undoubtedly have dimensions of both), but are in fact also a logical expression of a body theology and a participatory theory of knowledge.

Third, there is an awakening in contemporary man to new meanings for old words: "freedom" and "the future." On the one hand, perhaps we are discovering what a tenuous gift freedom is after the euphoria of the last years of the modern period. On the other hand, as Gilkey says, Hegel and his philosophy of history has probably done more to shape the mind of contemporary man than anyone else.[17] History holds out the promise of a future, and the future gives man the possibility of autonomy (which is the fourth characteristic of contemporary thought listed by Gilkey).[18] Churchmen cannot ignore the charge of the Marxists that religion is the opiate of the people; for without a doubt it has been so employed, particularly in modern times. The tendency of modern ministry was to call upon people to endure the present misery in hope of heaven, and to offer some an emotional outlet that made oppression and lonely drudgery (as in the factories or on the American frontier) more tolerable. In responding to this, Christianity is faced with recapturing the meaning of the God of history that was lost over sixteen hundred years ago; but to recapture it devoid of a Greek dualism.

The Marxist accusation has particularly reawakened Western man to the theodicy question: How can God justify evil? or How are we to be consoled for the misery of living?

Marxism answers these questions in terms of a promise of freedom at the end of history. The drug culture says that it will simply "cop out" and die "high." Rieff suggests that we ignore the question and it will go away.[19] Ernest Becker, a social psychologist, has the interesting solution that we turn the question from a plea for a theodicy to a demand for an anthropodicy. If man is the captive of evil, we ought to be aware of our power as man to "create free, confident, self-aware individuals," who can "unite an ontology of natural revelation with a reliance of reason," and give to man the autonomy he seeks.[20] Becker's argument in all his books and articles is that man is free: he only needs to throw off the oppressive notions of people like Freud, Darwin, Ardrey, etc., and seize his freedom.

The Western obsession with planning is one practical expression of Becker's theory. Daniel Bell in *The Year* 2000, a project of the Hudson Institute, suggests that we want to look ahead because of the nearness of the millennial year 2000, the lure of space, the recurrence of an impulse toward omnipotence, and, most important, because of a need for economic planning.[21] Behind this lies the keen awareness that man can no longer leave things to happenstance, lest, for example, we find ourselves, as Paul Ehrlich suggests, with sixty people for every square yard of earth.[22]

Fourth, this opens the question of the impact of technology and the second industrial revolution (the first having brought to an end the modern period). As I sit and write this page, I look out on a scene first inhabited by my fellow churchmen about 130 years ago. To live here then a man had to build his own house, grow his own crops, dig his own well, wash his own clothes by hand in the lake below, chop vast quantities of wood (it regularly gets to 20 below zero in this part of Wisconsin), shovel his own snow, trim and clean his own lamps, and on rare occasions ride by horse the day's journey to the little village of Milwaukee to get supplies. Now none of these things are problems to me. I do none of these chores, and can get to Milwaukee in twenty-five minutes or telephone there instantaneously.

McLuhan has very aptly pointed out to us the radical difference our technology and particularly our electronic communications media have made in our lives. Not only do we have the ability to be in instant communication with the world, but we also have the time to participate in life over and above what it takes to stay alive. This, except for the very wealthy, is a contemporary phenomenon. But it raises an acute problem of what to do with our growing leisure time. One of the characteristics of our age, pointed out back in the fifties by Paul Elmen, is boredom.[23] Unless we are trained to use leisure for what I have called "participation in life," we are threatened with all the problems that come with a sense of uselessness and its incumbent frustrations. How much alcoholism, drug addiction, adultery, suicide (conscious or unconscious) is the result of too much time and too little purpose?

It is out of response, perhaps, to the opportunity and problem of leisure time that a call is being made for contemporary man to discover the meaning of art and play. We would be greatly taxed to find two ideas more alien to the modern middle class mind than art and play for their own sake as descriptive of the necessary dimensions of the true *humanus*. McLuhan says that the person most needed in his "global village" is the artist, the person who is "integrally aware." [24] Humanistic psychology often places at the pinnacle of human maturation the artist, the person who possesses the kind of creativity "best exemplified by the improvisation, as in jazz or in childlike paintings." [25] Even Rieff has suggested art as an appropriate therapeutic activity for his "psychological man." [26] It was twenty years ago that Johan Huizinga undertook to explore the element of play in human nature, and since that time there has been a growing exploration by psychologists, philosophers, and theologians of the necessity of play for the fullness of humanity.[27] These two elements—art and play—the positive side of the technological revolution, offer to ministry opportunities very different from those provided by the dour bourgeoisie of preceding centuries. I hope this becomes apparent as we explore the relationship of imagination in ministry to hope and the future.

My intention is not to suggest that the four elements that are distinctive to the contemporary period as opposed to the modern just discussed—loss of universal coherence, a different model of knowledge, a renewed sense of freedom and the future, and the impact of technology—are generally to be credited to the "loss" or "gain" column. They are an attempt to describe what appears to be characteristic of the prevailing tenor of our age, and are not necessarily *consciously* held by the majority of people. They do, however, help constitute the reality that is all of ours in one way or another.

Therefore, this rather lengthy and closely documented introduction forms a necessary prolegomenon to the analysis of contemporary forms of ministerial function. My intention now is to examine out of this background (1) the present-day parish ministry, (2) the persistence of the image of the post-Reformation parson, and (3) three contemporary experiments in reaction in the psychological, social psychological, and sociological models. The question we must continue to ask is whether our ministry effectively confronts us in this present culture with the transcendent power of God in a form that has promise for man as he perceives reality. My contention will be that on the whole we have failed, through a combination of factors such as a lack of imagination and courage, and the age-old trap of idolatry.

## chapter 7

# THE
# TEAHOUSE
# ON
# ELM STREET

When the vast majority of the present clergy of the Episcopal Church first began their educational preparation for the ministry, they wanted to be parish priests.[1] Their reasons for desiring this were, largely, either because it was all they knew or because they thought the parish offered opportunities for personal relationships with people.[2] In 1968, 64.5 percent (7,421) of the clergy of the Episcopal Church were serving in parochial cures compared to 69.2 percent (7,697) in 1966. Of the active clergy, 72.6 percent were in this number. "From 1966 to 1968, the number of non-parochial clergymen (those in non-parochial ministries, secularly employed, retired, and 'others') increased by 666 persons." There was a loss in parochial clergy of 1.9 percent.[3] Not even two-thirds of the clergy of the Episcopal Church now serve parishes, and the number and percentage are decreasing. There is every reason to believe that the situation is relatively the same in many other denominations. What is the cause?

One point is that the number of congregations has declined by 9 percent (770) in the last fifty years.[4] This reduction in numbers promises to continue. James L. Lowery has made a very good case for maintaining that a viable congregation in the Episcopal Church—and the same is true elsewhere—consists of no less than two hundred communicants or just under one hundred pledging units and a budget of $20,000.[5] By "viable" Lowery means a congregation according to current canonical standards capable of supporting a priest at subsistence level and "keeping the doors open." It does *not* mean a congregation in which all ministerial functions are vital. Of all congregations in the Episcopal Church in 1967, 62 percent were under this level, and the figure for 1952 was approximately the same. These 4,512 congregations, which had 14 percent of the total church population, were served by 45 percent of the Episcopal clergy (2,339).[6]

Figures such as these make clear, first of all, that there is a growing mathematical gap between ministry and parish; that is, there are more people who consider themselves trained "to minister" than there are parishes in which to exercise this ministry. Furthermore, there is an attitudinal change in that many do not see the parish as the only or even primary focus for ministry. It is my conviction that this attitude is completely foreign to the average layman, for whom the parish is the only "real" place for the overt life of the Church. He is a member of a congregation, which he has joined in a number of possible ways and which he identifies with his pastor, and he sees *its life as the ministry* of the Church. It does not matter to him that it can be argued that it has been this way for only a thousand years or so, or that the contemporary shape of congregational life he takes for granted is really an expression of the inept groping of the parish for purpose.

Yet the truth is that today this is just what congregational life is: *a search for purpose.* From where I live at Nashotah House, founded in 1841 as a training school for mission priests, there are or have been until recently seven or eight Episcopal churches within walking distance or an easy horseback ride. Not one of these churches began with anything but a building for the liturgy. If a parish house exists now, it is an addition since 1900. Visit the Episcopal churches of New York City, and you will find historic congregations often within walking distance of one another, worshiping in spacious sanctuaries, wedged between other buildings, constructed obviously without any prior thought to the needs of a parish house. Today we build "churches" on four- and five-acre plots, only miles from the adjoining parish, and start with a "multipurpose building," wistfully dreaming of a time when perhaps we might complete our "final church."

Nancy Master, in a doctoral dissertation now almost completed, has studied the rise of the Episcopal parish house from 1865 to 1910.[7] Focusing her attention upon noteworthy parishes such as St. George's, New York City; St. John's, Washington, D.C.; Christ Church, Louisville, Kentucky; Christ Church, Cincinnati, Ohio; Christ Church, Dayton, Ohio; St. John's, Detroit; and St. Mark's, Grand Rapids, Michigan, Master maintains that the parish-house movement is principally a post-Civil War phenomenon beginning in the East. Although there was a parallel movement in England at the same time (e.g. Toynbee House was founded in 1882 in London), the American development was an indigenous response to *social needs*. William Augustus Muhlenberg, a prophetic figure in the Episcopal Church, was responsible for building a parish house at Holy Communion, New York City, and St. Mark's, Philadelphia, acquired a parish house in the 1840s; but the real spurt of construction occurred between 1880 and 1910, with the Episcopal Church setting an example for other denominations. These structures were five or six stories high and had classrooms, an assembly hall, a kitchen, a gym, parlors, and even billiard rooms, all provided with the intention of ministering to the physical, recreational, and educational needs of immigrants and laboring people. They were intended only secondarily for their own members!

The great pioneer in this development in the Episcopal Church was the rector of St. George's, New York City, W. S. Rainsford. It was his way of meeting, rather than running from, the challenge of the inner city. It is important to note that Rainsford was committed to the Social Gospel, and that the parish-house movement was in its first phase a part of this pastoral and theological point of view. For in its second phase, after World War I, when the Social Gospel fell into bad repute, the parish house came to be used for very different and, in my mind, less defensible purposes.

The initial development of the parish house, albeit in itself not necessarily bad, is symptomatic of the attempt of the local congregation at the end of the modern period and the beginning of the contemporary, to find its raison d'être. The power of the sacramental word was on the wane. A post-Enlightenment Romantic age had, often in studied anachronisms, embraced the sacramental rite. But the appeal was largely to the aesthetical sensitivities of the highly educated or to the emotions of the economically depressed, without ever really catching the imagination of the practical and sometimes sceptical mind of the industrial and mercantile classes. The nineteenth-century middle-class parson, with some notable exceptions, found it difficult to function as a sacramental person. Religion of the period tended toward either a sterile intellectualism or a puerile emotionalism, and never really freed the person to find the person of God.

The Church had been abruptly thrust out of the political and social spheres in what Martin Marty describes as the "modern schism," and in seeking some organizing principle for its ministry, turned to the *parish program*. What in effect happened was that a number of talented, committed, and educated people assumed leadership in the Church just at the time the Church lost *its* leadership in society. The energy an Augustine would have expended in leading men from one culture to another, that Hildebrand utilized in changing the political structure of Western Europe, and that Luther spent in establishing the foundation of modern culture—such energy was now turned to directing the Church's moral witness to the needs of the industrial society, even while the Christian symbols about which the Church leaders rallied were fast losing their power in the minds of men.

Examples of such efforts would include Christian Socialism, begun in England in 1848 under F. D. Maurice (1805–

1872), Charles Kingsley (1819–1875), and others as a mild protest against obvious social injustice. Its American equivalent expressed concern for Indians and working men, and in 1872 the Christian Labour Union was formed. In 1887 the (Episcopal) Church Association for the Advancement of the Interests of Labor was created. Leadership for work among those captured in the inhumanity of industry included such strange bedfellows as Fr. J. O. S. Huntington (1854–1935), founder of the Order of the Holy Cross, and Leighton Williams of the Amity Baptist Church; other related movements included the Women's Christian Temperance Union, founded in 1874 out of the Chautauqua movement. Liberal religion inspired Dorothea Dix (1802–1887), who worked on behalf of the mentally ill; Clara Barton (1821–1912), who founded the American Red Cross; and Susan B. Anthony (1820–1906), one of the great leaders of the women's suffrage movement.

This surge of organized outreach achieved a theological status in the Social Gospel, which sought in various ways to bring the Kingdom to pass on this earth. Washington Gladden (1836–1918), who is considered its father, preached a religion of love for justice and service. Walter Rauschenbusch (1861–1918), its greatest prophet, taught the transformation of the social order. It is interesting that both these men, and others like them, came out of a Pietist background; yet as the gulf between the Church and the State became truly apparent for the first time in fifteen hundred years, they turned their attention to man's social self and to the present. They called upon the Church to speak and work in a way that was reminiscent of the Old Testament prophets. The irony was that, as they now had the perspective to see the hypocrisy of the world in which we had lived so comfortably for so long, their message had at the same time lost its power to move that society. As World War I passed, the Social Gospel became identified in the minds of many with pacifism, the dreaded radicalism of state ownership, and the labor movement. Many a Christian consequently lost his nerve and began to look for areas of ministry that were not so controversial. (David O. Moberg, in "Evangelical Christians in Contemporary Society: How to Reverse the Great Reversal" (a mimeographed paper published by the Theology Commission of the National Association of Evangelicals, 1969), cites a term for the change in attitude among Evangelicals concerning social issues after 1910 as the "great reversal." He attributes a move among theological conservatives away from social action to privatism as caused by a hardening of theological lines between conservatives and liberals, a draining of energy into the evolution question, a belief that Prohibition would solve all social ills, and a new premillenial spirit. Moberg's paper confirms our observations about the radical shift in the parish-house movement.)

There had always been, along with the social concerns of the Church since 1850, a program directed more toward the personal needs of individuals. As we have already seen, the Sunday School reached a high form of development and popularity in the late nineteenth and early twentieth centuries. At that time, the women's missionary organizations, capitalizing on what Stephen Neill has called "the heyday of colonialism," [8] spent many long meetings studying the conversion of the heathen. In the Episcopal Church the Women's Auxiliary to the Foreign Missions Board was founded in 1868, and in 1877 the Girls Friendly Organization was brought from England to the United States to help the working girl. The Order of the Daughters of the King and the Church Mission of Help had the same purpose. The Brotherhood of St. Andrew sought to enlist men in the service of our Lord. Devotional and educational organizations, many with a strong polemical purpose such as the Confraternity of the Blessed Sacrament and the Evangelical Education Society, met with enthusiastic response. Other denominations had their equivalents. The Church as a whole assisted with the Scouting movement after its founding in 1912. The establishment of religious orders in Anglicanism, as well as their rapid growth in the Roman Church, and the dedicated work of many Protestant clergymen and laymen, contributed substantially to the care of the sick and made up the deficiencies of public education.

But there has always been a growing tendency for organizations to exist for their own sake. Especially as truly creative and helpful work has become more and more expensive, bold efforts to meet real needs have become suspect, the pluralistic society less and less expectant of the Church, and the State increasingly willing to assume responsibility for the welfare of the people. It is not altogether unfair to say that many a parish church in the last fifty years has been unwilling to play the same unpopular role that crucified Christ and has turned its attention from meeting needs outside itself to those within itself. It has tended to establish an organizational structure that parallels the secular, either because a complicated "flow chart" or a crowded bulletin board demonstrates success (what clergyman has not heard his vestry ask, "What are we *doing* here at Trinity Church?"); or because there is a *selectivity* of companions in church functions that is not always present in secular organizations. There is perhaps also a genuine belief that we honor God a little more if we sponsor a baseball team in the name of Trinity Church rather than in that of the Downtown Kiwanis Club. A classic illustration of this mentality comes from a recruiting letter of a Roman Catholic organization in Richmond, Virginia.

The Knights of Columbus was formed some 87 years ago to meet the challenges of those times and ever since has adapted to meet every new challenge confronting it. . . .

If you would like to see how we are meeting today's challenges we would be most happy to show you. We are pleased to invite all men in the parish to an Open House to be held in St. Edward's parish center. . . . The highlight of the evening will be the showing of the movies of the 1969 Notre Dame football season including the Cotton Bowl game against Texas. If, at this time, you would like to participate in the task of meeting these challenges, we would welcome the opportunity of accepting your application for membership into our Council.[9]

The contemporary parish is for most people, I believe, either consciously or unconsciously a voluntary organization which people choose to join in order to meet certain personal expectations. (This is not, of course, its only possible socio-logical description.) It is not to the common mind the local manifestation of the Body of Christ to which people are called to their true end. This anomaly has never been more evident than it is now.

Documentation of this phenomenon is ample and is carried in a number of "classical" studies. J. R. Seeley and his colleagues, in a study of a Toronto suburb in the mid-fifties, described the parishes there as providing "worship and recreation," and attracting the *tentative* loyalty of people who think their children ought to be "exposed" to religion. The school, however, is the real integrating force in the community, not the Church.[10] Then, shortly after Seeley's study, Gibson Winter analyzed the identification of the Protestant Church with the *new* middle class and the exodus to the suburbs in what he called the "organization church" or the "introverted church." His thesis was that it required for existence a "socially homogeneous membership,"[11] and that it is "a vehicle of the social identity of middle-class people."[12] The guilt of the members (and who is not guilty?) is worked out "through sacrificial action for the organization."[13] He spoke of "the trivialization of the religious enterprise,"[14] and then went on to add this damning comment: "The introverted church is one which puts its own survival before its mission, its own identity above its task, its internal concerns before its apostolate, its rituals before its ministry."[15] Obviously not all parishes are middle class. There are the ethnic, black, and sectarian congregations. But neither do they, according to Winter, break out of this introverted pattern.

Thirdly, Robert Bellah, in a frequently reprinted article, "Civil Religion in America," described a religious reality that has emerged from the experience of the American people. It is not to be identified with Christianity in some kind of classic form but is rather the belief that the American vision and God are in some sense synonymous, though Bellah insists that at its best American civil religion is capable of real prophetic judgment upon American policy.[16] At present, however, the "God" of the average member of the "civil religion" does not seem to be equal to this task. As one gracious native of Mississippi explained to me shortly after the 1954 Supreme Court decision, "I'm afraid I'll have to choose the 'American way of life' [i.e. his personal ideology] over Christianity, if it comes to that."

Certainly a great many American Christians do not wish to be faced with such a choice. That is not their purpose in being churchmen *and* Americans.[17] The "God" of their civil religion, which assures them of some divine authority in the American dream, is the same comforting deity that offers the *needed* additional consolation on Sunday morning that in this cruel, impersonal, and anxiety-ridden world they are important. Charles Glock and his associates offer in this light my fourth "documentation" of the personal expectations of American Christians. They show considerable evidence that the person most likely to be heavily involved in church life is the woman over fifty, without family, from a lower economic class. It is just these characteristics, they remind us, that lack status in our society.[18] There are, however, other researchers such as Earl Main who question how universally true this judgment is. Main found different results for age, marital status, and social class as related to church participation than did Glock.[19]

All in all, Seeley, Winter, Bellah, and Glock give some clear indication that, despite efforts between 1850 and 1914 for the Church to stand apart and yet to speak effectively to society, there has been over the past fifty years a willingness on the part of most Christian congregations to become *spiritual ghettos*. Compared to the world at large, the parish now talks a strange language, from another reality that is devoid of content. It lives by ideals no one would dream of exercising anywhere else, and provides an acceptance that makes no demands. This is what Bonhoeffer called "cheap grace." It has become this because many a layman, despite some contrary rhetoric, really wants it this way and because the clergy are either willing to go along or are too confused or frightened to fight. We can be thankful for the courageous exceptions from both quarters, clerical and lay.

I must emphasize that the "ghetto quality" of the parish church becomes evident only when we take its inherited cognitive notions concerning the traditional parish seriously. The only people who do so are, by and large, some of the clergy. If they choose to live cognitively both in the Church and the world, they are doomed to an intellectual schizophrenia. Traditional parish images assume a universal coherence and subject-object epistemology that the world has long since abandoned (my first two points in Chapter 6). The contemporary culture demands a concern for the future and for technology to which inherited patterns of ministry say little or nothing (my last two points). If the noetic life of the parish church is accepted as "rite without content," as I suspect it is by more and more laymen, then it is no "ghetto," but a sort of "teahouse" to which the overwrought contemporary man retires to find peace and assurance, to view life in the unreal light of a Gospel of consolation that is intentionally divorced from the real world outside.

What is happening, however, is that although some clergy are willing to be chaplains to a ghetto or perform a "geisha" function, more and more are what Jeffrey Hadden calls the "new breed." These men would recall the parish church with new vigor to the prophetic function it tried between 1850 and 1914. I shall speak further of this in another chapter, but I want now to illustrate something of the dilemma of the parish itself in the light of Hadden's thesis.

Hadden's belief, expounded in his book *The Gathering Storm in the Churches*, is that there is a threefold crisis developing in this country over (1) the meaning and purpose of the Church, (2) religious belief, and (3) authority within the Church.[20] There is no doubt that initial lay perplexity over clerical involvement in what laymen think are matters outside the concern of organized religion has now taken a more defined thrust. The laity is angry, and a widening clergy-lay gap is expressed in a drop in church attendance,[21] a lessening in the belief in the importance of religion, a loss of prestige by the clergyman,[22] a withholding of funds,[23] and a lay effort to assume command of the Church. This has been fed by a growing disbelief in the traditional teachings on the part of many Christians.[24] The fact of disbelief is not a source of clergy-lay disparity, for it is shared by both. What has happened is that with no common faith to which to appeal, there is little basis for a lessening of tension between clergy and laity.[25] (My belief is that knowledge follows action and action follows faith. A common belief or faith is, therefore, fundamental to a common purpose.)

Where, despite the trend, theological fundamentalism or conservatism does occur, it seems to be related to political conservatism and a rigid moralism.[26] Talcott Parsons has described in "Religion in a Modern Pluralistic Society" what even the casual observer of the national scene can note; namely that to maintain his position the fundamentalist must narrow his acceptance of differentiation in religion. This intolerance is accompanied by a "deflation" of conscience as seen in a simplified, rigid morality and an identification with a resistance to social change found in the far Right.[27] Why this is so it would be hard to say. Glock and his associates offer a hint when they observe of Episcopalians that those highly involved in the Church often consider the miraculous power of individual faith an alternative to a corporate prophetic action.[28] For example, on one occasion while I was chaplain at Louisiana State University we had two Episcopal priests in attendance for Religious Emphasis Week (a gimmick particularly popular in campus ministries during the fifties), Malcolm Boyd and Herbert Bicknell, O.H.C. Fr. Boyd was speaking to large crowds of students on the race question (it was

1958) and Fr. Bicknell was leading a school of prayer. Both were quite in accord with what the other was doing, but more than one layman said to me, "If Fr. Boyd would stop stirring up trouble and let us listen to Fr. Bicknell, we can learn how to pray and stop worrying about integration!" But all this certainly does not tell us *why* some people line up along the conservative-rightist-pietist axis, and others along the liberal-socialist-activist axis.

The alliance between the Church and the middle class of the last decades of the modern period provides a further insight into this question. The parish was staffed by clergymen and laymen for whom there was a clear value system—duty, family, work—and behind which there was a simple, but coherent, theology demanding the loyalty of all. The middle class that fills the suburban parish today has little, if any, continuity with that group, being the affluent product of an upwardly mobile technological society and lacking the roots, time, and cognitive skills to develop a defined value system, based upon a philosophy or theology consistent with their present reality. Instead there is a slow but clear drift away from traditional theological formulation. But only among a few, which includes those likely to choose the ministry as a career, has there been a willingness to work through a *re*formulation of theology. This is not to say, by any means, that this is what everyone coming to seminary is seeking to do. Quite the opposite can be the case. But no matter whether we are recapturing an old theology or developing a new, it has had the effect (1) of giving no common basis for the restructuring of the purpose of the parish,[29] and (2) of alienating the clergy and the few laymen who are attempting to build a contemporary theological expression of their faith from the clergy, and what appears to be a solid proportion of the laity, who would prefer the ghetto or the teahouse.

The question can be justifiably asked at this point, if my analysis of a Church populated by a *new* middle class is accurate, how is it that we are able to recruit clergy from this group. My own experience, which is limited to the Episcopal

Church, is that men coming to seminary out of this environment have either experienced a conversion or a revulsion. Those who are converted make up Hadden's "new breed." Those who have been repelled often are willing to settle for the ghetto. It is only the tired pastor, defeated by no rewards for fighting hardened hearts, who accepts the teahouse.

The effect of all this in the typical parish has been demonstrated in at least two separate studies of parishes faced with efforts for community organization. In *The Edge of the Ghetto* John Fish and others describe what happened to six parishes in the Organization for the Southwest Community of Chicago; in *The Schizophrenic Church* Robert Lee and Russell Galloway record the involvement of six Presbyterian churches in the Commission on Race and Religion of the San Francisco Presbytery in a community organization project directed by Saul Alinsky and the Industrial Areas Foundation (IAF). What is very apparent in both these analyses is that there is a clear-cut polarity within most parishes leading to the possible conclusion that different factions serve different Gods.[30] This lack of a dominant and reasonably defined common loyalty within the parish has created a situation where parties have now retreated to their "fortifications," and can only scream invectives at one another. It does not have to be this way if such polarities are held in a community for whom there is an overriding reason to work together. It is absence in many cases of that "reason" that is disturbing.

The paralysis of the parish has only in the last few years reached an acute stage. Its roots are more than a hundred years old. As long ago as 1925 the Roman Catholic Church in Germany was raising questions about the "parish principle" (*Pfaarprinzip*). *The issue is simply this: can the parish in its present form as inherited from the past still function as a locus for the vital and necessary ministerial functions of the Church?* Hans J. Margull, who speaks of the parish (the "pastor's church" is his term) of the past as a *"come-structure,"* says it was "our fathers' correct answer to the challenge of being the Church in their historical hour. There is another historical hour today, and we are compelled to give our own and a new answer in this hour." [31] When Margull and others such as Hans Schmidt and Colin Williams attack the parish structure, central to their concern is the concept of the *residential* church, the point being that *people do not live where they live.* Contemporary people do not think of themselves, they say, as persons of a particular place. Rather, their identity is tied up with how they spend their time (work, education, recreation). It is for this reason that Margull and others are not calling for an abolition of structure, but for new structures that are related to people where they truly live.

There is another side to what these thinkers argue so convincingly, for I am not at all sure that the problems of the parish relate to its organizing principle; that is, whether it is residence or occupation of time. This will have to come up later. For the moment, it is important that we give ear to the defenders of the parish principle in terms of a need for structure so that in the last half of this chapter the discussion of the efforts to reform the parish can be considered worthy of attention.

Perhaps one of the most vocal exponents of the relevancy of the residential parish church today is Charles Stinnette, who is a colleague of Gibson Winter at the University of Chicago. In an article entitled "The Parish, the World, and Pastoral Care," Stinnette does not shrink from acknowledging the failures of the contemporary parish. It has, he notes, been closed to the world, resistant to change, highly clerical, and blind to the creative use of power and conflict.[32] But to do away with the parish is to *overdo* sociological analysis, Stinnette would claim, and to fail to see the role of the parish as a natural community enabling people to become participants in Christ's action in the world. There is more to religious meaning than the adult, public sectors of life.[33]

In one way or another, practically every defender of the parish first describes it as a sacramental localized expression of the unity of the whole man within himself and to God. Joseph M. Connolly goes on to speak of the presence of the priest as "presiding person" as the organizing principle of this unity.[34] The parish is the visible expression of the Church as the Body of Christ. Second, there is a general consensus that the parish is the best possible foundation for mission, which I think is more a hope than a fact. Certainly it is true, as both Charles Bayer and Gaylord Noyce say, that parishes have the people necessary for mission.[35] However, this pragmatic approach does not resolve the equally real problem of directing that number of people from a "come-structure" into a "go-structure." Finally, there is the opinion of a number of theologians that in the worship and teaching of the parish real community is found and growth in holiness is achieved which would be impossible without such structure. Beyond these three points—sacrament (nature), mission (dynamic), sanctification (goal)—other reasons for the existence of the parish are expressed, but not with the weight of common agreement. But perhaps these are sufficient; for they constitute a further explication of an observation of Hadden with which I firmly agree:

Those clergy who are today speaking of an *institutionless* Christianity are perhaps the most guilty of abdicating responsibility, for the very fact that they speak in these terms would seem to suggest that they understand the implications of the conflict. But I do not believe they understand the implications of Christianity without an institutional base.[36]

There is no other way known to man to direct the ministry of the Church *effectively* in terms of its nature, dynamic, and goal than through *some* kind of structure. This is what Christianity is all about.

In the past generation there have been at least four attempts within the parish structure to revitalize the local congregation—and perhaps a fifth, which is really a counter-movement ending up the same place—to which I wish to speak: experiments in Christian Education, the Liturgical Movement, the Neo-Pentecostal Movement, the grass-roots Ecumenical Movement, and fifth, the functional alternative to the residential parish. These are attempts to recognize the need for structure, but at the same time are also attempts at its renewal.

Prior to World War II Christian Education in the more conservative traditions suffered from a euphoric triumphalism, a naïve and pedantic methodology, and small vision. In the liberal denominations there was more interest in methodology, and under the leadership of George Albert Coe they were rather short on content and long on social adjustment. The war made apparent to many how ignorant the average young person was about his religion, and it was assumed that if the Church were to keep them they would have to *know more*. This same confusion between information and commitment (knowing *about* someone and *knowing* someone) had inspired the foundation of the America Church Sunday School Institute in the Episcopal Church in 1875, in order to stop the loss of children to the Church (an interesting turnabout, since the 1865 General Convention described Sunday Schools as "unchurchly"). The new interest in good Christian Education took essentially two directions: one was centered on the current popularity of biblical theology (who can forget the innumerable discussions of Suzanne de Dietrich's presentation of the "mighty acts of God"?), and the other took a psychological bent, under the inspiration of Martin Buber and Kurt Lewin. The second direction has been longer lasting, enduring the fierce debate provoked by Parish Life Conferences, Group Life Labs, and the early versions of the Seabury Series in the Episcopal Church and its equivalents in others.

Whereas Christian Education is these days no longer "stage center" in parochial, diocesan, and national controversy, its proponents have not despaired of the vision of a better educated community. Much of what was considered "heretical" twenty years ago is now commonplace among most people. The insights are more sophisticated, the methodology more refined and less polemical, and leaders such as Jerome Bruner, Ronald Goldman, and Gabriel Moran people to be reckoned with. With the popularity in the past ten years of Roman Catholic catechetical methods, ecumenical programs have become more acceptable, and there is a feeling that improved methods and materials lie ahead of us.

But also the movement is less messianic. We know that morality, much less commitment to Christ, is not taught. It is caught. Through the individual's association with family, peers, teachers—all of the "significant others" of the socialization process—attitudes and values become a part of his person. No Christian Education program, much less one that consumes only forty-five minutes a week and employs unskilled teachers (no matter how devoted), is going to reconstruct the emotional and intellectual investments of its subjects. There are possibilities, to which I shall speak in Part III, for the reconstruction of small groups of Christians through a pedagogical method; but time and personnel make it impossible to consider this an answer to the problem of revitalizing the parish. It is equally true that people who expect the parish to serve as a source of moral teaching, under the illusion that it previously served in this capacity in an era where there was an almost universal commitment to an identifiable ethical standard, should differentiate between information and commitment and be aware of the dangers involved in a panic-stricken attempt to push the former in the belief that it will achieve the latter.

The origins of the Liturgical Movement lie in mid-nineteenth century European Roman Catholicism. Its principal commitment has always been to the centrality of the Eucharist in the parish community. The great theologian of the movement, Dom Odo Casel (1886–1948), devoted his life to promoting a greater understanding of the meaning of the Eucharist as a participation in the mystery of the salvific life of Christ, and he genuinely sought to serve this end in every way he could. It is regrettable that for several generations he and others like him failed to perceive what Charles Davis describes as the "pastoral problems of liturgical revival." [37] Their approach was steeped in a romantic pursuit of the pure rite in the past, and they failed to see that an anthropological and theological methodology would have been a far better tool in their quest than the historical.

The impact of liturgical revival became generally apparent on the parish level after World War II, although the publication in 1937 of *The Parish Communion,* edited by A. G. Hebert, was a noteworthy event in the Church of England. There is no need to recount here in detail the radical change that the last twenty years has brought not only to the Roman Catholic liturgy but to that of other liturgical churches as well. Whether or not the change in the forms of liturgy— official, trial, or unofficial—that proliferate within the Church have succeeded in renewing the life of the parish is a matter inaccessible to any final or universal judgment. They have certainly made some difference, which has brought us face-to-face as never before with the question of what happens to people when they attend the liturgy. The problem needs much more study, for within it lies the whole debate about the function of rite *vis-à-vis* the Christian community. For the moment I would identify three possibilities.

The first possible value within liturgy relates to what the psychiatrist Eric Berne called "stroking." [38] Many want liturgy to make them feel comfortable. We all need the maternal caress. For some exceedingly neurotic people, Leo Salzman says, "ritual is an attempt to control the individual's behavior by focusing his attention on the ritual, thereby distracting interest away from other [anxiety producing] matters. In addition, it may be a symbolic performance in which the individual controls those elements which he feels may go out of control." [39] The most effective kind of ritual for this purpose is *repetitious, familiar,* and *without content.* Since the purpose of the Liturgical Movement is to remove the "vain repetitions" and to provide a clear content that calls for a new, unfamiliar life, we can understand some of the cries of anguish that liturgical revision have produced.

A second value is that most often heralded by the proponents of liturgical revival themselves: the Eucharist constitutes the Christian community. To put it another way, it effects cultural change. It has been argued persuasively that the purpose of the Eucharist is "forming a family of God." [40] The Eucharist has an obvious parallel to the family meal, as well as the marital bed, which are *means to* greater family solidarity and conjugal union.

After a generation of such teaching, however, we still find many parishes introverted and split asunder despite a weekly sharing in the eucharistic offering. This has provoked the charge that the Liturgical Movement has failed. A particular case in point was an article by Daniel Callahan in the *National Catholic Reporter* of August 9, 1967, called "Putting the Liturgy in Its Place" in which the author said that in fact the liturgy was more a celebration of what had come about otherwise than a means of creating it. This is to say that liturgy is a function of society or community. Richard Neuhaus in an editorial in *Una Sancta*, picked up by *Worship*, wrote in response to Callahan: "The power to engage and sustain us in the redeeming work of God may come from many encounters, sacred or secular, personal or institutional. Word and sacrament are decidedly not the exclusive focus or power of Christian living." [41] This from the center of the movement is a clear indication that it cannot and does not claim to be that which shall alone renew the parish, but is the context in which all our gifts, and all our failures, are shared.

The Neo-Pentecostal Movement (which must be distinguished from the separatist Pentecostal Movement, as in the Church of God) is a remarkable phenomenon that has spread for the last ten years among Roman Catholics, Episcopalians, Presbyterians, and many other members of traditional denominations. It focuses upon the belief that the power of God is immediately available to transform the lives of Christians, and is experienced in what is called "the Baptism of the Holy Spirit." This is an event of personal renewal, subjectively experienced, which frequently manifests itself in "speaking in tongues" or glossolalia. Those who have had this experience or seek it generally form complementary groups to the routine life of their parish, and find in these a very deep and satisfying relationship in Christ and one another. There is no doubt that the movement stands in the Pietist tradition, and that it is an attempt at parish renewal. In 1961 Dennis Bennett, its early leader in the Episcopal Church, explained in a sermon how prior to "Baptism in the Holy Spirit" his parish work was "like taxiing down the runway and never taking off." Now, he said, he and his parish "took off" every week.

The movement frightens many Christians, for the freedom it creates in people is threatening to our own feelings of what would happen if we "let go and let somebody [maybe God?] take over." There is no evidence to support the easy charge that such people are "mentally ill." Virginia H. Hine, a sociologist who has studied the movement closely, says that there is some indication that glossolalia itself is learned behavior of generally devout Christians who are seeking a deeper religious commitment. It has never been, however, an exclusively Christian phenomenon. In terms of function, she says that Neo-Pentecostalism is associated with a fundamentalist ideology, a change in personal attitude and social behavior (there is a great deepening of interpersonal relations), and a cognitive reorganization on the basis of group ideals.[42] Elsewhere Hine and Gerlach describe how the movement grows on the basis of an acephalous organization, face-to-face recruitment along lines of preexisting significant social relationships, commitment generated through experience, a change-oriented ideology, and real or perceived opposition.[43] Others, such as Kilian McDonnell, William Samarin, and Loma Kendall point out that glossolalia itself is really a form of prayer, that the movement has awakened many Christians to the meaning of their baptism, that it has closed for them the ideal-real gap and restored religious experience to its rightful place, and has created a new sense of trust in God.[44]

It is clear that the Neo-Pentecostal Movement has worked

a truly transforming ministry among many people. I do not think, however, that it will ever become the primary tool in parish renewal and the revitalization of ministerial function. First, it appears particularly related to one type of personality. Whereas I doubt that I would use as strong language as Lapsley and Simpson, who describe Pentacostals as "uncommonly troubled people," [45] it has been my observation that it attracts persons with a low frustration tolerance. This is illustrated by the movement's very effective work with drug addicts, who find ambiguity very difficult to bear. On occasion glossolalia is described in terms of "taking a trip," [46] and the comparison is not without significance. Second, in its desire for assurance and consequent fundamentalist bias, the Neo-Pentecostal movement is often guilty of "tunnel vision." Intellectual problems are ridiculed or preached at, rather than met on their own ground.[47] Social concern is frequently swallowed up in a simplistic privatism and eschatology.[48] Third, without blaming the Neo-Pentecostal movement itself, there is a tendency within it to divide a parish into the "do's" and "do not's." It can be overtly gnostic. Schism may be too big a price for the value received.

This is not to deny that the Neo-Pentecostal movement has changed people's lives for the good, and that its helpfulness can outweigh its harm in given situations. It does appear to me that the movement requires its members to withdraw into a cognitive subsystem. Not everyone is willing to do that in order to acquire its benefits, and therefore I would consider it a highly impractical means of total parish renewal. This is, however, no condemnation of the sincerity of those involved or a repudiation of the values received.

Fifteen years ago the most controversial efforts at parish renewal centered in the grass-roots Ecumenical Movement; that is, the merger of small, competing congregations of different denominational affiliation into cooperative parishes. The intention was to pool resources, in an area that did not promise great growth to either, in order to serve the community better.

The obvious conviction was that differences in doctrine, polity, and liturgy could be surrendered or compromised for the sake of a higher common goal.

Probably best known in the Episcopal Church was the establishment of the Indian Hill joint Presbyterian-Episcopal church in the Diocese of Southern Ohio in 1948. This parish was and still is served by an Episcopal priest, whereas an earlier merger in the same diocese between the West Cincinnati Presbyterian Church and St. Barnabas Episcopal Church had a Presbyterian minister as its pastor. The Indian Hill experiment was strongly attacked in the church press in 1952, when with the completion of its building it came to national attention. A *Living Church* editorial called it an "outright departure from the integrity of its [the Episcopal Church's] Faith and life," [49] and several dioceses passed resolutions against it. A later article in the *Living Church*, written in 1967 by the present pastor of the church, leaves the reader in these days of novelty with the decided impression that it was a rather conservative and quite conventional sort of compromise.[50]

Marvin Judy has done an analysis of the problems of the small parish in a nonmetropolitan area in which he does show how it is possible for various forms of cooperation to take place between struggling congregations of both the same denomination and different ones. In a very brief discussion of the latter situation, he describes the "yoked field" (one pastor serves two churches of different denominations) and the "federated church" (churches of different denominations are joined in one parish under one pastor).[51] He tells us that this is a growing phenomenon, but about the only evaluation he or anyone else can give is to say that where the differences are not too important in the first place, it produces a stronger parish; where they are, it is no solution.

Another way of getting at this problem is through a "comity agreement," where in new suburbs church leaders will agree that only one denomination will go in and establish a mission. Some years ago, when the Diocese of Massachusetts

(Episcopal) entered into such an agreement, a great furor was raised by those who protested the limitation upon the Church's ministry. It is worth noting that such plans are often accepted in the foreign mission field, although attacked at home. Perhaps this is because of the strong emotional factor on the domestic scene, where some members of one denomination have previously rejected their childhood church, and do not wish to be forced back into it because of a comity agreement. Their new church under these circumstances would appear to betray them. Beyond this, it can be argued that it is a simple matter of truth, which one has and the other does not, and we cannot enter into an agreement with error.

This solution is obviously fraught with many difficulties, and its viability exists in inverse proportion to the degree of commitment to a particular theological position. William Whyte has described another way popular in the 1950s of going at the same question: the pan-Protestant community church, which has no prior denominational affiliation.[52] As he tells it, the appeal of such a congregation is community service and not commitment to a unique value-structure. Consequently, what is done tends to have no roots except superficial goodwill. It has no place from which to speak prophetically to its membership, since it is a creature of its membership and nothing else. Consequently, there is little hope that this element of the movement can offer much to parish renewal, more than an opting out on the real issues facing the Church.

The only place where the grass-roots ecumenical dimensions of parish renewal really seem to have some integrity and strength is as a part of the functional alternative to the traditional, denominational residential parish. I refer here not just to the underground church, but to congregations such as the Berkeley Free Church, the East Harlem Protestant Parish, the Church of the Savior in Washington, D.C., the Boston Industrial Mission, the Ecumenical Institute in Chicago, and many more. The directory of the Liberated Church in America, "Win With Love," as of the October 1970 issue of the same, had 401 entries in the United States. This does not include groups such as the Church of the Savior or the Boston Industrial Mission, but it does include some canonically established Episcopal parishes. Rudiger Reitz has described this movement as committed to "a 'theology of action,' the central message of which is God *is* mission." [53] It is necessary to understand why Reitz defines it as a "structural protest against institutionalism," [54] because the distinction is important. The latter speaks of the Church as conceiving of its own life as an end in itself, rather than what is implied in the former—organization for the sake of the Gospel.

What is happening is a break from the "establishment," which has much in common with the entire counterculture. The four areas in which this movement sees itself organizing are: ghetto poverty, alienated youth, the peace movement, and liturgical renewal. The themes that prevail are peace, liberation, and love. There is a close tie between the New Mobilization, the Believers Church Conference, and on a marginal basis various consultations on the underground church. John Pairman Brown, now attached to the Berkeley Free Church, has in personal correspondence described what he does as "'far from intending to deviate' from the new thing which is spontaneously happening all over 'more than the local circumstances require.' (Namely, being a hippy street ministry.)"

Yet it would be a mistake to understand this as an escape from form. It is more a *restructuring* of the Christian life around different priorities. Take for example the Church of the Savior. It is not easy to be a member of this group; it requires two years of membership training, a definite financial commitment, and a willingness to give much time to the projects of the congregation. They have been able to maintain this degree of commitment in the past, however, in part by separating themselves from any denominational allegiance, figuring that the "baggage" imposed by such ties inhibits the formation of a truly believing body.

It is impossible in this study to chronicle all the variations within this movement or even to characterize the total phenomenon more than I have. Those interested should read

*The Underground Church*, edited by Malcolm Boyd; Robert S. Lecky and H. Elliott Wright, *Can These Dry Bones Live?*; and the book already mentioned by Rudiger Reitz, *The Church in Experiment.*[55] The question remains, even after exploring what is happening, whether such a restructuring promises to renew the Church. Lecky and Wright, in a very bitter book, think not. "For many agonized minds who feel compelled to push renewal when hope is gone, a church-non-church attitude would be the honest course. A church-non-church stance requires rather dramatic shifts away from the renewalist approach of updating organizations [e.g. the Underground Church and unifying dominions [e.g. the Consultation on Church Unity or COCU]." [56] I myself am inclined to think that Lecky and Wright expect too much and see too little.

But beyond this, we have to realize that any effort at revitalization of a culture, and this is essentially what the movement is attempting, first presents itself in an absolute form. If it is going to have a lasting effect upon the culture, it must, through dialogue with it, adapt itself to a working relationship.[57] This has not, in effect, happened yet. We can hope it does, and in this study I am very dependent upon its occurring, if some of my projections ever come to pass.

In this discussion of the parish my effort has been to show something of the very serious situation in which the local congregation finds itself today (often without knowing it); and at the same time to plead that we not despair of institutional Christianity. Our incarnational faith requires in some sense an institutional expression. Yet we find ourselves functioning in a deep dilemma, torn between our principal contributors who want to maintain the parish as their local teahouse, and a vanguard of articulate and committed prophets offering various solutions for the effective ministry of the Christian community. I do not think that it is easy to dismiss either faction, and yet I find it almost impossible to reconcile them.

## chapter 8

# STUPOR AUT
# STUPIDUS MUNDI

The nineteenth-century Anglican middle-class parson, armed with his university degree and no longer the nonresident holder of plural benefices, was known as the *stupor mundi*, the "wonder of the world." Today it might be more accurate to speak of the same person as the *stupidus mundi*, the "stunned of the world." In the English or American village of a hundred years ago, where the heirs of the classical Reformation commanded the respect, if not the whole-hearted allegiance, of the community, the Presbyterian, Congregationalist, or Anglican clergyman ranked somewhere between the squire/local industrialist/judge and the schoolmaster. The clergyman was a little better educated than the former, but did not have quite the same financial leverage, whereas his learning was more "humane" than the schoolmaster's, and he probably came from a "better" family. Later the town doctor made it a "quadumvirate." Today the clergyman is as well educated as he ever was—90 percent of the Episcopal clergy in 1967 had seminary degrees, an equal number having a baccalaureate from a college or university, and 10 percent having masters' degrees[1]—and yet every indication is that his image is slipping badly. A Gallup poll indicates that in 1967 only 8 percent of the population recommended the role of clergyman as the preferred profession, far behind that of doctor, engineer-builder, professor-teacher, and on a par with the lawyer, business executive, and a government career.[2] Other surveys indicate an even lower ranking.

In addition the exodus of clergy from a stipendiary function within the institutional Church is growing and is causing alarm in many quarters. According to Vatican sources, from 1963 to 1968 7,137 Roman Catholic priests asked to be dispensed from ordination vows; and in the first two-and-a-half months of 1969, 675 so applied. The 1963–68 figures amounted to 1.28 percent of the Roman Catholic secular clergy and 2.31 percent of the Roman Catholic religious in the world, but only 0.98 percent of the seculars in the United States.[3] This is a conservative set of figures. The National Association of Pastoral Renewal estimates that 1,183 priests in the United States left from January 1, 1966, to September 1968.[4] An even higher estimate is 2,700 priests in 1968.[5] In the Episcopal Church, where canonical acknowledgment of this growing trend in the Church was made at South Bend in 1969 (Canons 44 and 63), the number of secularly employed presbyters supplying churches grew from 162 to 322 in the period from 1966 to 1968; secularly employed, not supplying, presbyters grew from 296 to 397; and the number of "noncategorized" presbyters grew from 33 to 130. These three groups equal 7.9 percent of the total presbyters of the Episcopal Church, and they represent a three-year growth from 4.7 percent.[6] Estimates of Protestant clergy are harder to come by,[7] but authorities agree that departures have increased dramatically over the past few years. Jud's study of United Church of Christ ex-pastors began with 383 names, out of roughly 7,000 clergy in that church.[8] Obviously there is a trend; though we should keep in mind that the percentage of men and women leaving is probably less than in occupational changes generally, and our concern reflects in part a naïve view of clerical commitment. I am confident that the prediction made by John Wesley Downing, an Episcopal priest helping ex-pastors adjust to the secular life, that by 1975 half of the nation's 450,000 clergy will have opted out is absurd.[9]

What is happening?

In the first place, there has been a shift from one or two clearly defined ideas of what it is to be a clergyman, depending on whether the emphasis is Catholic or Protestant—the representative of the authority of God's Church or the preacher of the Word—to a different and poorly defined role. I have written of Cunningham's description of the "physician of the soul." [10] In the same spirit H. Richard Niebuhr spoke of the emerging "pastoral director" as the new pattern of ministry. No longer does the clergyman operate *primarily* from a pulpit or at an altar, he said, but from his study. He likened this role —and this point is very suggestive and one upon which I shall build later—to the ancient bishop, whose task was not so much to oversee a far-flung diocese as to "edify" the local congregation.[11] It is interesting that in one sense Niebuhr could not predict the future, for he described at length the growing "communal authority of the minister of our time." [12]

In a 1967 survey of Episcopal clergy the clear evidence was that pastoral counseling was considered the most important function of the priest.[13] This relates to the fact that 36 percent of Episcopal clergy say that "serving, helping, relating to other people" is what particularly attracted them to the priesthood.[14] It received negative support in that 66 percent of the clergy say they got too little psychology and counseling instruction in seminary,[15] and that the kind of continuing education they want tends to be more in this direction than anything else.[16]

But there are several notes of ambiguity in all this. In Samuel Blizzard's oft-quoted study, non-Roman Catholic clergy rated *preaching as the most important thing they did;* although they enjoyed counseling more, and they spent most of their time administering.[17] Whether fifteen years later the results would be the same is uncertain; but evidently in 1956 there was some carry-over from a more traditional view. It is also interesting that when vestries of Episcopal parishes are asked what is most characteristic of the ideal clergyman, the principal difference from the clergy's understanding of themselves is that they put more emphasis upon administration (11 percent compared to 7 percent) and teaching stands out way above the rest (22 percent compared to 14 percent).[18] My suspicion is that the average vestryman thinks of preaching as teaching.

Furthermore, if I may offer by title a matter I will discuss at some length in the next chapter, in the shift from preacher of the Word or representative of the authority of the Church to "physician of souls" or "pastoral director" I believe we have moved from a clearly defined, discrete job description to something that is confused and uncertain. When Episcopal clergy were asked to describe what it meant to do pastoral counseling they suggested that it was being "a good listener" (64.5 percent), "a spiritual director" (46.6 percent), and an "adviser" (36.9 percent).[19] With the possible exception of the second (see chapter 10), all such descriptions lack a sense of immediate professional identity. When it is someone's job to tell people what God is saying in his Bible or Church, particularly when the people are not too aware of the ambiguities involved, there is no question as to what the person is doing. But I am not so sure that this is true of the clergyman sitting in his study, listening, directing, or advising. At least only 22 percent of Episcopal clergy rate themselves as "highly satisfactory" at "resolving personal problems of the laity," though it is true another 50 percent consider themselves "somewhat satisfactory."[20] Perhaps this relates to the study of ex-pastors of the United Church of Christ, where it was found that although there is no one overwhelming reason why men leave the parish ministry, the leading reason (17.1 percent) was a "sense of personal and professional inadequacy."[21]

At the same time, most clergy are sensitive to the fact that the traditional sermon is a problematic tool of ministry today, and that it is no solution to return to Charles Spurgeon, Phillips Brooks, or John Henry Newman. Perhaps no one has pointed this out recently with such vigor as Clyde Reid, who says, "Our understanding of the nature of communication now helps us realize how futile this effort is when preaching is relied upon as the major communication tool."[22] Not everyone agrees with Reid; but after listening to innumerable tapes of lay "feedback" on sermons, I am convinced that it takes a truly remarkable preacher today to get his message across in a coherent form without either having the congregation accept it as "rite without content" (there are preachers who argue it is not *what* you say, but *how* you say it!) or raising their anxieties to the point where they can hear nothing. We are not an audient people, who can sit still for such a "hot" medium as the usual Sunday sermon. There can be no retreat to preaching the Word or speaking for "holy Mother Church" as the characteristic role of the clergyman.

An alternative to retreat is to move beyond the role of "physician of souls" or "pastor director." This is what the "new breed," of which Cox and Hadden speak, have done. In 1966 I attended a national consultation on the campus ministry sponsored by the Episcopal Church. For a number of years prior to that time I had devoted a good bit of my energy to organizing an interdenominational counseling service on a campus of 18,000 students, where there was less than minimal psychiatric and psychological service offered. I remember my discomfort at this meeting upon being told I was failing in my role as a university chaplain. My task was to be a "change agent." Hadden points out that for a number of years the radical clergy, so-called "change agents," had been absorbed by the college chaplaincies and kept away from staid parishes, but now the supply of such people has far exceeded the demand of the academic community and they are spilling over into the parishes.[23] I am sure this is true. But I suspect that the vast majority of clergy do not yet, and may never, conceive of the "change agent" as their characteristic role. The laity do not even dream of it! In a survey of Episcopal priests in 1967 only 2 percent of the parochial clergy and 4.3 percent of the need-centered clergy (4.4 percent in college chaplaincies and 12 percent in inner-city work) saw it as their most important function. Most rated it fifth, just ahead of administration.[24] Aside from this, there are some ambiguities in this role, as well as that of "pastor director," to which I shall speak in the next chapter.

The first thing happening to the clergyman today, I would say therefore, is that in losing the modern image of the pastorate he has not been able to gain a clear contemporary image. He cannot go back in good conscience, but he is unable to live happily with the present options. A humorous illustration of this kind of "role dilemma" ("What do I do to make myself important?") is this item from the bulletin of an older priest in a country parish. The rector, who had a "late vocation," had previously served as a male nurse.

This month of October has been designated Diabetes Detection month, and the Rector, himself a Diabetic, offers this service to anyone who desires it. Just follow this proceedure [sic]:

1—collect a specimen of urine in a clean bottle and attach your name firmly by tape to this bottle

2—bring me the specimen and I will run the sugar test and report to you what I find.

If the specimen is negative you have nothing to worry about, but if it turns out positive you would do well to consult your Doctor without delay. Diabetes is an insedious [sic] disease and can cause very serious trouble if it is present and undetected. So do not take a chance—the test will cost you nothing, and I will be happy to be of service.

I consider this a classic.

Second, there is the matter of clerical training. The Church has been a long time deciding what theological education is. Generally speaking, the curriculum of a seminary differs from that of a university not because seminaries have changed, but because universities have changed. As we have seen, between the demise of the rhetors schools in the fifth century and the post-Enlightenment state universities in the late eighteenth and early nineteenth centuries, education served the Church. This has been particularly true, as Mark

Curtis points out, since the sixteenth century where in England Oxford and Cambridge not only trained clergy but had "the additional duty of cultivating proper religious ideas and habits in the young gentlemen who invaded them." [25] This was a uniquely Reformation inheritance, however, and religious instruction was generally extrastatutory. Only since World War II has the theology curriculum that evolved in the universities through those fifteen hundred years and particularly in the last four hundred (having been more or less "ghettoized" in seminaries beginning in the early nineteenth) been effectively challenged. In an age where professionals boast special skills, it is a little difficult to say that a person is qualified to be a clergyman because he has a good, seventeenth-century higher education, with a "major in divinity." As one priest, now secularly employed, told me, the time has come when the clergyman can no longer trade on the image of being "a well-educated, gentile person."

In the year 1855–56 a student attending Nashotah House studied Bible, History, and Hebrew in his junior year; Bible, Systematic Theology, Polity, and History in his middler year; and Systematic Theology, History, and Pastoral Theology in his senior year. It was assumed that he had Ethics, Classics, Logic, and English before he came (and a preparatory department provided it, if he had not). This was very adequate training for men destined to preach the kind of solid, literary sermons expected of an Episcopal priest. For what else did it equip him? The clue should lie in Pastoral Theology where the art of priesthood is expounded; and since we are also provided with a book list in the announcements for that year, we are able to discover that the students read *five* books on preaching, *three* on the Book of Common Prayer, the Constitutions and Canons of the Episcopal Church, and something called "Wilson's Parochialia." This last named turns out to be by the Bishop of Sodor and Man, written in 1708 (the equivalent in 1970 of using a book written in 1823). It concerns itself with preparing young people for Confirmation and the Lord's

Supper, expounds the implication of Family Prayer (including how to raise children, and how to treat the poor, servants, formal Christians, and evil livers), and discusses the method of visiting the sick. It concludes with a form of personal examination and confession.[26] It can be read in an evening, and consists of the common, pious, good sense of the day.

As I compare with those days what the institution in which I teach, and most of our other seminaries, offers its students in 1970, I find the change in the Bible-History-Theology core is minimal. Obviously the texts are different, maybe even the content is altered (in the second quarter of this century particular effort was made to bring seminaries up to graduate level), but the spirit is more or less the same. The change has, *perhaps*, taken place in Pastoral Theology. I say this in a very tentative way because the text used when I was in seminary in the early fifties, *Priesthood in Action* by Wallace E. Conkling, was very similar to Wilson's *Parochialia*, only filtered through the Catholic Revival (in Anglicanism) and the parish-house movement. It was equally lacking in substance. Yet since 1945 there has been the growing movement in clinical pastoral education and field education to develop not just knowledge, but skills, human growth, and commitment— those four qualities which Charles Feilding in his well-known "Education for Ministry" describes as essential for professional theological education.[27] Whether clinical pastoral education and field education will take over for the more academic concerns of pastoral theology, or for that matter should, is debatable; but the point is that the focus of effort to provide the training of men for a clearly defined professional role has centered here. Well it might! In the report of the Temporary Commission on Continuing Education of the United Presbyterian Church, more than 90 percent of the clergy reported field education was helpful to them, even when poorly done— a very impressive statistic.[28]

But the problem remains. For even where there is good will (and this is not a universal condition) among the facul-

ties in the more traditional disciplines of Bible-History-Theology, there is little understanding of how these academic subjects can relate in a specific manner to field education, and this
inhibits the development of an integrated clerical role. This is
a problem with which Owen Thomas, professor of Theology
at the Episcopal Theological Seminary in Cambridge, Massachusetts, has experimented for years. Of the prevailing dichotomy between the traditional and practical disciplines, Thomas
says, "The fundamental source of it is the failure on *both sides*
to face the basic question about what the church and its members should be and do today. The traditional disciplines often
do not get to this question and the practical disciplines assume
that it has been answered." [29] I think this is quite true, particularly since the purpose of this book is to speak to that very
question for our times.

It is important to see that although the charge is frequently made that faculties representing Bible-History-Theology are hopelessly obscurantist—and there is just enough
truth to this to feed the notion—it is equally important to
perceive that all types of field education (including clinical
pastoral education) are both lacking in adequately trained
supervisors and theologically inept to an alarming degree. It
is well known that parish field education is woefully short of
trained supervision, and even in the program of the Association for Clinical Pastoral Education any seminary director of
field education learns that there are men to be avoided. The
prevailing concept in all field education is that we train men to
do "theological reflection." I would heartily concur with James
Bergland, who points out in listing five problem areas what
a very difficult thing this is for seminary faculties and clinical
supervisors as well as their students. He says (1) our religious
imagination has been objectively "traumatized"; (2) in Western thinking perception tends to be one-dimensional; (3) there
is a lack of an interdisciplinary theological style; (4) we are
inadequately educated for this kind of thinking; and (5) we
cannot limit (as the discipline attempts to do) reflection to

immediate experience.[30] The truth of these statements has been demonstrated for me in three years of seminars with seminarians and in a number of conferences of field educators, all devoted to "theological reflection."

The average pastor complains that his theological education did not equip him to do a defined job, and the tragedy is that even when the seminary tries to break out of fifteen hundred years of tradition, it is not sure where to go and how to do it. Areas in which the Episcopal priest reports that he got *too little* education are predominantly Christian Education (68 percent), Social Problems (71 percent), Pastoral Care (60 percent), Administrative and Organizational Techniques (65 percent), Public Relations (66 percent), Communications (71 percent), and, as I reported before, Psychology and Counseling (66 percent).[31] I am not at all sure that the seminary knows how or has the ability to offer the kind of training these statistics plead for. Perhaps Maynard Moore, a student at Union in New York, is right: "The inadequacy . . . of theological education lies in its taking for granted inherited relationships between seminaries and churches and its passing over some important questions that have to do with the function of the Church in contemporary society." [32]

Yet does the solution lie in what Moore and others propose: a functional model of theological education? Just recently a "Seminary of the Streets" has been underwritten by Trinity Church, Wall Street, under the direction of John D. Swanson; in the program men will leave the traditional seminary for a year to live and learn in the slums of the Lower East Side of New York. Undoubtedly this break from the usual pattern of three years in an artificial community is a step in the right direction. I am not sure, however, but that it is not still an avoidance of the *real issue*: the relating of Bible-History-Theology to ministerial function in such a way that they inform and shape one another. Charles Feilding points out that the summer of clinical pastoral education can be a "cop out" on the part of the seminary in facing the issues of ecu-

menical and functional theology.[33] What is the difference between three months and a year; and how do we remove the
gulf between a seminary that produces educated men and one
that develops skilled professionals?

A third area that has a causal relation to the image and
morale of the clergyman is the support system within the ministry. What happens to the pastor, equipped with a vaguely
defined job description, trained in a poorly integrated system,
once he finds himself functioning as minister?

The first thing he will discover is that *all ministerial functions rest on him.* Whereas from time to time we pay lip service to the apostolate of the laity, and we speak vigorously of
the threefold nature of Holy Orders, all the discussions of
ministry by Blizzard, Hiltner, Fichter, Hadden, Feilding, etc.,
assume that ministerial function and the role of the presbyter/
pastor are almost entirely congruent. This is the result of the
modern equation of education with function, the development
of the parish program, the ensuing need to "ramrod" the organization, and the notion of ministry as profession. The fact
that Trent reflects a historic suspicion of the layman and the
*Eigenkirchen* does not help the matter from the viewpoint of
Roman Catholic canon law.

The pastor carries out this role in what is primarily a
*congregational* setting. In a pluralistic culture, with the size of
denominational administrative units running sometimes in
excess of a state, it is extremely difficult for the average pastor
to have a strong sense of his place beyond the immediate congregation. Some might question this statement. In Jud's study
the point is made that ministers in the United Church of
Christ are not subject to much hierarchical discipline, but that
denominational executives are important because they offer
the best possibility of a move upward.[34] In the Episcopal
Church, where the organization is to a certain extent more
hierarchically oriented (although this can be easily exaggerated), 25 percent of the priests state that they value their
bishop's judgment more than anyone else's, followed by that

of the vestry, some members of the congregation, their wives, and fellow Episcopal clergy.[35] Furthermore, after his wife (36 percent) the Episcopal priest believes that his bishop would support him most in a controversial issue (20 percent).[36] Yet I think it is possible to see some of this grounded on what theologically *should* be true rather than what is true. It is interesting that when vestrymen in the Episcopal Church were asked who besides themselves they considered had the most influence on the decisions of their rector or vicar, 24 percent answered "some members of the vestry" and only 6 percent answered "the bishop"; 49 percent could not answer the question![37]

I would argue that the "significant others" (after the theory of George Herbert Mead) for the pastor are the members of his congregation, and particularly his vestry or its equivalent. Frequently the maintenance of his integrity demands of him alienation from this group, and he must pay the price of loneliness and depression.[38] Of Episcopal clergy, 31 percent say the congregation limits their ability to perform their clerical functions. An illuminating point made in the United Presbyterian survey is the clear difference between the kinds of pastoral skills sought by the clergyman and those expected by the layman.[39]

More often, I would say, the pastor has not clarified his theology and self-image to the point where issues can be defined between himself and his parish, *and he becomes a function of his congregation.* When challenged, this is explained in terms of "maintaining the pastoral relationship"—a point that has just enough truth to make it an insidious trap. But it is remarkable how many a clergyman fulfills the *congregation's* image of the pastor, which is utterly incongruent with the Gospel's. This is not infrequently carried to the point of regularly decorating the social page, being seen frequently at the bars of the better country clubs, filling time with very "busy work" that is calculated to impress, and keeping peace at the price of the curate's integrity and the occasional Christian's good conscience. I was only recently reminded of this terrible seduction when one of our graduating seniors returned from a job interview in a parish of over fifteen hundred communicants to report that upon asking what kind of counseling they did there the rector replied in utter amazement, "Counseling? We have no problems here!"

It is very clear that the primary hold of the congregation and especially the vestry over the clergyman is that they pay his salary. This leads us to reflect upon the financial support of the clergyman. In the Episcopal Church in 1967 the median cash salary was $6,000; and with fringe benefits (house, car allowance, utilities) the median salary was $7,500.[40] This is considerably less than professional technical workers and craftsmen, and somewhat less than salespeople. The mean income of an Episcopal priest is $8,101. This is lower than the mean average on the first level of chief accountants, personnel directors, attorneys, managers of office services, and engineers, all of whom may anticipate growth in earnings to between $19,000 and $27,000. Only 1 percent of the Episcopal clergy make more than $15,000.[41] How this compares with Protestant clergy is hard to say, though in 1963 an NCCC survey revealed that Episcopal salaries ran 4 percent higher than the overall average. Although Roman Catholic priests get much less "on paper," there is no question that celibates are in fact better off in purchasing power. Viewed historically, the financial remuneration of clergy is probably better today than ever before, with possibly such exceptions as the early seventeenth-century Scottish Church. Considered relative to the cultural ideals and other employment, however, the situation is degrading and destructive of morale in a manner that cannot be exaggerated.

Asked what the three kinds of deprivations most frequently encountered by the families of clergy are, one out of four Episcopal priests named economic problems.[42] Their wives agreed. However, in Jud's study of UCC ministers it is interesting to note that in rating reasons related to why men leave the active ministry, money is a very important factor for only 12.2 percent. My impression is that financial difficulties rankle, inhibit effectiveness, and destroy integrity. The average layman does not realize how much many clergy bitterly resent their poor pay, living in someone else's house, and having to depend on the largesse of the 10 percent discount. *The simple fact is that in our affluent society genteel poverty has no discernible positive value*, ascetical or emotional, and only symbolizes lack of community value for services performed. It is only out of deep commitment and perhaps fear that he is trained to do nothing else that the average clergyman is willing to sacrifice his integrity for a salary comparable to that earned by someone with less than a college degree.

One thing we may expect in regard to this situation is growing "moonlighting," which may not be a bad development. Another increasing practice will be that more wives will take paid jobs. Now one out of three wives of Episcopal clergy contribute to the family income. This too has created deep resentment on the part of the wife as well as her husband. We must keep in mind that the average clergyman's wife is his strongest source of moral support.[43]

Another difficulty is the general feeling of many clergy that they are "put on a pedestal" and dehumanized in order to render them an *ineffective ideal*. Charles Smith, in his *How to Become a Bishop Without Being Religious*, did a beautiful job of ridiculing the layman's notion of his pastor as a "third gender" (neuter).[44] Many readers probably did not realize the pointed nature of the remarks behind his gracious humor. Thirteen percent of the Episcopal clergy listed this ambiguous social role as a deprivation in their life.[45] I suspect a greater percentage in all denominations are becoming increasingly aware of the implicit assumption carried with this isolation; namely, that the clergyman does not understand what it is to live in the "rough and tumble world," and therefore has no right to speak to it. It was on this basis that a group of clergy were attacked on the question of civil rights in the public press in the early sixties in Baton Rouge, Louisiana. A sensitivity to this phenomenon is driving many Roman Catholic and Anglican clergy out of a distinctive clerical garb, which in our society, rather than being a witness to a denial of the flesh *within* a culture that acknowledges its true ascetic end, effects an *isolation and eccentricity* that confirms our culture's conviction of our naïvete. Fr. Martin Thornton, whose "Catholicity" only the ignorant would question, is probably accurate when he writes:

There would appear to me to be very strong arguments against any kind of distinctive clerical badge . . . In my own experience (for what it is worth) it is extremely difficult to maintain recollective love, to respect and intercede, to try to serve humbly and without ostentation, when everyone is looking at you; when a few of the faithful think, quite wrongly, that you appear to be very holy, and when the rest, quite rightly, think you look idiotic.[46]

Perhaps the most reasoned argument in favor of the distinctiveness of the pastor in general and for the use of clerical garb in particular is that made by the Presbyterian, David C. Jacobsen, in *The Positive Use of the Minister's Role*.[47] Basically he is arguing for the role of the pastor as representative of the visible Church and all the positive values attached to that image. I would say, however, that he is probably overrating the current image of the Church in our culture and underestimating the perversity of the "using" of Church and minister for sub-Christian ends.

An example of such "using" would be the clergy's complaint that they are "running a show," in which the congregation seeks more to be entertained than edified. Competing with all kinds of media, attendance and participation is dependent upon the parson's success in offering something better than TV. One young pastor, seeking to get out of the parochial ministry, assured me that for a number of years he had been one of the most "successful rectors" in his diocese (and I have no reason to doubt his assessment). But he remarked sadly, "I ran out of tricks." As a student at the Philadelphia Divinity School it was my delight to read weekly the amazing advertisements of the rector of Christ and St. Michael's Episcopal Church, Germantown, Pennsylvania, in the Philadelphia papers. Hamilton Aulenbach, just recently retired, was able to build a ministry upon a succession of imaginative gimmicks. But there is only one of him, and probably room for very few of his kind in the Church. Furthermore, I'm inclined to agree with R. K. Yerkes' observation that he could do just as well "with a barrel of whiskey in the narthex."

Finally, in regard to the support of the clergy, it must be admitted that there is a leadership vacuum. At the risk of seeming uncharitable, it has to be said that advancement in most denominations goes to men who are "safe" and "statistically successful." There are notable exceptions to this, and most of them get thoroughly vilified in letters to the editors and even editorials of the church press, not to mention being crucified daily in "bull sessions" in rectories, seminary dorms, and church conferences. But for the majority conformity comes before creativity, expediency before imagination, and fear before thought. Clergy plead for directives from their superiors, not so much because they want something with which to "club" their people, although some desire this as well, but rather so they can have some sense that the Church is moving in dialogue with the times. My impression is that we have strangely managed to antagonize more people lately while saying less of any kind of imaginative substance than would seem possible. There is particularly a lack of theological reflection that can command the thought of those Christians who really want to let reason rather than emotion guide their commitments.

Fourth, the ebbing of the clerical image and loss of morale is related to a growing confusion in theological conviction and devotional commitment. I lump these two together not only because systematic and ascetical theology are intimately related, but also because there is a justifiable abandonment of some notions that prevailed in previous years, but a regrettable failure to retain the core of truth in both of these disciplines.

A hundred years ago the average clergyman still had a fairly solid common, cognitive, assumptive base with the laity upon which to rest his vocational image. It was generally believed man possessed in some sense a defective nature, incapable of fellowship with God as a result of his biological descent from Adam. As a result, if he was left to his own devices he would after death go to a place called hell, ruled by Satan, where he would suffer eternal punishment. Yet since God the Father created and loved man, he sent his Son, conceived by the Holy Spirit of the Virgin Mary, to suffer a vicarious death upon the Cross and to free man from Satan's power. The success of his mission was proclaimed in his historical resurrection from the tomb, and his ascension into heaven to intercede for man. Man might share in the power of the Cross through the agency of the Holy Spirit either by an act of faith (Protestantism) or by his life in the Church and its sacraments (Catholicism). There was usually a sort of implicit and chronic Manichaeanism in all of this. Sin was identified with the flesh, and God with our spiritual self. Perhaps this all can be summed up in the literal interpretation of "Christ crucified, risen, coming again." [48]

The problem is that the majority of Christians (with the notable exceptions of groups such as the Missouri Synod Lutherans, the various Baptist bodies, and the sects), do not believe just like this anymore, be they lay or clerical. For example, only 3 percent of Episcopal clergy believe that Adam and Eve were historical, only 5 percent that the Scriptures can be a source of historical, geographical, and other secular information, and only 45 percent that man is guilty of original sin.[49] There were those who wanted to try Bishop James A. Pike for heresy. If they made the biological miracle of the Virgin Birth an issue (there were other issues more important), they would have had to try 44 percent of Episcopal priests with him! Episcopal priests do a little better with the physical resurrection of

Jesus, inasmuch as 70 percent believe in this pivotal teaching of the Church.[50] It is particularly interesting for us that in the Episcopal Church, where the notion of priestly "character" seems to have prevailed for some time, only one out of three consider themselves "different after ordination" ontologically.[51] There is no denomination upon whose clergy the twentieth-century discussion of myth and symbol—not only in accordance with Bultmann, but also Tillich, Ricoeur, Barfield, Ebeling and many others—has made a greater impact than the Episcopal Church.[52]

According to Stark and Glock the Episcopal Church is, together with the Congregationalists and Methodists, a "liberal Protestant church." The "moderate Protestant churches" are the Disciples of Christ, the Presbyterians, the American Lutherans, and the American Baptists. The "conservative Protestant churches" are the Missouri Synod Lutherans, the Southern Baptists, and the various sects. The Roman Catholics appear to fall somewhere in the center to the right edge of the "moderate" group in their "orthodoxy index." The basic point Stark and Glock are making, however, "is that the overwhelming proportion of Americans today do not adhere to a pristine orthodoxy." Less than a third overall were firmly committed to these three beliefs: "that there is a life beyond death, that Jesus was born of a virgin, and that Jesus walked on the water" (which the authors argue are reliable indices of the individual's total commitment).[53] The clergy are very little different from the laity.

One way of meeting this situation is to reformulate our theological propositions in such a way that once more we will have a common cognitive base for Christian ministry. This is being attempted by a number of brilliant theologians, and it is my conviction that it is the only possible way to restore integrity to the Church's ministerial function. However, to date it is very difficult to command a sufficiently wide hearing to the theological disciplines on both a clerical and lay level even to begin to establish such a foundation. Instead we are "tossed

by the waves and whirled about by every fresh gust of teaching" (Eph. 4:14).

Stark and Glock make the point that with the loss of
orthodoxy, clergy have attempted to substitute "ethicalism,"
which is the name they would give to the ideology of the "new
breed." This is undergirded by "conceptions of God as ultimate concern, as love, as poetry, as the divine essence in all
of us—the ground of our being . . . But," they ask, "how do
they [these concepts] differ from humanism?" [54] They do not
see us going back to conservative Christianity, and apparently
they do not give much hope for the "salability" of contemporary theological reformulations. Ethicalism, however, they say,
is negatively related to religious commitment (belief, practice,
experience, knowledge, and communal involvement) in Protestantism, and has only a slight positive relation in Roman
Catholicism; which leaves the Church and its clergy where? [55]
Their answer is not a little threatening to the "man of the
cloth."

The institutional shape of the religion of the future is as difficult
to predict as its theological content. Conceivably it may take a
public character, as suggested recently by Robert Bellah [see page
121], or the invisible form anticipated by Thomas Luckmann. Or
it may live on in a public witness conducted by priests with
parishes similar to religions in Asia. Quite possibly, religion in the
future will be very different from anything we can now anticipate.[56]

Needless to say, many find this kind of suggestion appall-
ing. When this thesis was first suggested in an article in *Trans-
action*, two letters from informed people came back with impassioned denials of the authors' conclusions (both letters
missing the basic point).[57] Yet one might ask if there is not an
occasional feeling on the part of the clergy that they already
are serving as some sort of "civil morale officer." Certainly military chaplains are frequently eased into this function, and all
of us know the experience, as my students at Louisiana State

University used to say, of "representing the God squad." Many a pastor works more as "surrogate parent" than anything else, and some enjoy acting as the "local guru." But my overall impression is that the average "successful clergyman" hides from the real thrust of the big question being asked by Stark and Glock.

I am not aware of any survey that has been made of the devotional life of the clergy. It would be rather like polling America's psychiatrists about their sexual habits. It is true that in seminaries, be they Roman, Anglican, or Protestant, where the corporate worship of the community is optional, students and faculty are often to be noted for their absence. Whether this carries over into the private ascetic life of the cleric is difficult to determine. In a study of devotionalism in the laity, Glock and Stark found that Protestants are more likely to pray privately than attend services regularly, whereas with Roman Catholics it is the other way around.[58] Only the Congregationalists and the Methodists were lower in devotional participation than the Episcopalians; and, despite some myth to the contrary, church attendance for Episcopalians was almost exactly the Protestant average.[59]

Yet the tradition in the Episcopal Church for the clergy is daily prayer in the form of the offices of Morning and Evening Prayer, and the religious orders, through various associate rules, have encouraged an ideal of private intercession, Bible reading, and meditation. I doubt that there is any group of secular clergy for whom the personal devotional life is more clearly spelled out than the Anglican although we are not unique in claiming that the primary support of the cleric is his devotional life. Yet I can remember well my surprise as a young priest to discover that the Roman Catholic secular priest has no such clear demand upon him, and certainly the Protestant tradition of Bible-centered prayer is much less specific and prescribed.

Martin Thornton, an Anglican ascetical theologian, argues that the nature of the cleric is to be a learned man who prays.[60] This is what the bishop requires of the candidate in the Ordering of Priests in the Book of Common Prayer (page 542). But spirituality is not just correlative to learning; it is dependent upon a sense of a transcendent, personal God. The failure of contemporary theology to feed the ascetical theologian viable images that convey this reality to him and to those whom he would lead to a new spirituality has undoubtedly frustrated the process. There are indications that the writings of Dietrich Bonhoeffer offer the greatest possibilities in the area of a renewed ascetical theology, particularly since it now appears that the average cleric has either lost interest in the German martyr or has become aware of the gross popular distortion of his meaning. However, insights such as Bonhoeffer's have not been carried over into a contemporary method of prayer as yet. Thornton's suggestion that it is better to read the Office on a bus than in a neo-gothic barn has the right instinct, but Cranmer is still not the answer.

We are at a loss here. My seminarians are dutiful in their chapel attendance, but many are frank to say they are bored. I shall always be grateful to my Presbyterian clinical supervisor, who rebuked a fellow student of mine, a Roman Catholic sister, for suggesting that one ought to pray only when one *felt* like it. But what are my own resources, and how am I going to respond to the layman who has found the meaning of prayer for the first time in Malcolm Boyd's *Are You Running with Me, Jesus?* and asks if I would substitute some of it for the Book of Common Prayer? Speaking as an Episcopalian, I am caught between boredom and discipline, contemporaneity and indecorousness; and I suspect I am typical of the vast majority of my fellow clerics, for whom there seem to be no answers.

These four reasons why the image of the pastor is diminished today and why men are leaving the stipendiary ministry —ambiguity of role, disintegrated education, loss of personal integrity, and a moribund systematic and ascetical theology— certainly do not capture all the facets of the problem. For one thing I have not discussed family problems among the married clergy and the desire for a wife among the celibate clergy. But there is one thing that impresses anyone who explores the "clerical exodus" or just the problem of morale: "loss of faith" is not generally the problem. I have carefully spoken of men leaving the "stipendiary ministry," *not* the "ministry." Many who are now secularly employed consider themselves better "ministers" than before. The problem is with structures, identity of professional role, cognitive patterns; not with belief in Jesus as "the man for others," "the new being," "faith come to expression," or the "proleptic event of the eschaton." This is a very different situation than existed after World War I.

Having said this, it is necessary to conclude this chapter with some discussion of the quality of the men themselves as they enter the life of ministry. I have been impressed recently by very candid comments of prominent laymen who have described the quality of candidates as, generally speaking, anywhere from just poor to catastrophic. Their charges run from emotional imbalance through acute insensitivity, laziness and stupidity, to chronic naïvete. They may well say this to individuals like me because the blame is frequently laid on seminaries.

In this light, perhaps nothing aroused as much emotion in the 1967 report to the Episcopal Church on its theological education (the so-called "Pusey Report," which was actually prepared by the director of the study, Charles L. Taylor, and was called *Ministry for Tomorrow*), as its statement that the intellectual level of clergy and seminarians was poor. Of those in seminary, 43 percent had a C+ average or lower, and only 16 percent a B+ average or above.[61] There are those who seriously question the validity of these figures, and point out that in a selected group of clergy the average intelligence quotient runs between 120 and 129, which is considered "superior." Sometimes the response has been made in a negative form: high scholarly attainment does not guarantee a man will be a good pastor (which is true enough, but much less does stupidity). Recently I have heard a more explicitly anti-intellectual argument: the average, mediocre mind in our parishes needs intellectually mediocre clergy. If so, Taylor says that we are fulfilling this "need," since (he says) we have a predominance of intellectually mediocre students.

The solution to this problem, it is sometimes suggested, is that we need to inspire seminarians to better learning. There is no doubt that the faculty of our seminaries could improve their teaching techniques, preparation, and enthusiasm; but this is a very dangerous half-truth. For if we go about muttering *only* "mea culpas," we will miss a much more fundamental truth that an ambiguous calling has little attraction to mentally alert people, in the first place, and offers a very shaky base upon which to build a challenge to the mentally somnolent, in the second place.

A more important question, at which Taylor hints, is why men today are attracted to the ministry if all these other things are true. In attempting to answer that question it must be said that we have no *sure* data; it is very easy to do a severe injustice to many people of profound Christian conviction by simplistic answers; and it is very important that critics understand their own bias. Furthermore, it must be very clearly understood that if blame is to be laid for the intellectual or emotional problems of the clergy, the Church *as a whole* must assume the burden for creating a climate where those kinds of situations occur. At the same time, the *extreme defensiveness* among many seminarians and clergymen on the subject of the emotional needs that all of us are seeking to fulfill as clergymen, and the possibility that these inhibit the effectiveness of our ministry, does not add confidence to their claim of mental health. It is very important that we be willing to acknowledge that God can use all kinds of people, but also he expects us to use good sense in guiding one another into areas of service in which there is a likelihood that we can profit others and ourselves. A spirit of trust is desperately needed where the underlying factors that move men to seek ordination can be explored thoroughly and constructively.

Taylor observed that the motivations of many men who

leave other forms of employment to seek a stipendiary, ordained ministry (including over 50 percent of the Episcopal
clergy)[62] may have some negative connotations: a fleeing from
or reacting against rather than an embracing of a vocation long
sought and now found. He then went on to say "some" students in seminary are seeking therapy, "more" are simply alienated from the world, seeking protection, and an "encouraging number" are "reformers" and students of mature faith.[63]
Perhaps since this report the number of "reformers" has
grown, but my impression is that his analysis is accurate.

Another interesting question particularly confronting
Episcopalians arises from the fact that 52 percent of our clergy
are converts, more than half of whom came to us between the
ages of sixteen and twenty-five (when the identity crisis is at its
height). Reasons given for this are predominantly new possibilities in the Episcopal Church (34 percent), dissatisfaction
with their former church (19 percent), or a combination of
both (15 percent).[64] Apparently this phenomenon reaches
a proportion in the Episcopal Church unlike any other major
denomination. For example, among United Presbyterians, although 37 percent were not originally of that denomination,
only 14 percent were from other than "sister churches." [65]
Why is this recruitment of clergy from other denominations so
common in the Episcopal Church? We would like to think,
probably, that it is because of our conscious strengths, and that
may be so. It is interesting and worth some reflection, however,
that the Episcopal Church offers a highly structured liturgy,
a rational theology, reported good taste, an appearance of a
defined polity, and it has a married and reasonably well-paid
clergy.

Dunn, in an article written in 1965, said that a review of
all the studies performed in the past fifteen years confirmed
the notion that "religious and religious applicants [which
limits its value for secular clergy] show signs of defensive behavior typical of persons with neurotic tendencies." By this he

meant that they tended to be perfectionistic, worrisome, intro-versive, socially inept, and in some extreme cases isolated and withdrawn.[66] An analysis by Walter Kania argues that possibly the tests that have indicated these characteristics are wrong,[67] but a good many studies indicate evidence that some people who are anxious, guilt-ridden, introversive, obsessive, who find it difficult to accept hostile or sexual feelings in themselves, and who feel inferior, seek a vocation in the Church.[68] It may be conceived, consequently, as an ideal institution for passive-dependent people. The tragedy for such people is that this is less and less so, particularly where the Church is working with good effect. An even greater tragedy is that their erroneous im-pressions and neurotic expectancies are sometimes reinforced by their seminary training.[69]

Whether or not the stress that is created by this differ-entiation between expectancy and reality results in emotional illness poses a question for which we do not have the data. Margaretta Bowers, a New York psychiatrist who published in 1963 one of the earlier studies of the mental health of the clergy, *Conflicts of the Clergy*, seemed to suggest to many that it does. But Dr. Bowers as a clinician gets a highly biased sam-ple of clergy and may not offer the most reliable information. A report to the House of Bishops of the Episcopal Church some years ago on the mental health of the clergy gave some indication that we are faced with a critical problem; and it has been the contention of RACA, an organization dedicated to the treatment of alcoholic Episcopal clergy, that one form of mental illness, alcoholism, is in great need of attention among clergy.

We cannot deal here with the matter of psychotherapy for pastors, except to say that it is an acute problem. Somehow, to many pastors and to more laymen, for a clergyman to seek psychiatric help is the admission of a collapse of faith. This is absurd, but saying so does not remove the stigma many feel. It is almost as if the clergyman was not only thrust cognitively back into the seventeenth century, but that, unlike his people, he was expected to live in an era where mental illness was considered "possession."

The implication is that what I have said to this point relates primarily to the clergyman who seeks to be chaplain to the "ghetto" or "geisha" for a "teahouse." But it would be interesting to explore the unconscious motivations of the "new breed," whose hostility is more directed outward against structure and tradition and who abrogate reflection and mediation in favor of action and confrontation. Is this always a matter of acting out of rational conviction? Kenneth Keniston's study *Young Radicals* would warn us in general against psychologizing their activity;[70] but I think it would be equally unwise to disallow the possibility that some unconscious need was being met here that demanded this shape of their ministry, and left them frustrated and bored when it did not come to pass, but self-fulfilled when they "left in despair of the institution."

I want now to relate the figure of the contemporary clergyman to the total perspective I have developed in the first part of the book. What comes across most forcefully is the *discontinuity* of the pastor to the past tradition of the Church *and* to the present culture. The United Presbyterian study says that "all his [the cleric's] customary reference points have come under attack." [71] It is worse than that. For eighteen hundred years ministry was integrally related to the core of the community's total life: first to the persecuted Church and then to the entire society. Its teachings were the ultimate expression of its most cherished values and hopes. Its membership arose from the people and lived among the people, and yet possessed the "tools of transcendence."

The contemporary clergyman is a product of the middle class, not the "old," but the "new," which is itself a recent phenomenon. He embodies within himself the *detached* existence of that class, cut off from soil, value, and other members of the class. His loneliness, as he is trust into a peripheral role of therapy and socialization, is a function of mobile America and the depersonalization of technocracy. He is caught up in problems of maintaining a healthy family, paying his bills, and running a voluntary association—all of which are expressive of the basic question of integrity: *a man is what he does*. It is amazing that men still come to seminary and that so many do in fact touch the lives of their people for good. It is a testimony to the power of the Holy Spirit.

Perhaps I have spent too much time painting too gloomy a picture. For indeed in many Christian communities there is a sense of the pastor as the sacramental person, he who embodies in his presence with others the transcultural, transcendent person of God. But these instances are too few. In our groping we are caught up in ideals of ministry that cloud this image, and the very manner of recruiting and training men is calculated to make its fulfillment next to impossible. How can a young man, "sentenced" out of seminary to three years in a strange world (to him) of a small-town mission, be to the people a sacramental person? How can the "cardinal rector," determined to please his vestry in order to maintain his "accustomed standard of living," be a sacramental person? The whole thing is unrealistic.

True, amid all the urging for better organizations, we have not lost sight of the role of the sacramental rite and even the Word. Roman Catholics have occasionally gone overboard for the latter, triggering some Protestant warnings that the homily is not *the* answer. We need to become more aware of the relationship of Word to Person, and what we proclaim from our pulpits is ourselves, in Christ or in confusion. As for the rite, titillating romantic aesthetes enraptured with late medieval ecclesiastical haberdashery often reveal an immoral disregard for suffering humanity. But this is only the exaggerated expression of a failure to see where the roots of ritual lie in the life of man. Somehow it cannot remove him from his world, but must enable him to live in this world with meaning. The kind of pastorate we need is that which can wrestle with this understanding of the eternal value of Word and Rite, and not appear absurd to the world.

One way of touching upon the sensitive core of the whole problem is to think for a moment upon the need of the contemporary clergyman to *internalize* the symbols of his faith: to be, so to speak, an entirely self-contained, Christian person. He cannot, like the medieval or modern cleric, depend upon society to support him and feed him in his role. To a degree he cannot depend, as did the ancient bishop, upon his Christian community. He cannot even depend upon a coherent tradition of theology and spirituality. He has to do a great deal of it alone with a hidden God.

Perhaps this is too much to expect of anyone. Yet I cannot believe God will let his Church continue on its present way into oblivion. We can make a beginning by challenging a number of assumptions. But first we must look in much more detail at contemporary models of ministry, as opposed to inherited ones, and raise the question of what confidence we may place in them as solutions for the despair I have outlined here.

## chapter 9

# INSTANT PARSONS
# AND PROPHETS
# WITHOUT
# PORTFOLIO

Over the past fifty years the study
of ministry has been dominated by
the teachers of pastoral care. Preaching is on the defensive
(I periodically receive communications asking if we are still
offering homiletics at my seminary!), teaching has not been
able to catch the imagination of the average student,[1] liturgics
has become a branch of ecclesiastical history, administration
is what everyone despises and yet spends much of his time
doing, discipline is heard as a distant rumble (significantly
enough, from professors of pastoral care), and missions (evangelism) remind us too much of colonialism and triumphalism.
Only prophecy, but not by that name, stands to challenge the
assumption that "real ministry" is pastoral care.

James Ashbrook, whose new title at the affiliated institutions of Colgate-Rochester/Bexley Hall is Professor of Psychology and Theology (a significant switch from Professor of
Pastoral Theology), has captured the focus of this emphasis
in describing Seward Hiltner as the contemporary pioneer in
pastoral care, the work of William Clebsch and Charles Jaekle
as providing its historical base (*Pastoral Care in Historical
Perspective*), and Howard Clinebell as the most recent source
of its refined definition.[2]

In his *Preface to Pastoral Theology* Hiltner defines pastoral care as "shepherding."[3] This concept, which has become the "catchword" in Hiltnerian pastoral theology, he
divides into healing, sustaining, and guiding. "Shepherding"

itself, Hiltner tells us, is a " 'perspective' [which] enables us to think of the subject, or shepherd, as having and exercising an attitude or point of view or type of feeling that is basic to him and not just something tacked on. At the same time the subject is and has and feels more than this perspective." [4] Hiltner goes on to insist, in line with the situation as I have just described it, that pastoral care is not an "office" or discrete function, as I have spoken of it in this book, but a perspective that pervaded all of ministry. The theological reflection upon the experience of shepherding is operation-centered, not logic-centered, and is called pastoral theology. Other operation-centered areas are communicating and organizing, reflection upon which form evangelistic and ecclesiastical theology.

Other than the fact that this is a completely novel approach, I would offer these preliminary comments. Relating pastoral care and shepherding to the study of *poimenics* or its translation, "shepherding," is only remotely related to what Hiltner describes. I do not think, therefore, that he can get support for his radical departure from traditional ministerial forms in this manner, aside from the fact that *poimenics* is itself something of a novelty. This becomes particularly apparent when, search as we will, shepherding is never defined in any kind of logic-centered manner. To what end do we heal, sustain, and guide people? Hiltner talks about functional wholeness, comfort and encouragement, and moral resources;[5] but he says nothing about a distinctive Christian anthropology.

Clebsch and Jaekle, on the basis of historical analysis, refined Hiltner's description of pastoral care and spoke of healing, sustaining, guiding, and *reconciling*. The fourth is the most important, a discovery obviously aided by the growing concerns for racism and other forms of alienation, which Hiltner has never really worked into his system. Clinebell builds his exposition of the art of counseling upon this fourfold distinction of Clebsch and Jaekle. As he tells us, reconciliation includes discipline, which I consider a ministerial function different from pastoral care.[6] Here the tendency for pastoral care to become the overarching ministerial function is illustrated once again.

How these distinctions differ from my own description of eight ministerial functions, centered in the sacramental person, is at least in part to be understood by the difference in orientation between me and Seward Hiltner. I have begun from the presupposition that ministry is the function of the Church, as the *Ursakrament*, relating to the world of persons. This is a theological *a priori*. As such it is foreign to Hiltner, who begins from an empirical methodology, which is clinical and draws heavily upon psychology. Theology is *a posteriori* to the experience, which is defined by the discipline of the behavioral science. This assumption has had a sweeping effect upon the entire pastoral discipline since 1945. It lies at the heart of the so-called "psychological model" of ministry.

To understand in greater depth how the psychological model developed, it is necessary to go back to the 1920s and the slackening enthusiasm for the Social Gospel. In American Protestant theology it was a very unproductive period. Obviously the same cannot be said for Europe, since at this time Barth's *Commentary on Romans* (1919), Bultmann's *History of the Synoptic Tradition* (1923), and Brunner's *The Mediator* (1926) were all establishing the theological agenda for the years to come. In Roman Catholicism everyone was still in the grip of *Sacrotum Antistitum*, the *motu proprio* of Pius X, requiring of all Roman clergy the antimodernist oath. Liberal Protestant theology, which was almost no theology, held sway in this country without any really serious challenge. At this time Dietrich Bonhoeffer, studying at Union Theological Seminary in New York, wrote back to a friend in Germany:

A theology is not to be found here. I attend what are theoretically lectures . . . they clatter till all is blue without any factual foundation or any criteria of thought becoming visible. The students

. . . have not the faintest notion what dogmatic theology is all about . . . they intoxicate themselves with liberal and humanistic expressions, laugh at the fundamentalists, and basically they are not even a match for them.[7]

Into this vacuum moved the creative thought of two medical doctors, William Keller and Richard Cabot, followed by the enigmatic figure of Anton T. Boisen. Keller was a great believer in "social engineering," and worked out a plan with Samuel Mercer, the dean of Bexley Hall, designed to expose students there to various social-work programs in Cincinnati, in order that they be sensitive to their role as ministers in making a better world. The plan grew into the Graduate School of Applied Religion and was under the direction for some years of Joseph Fletcher, whose deep interest in social ethics, in addition to his clinical experience, gave the program its own distinctive orientation.

Richard Cabot, on the other hand, thought that there was much value in associating seminarians and clergy with the pure medical model, and began a clinical program at Massachusetts General Hospital. There he had as a student for a time Anton Boisen, who was an older man, vocationally confused for many years and recently a patient in a mental hospital. Boisen came to believe during his own treatment that the best theological training for clergy was the experience of people in crisis, the "living human documents" (a phrase now the unofficial motto of clinical pastoral education). He sought with Cabot to develop this theory, but soon broke with him because of his conviction of the psychogenic nature of mental illness. This was identified with psychoanalytic theory then, though Boisen certainly later was not a pure Freudian. Although in later years Boisen taught in seminary, did some supervision, and then was inactive in the movement, he is generally considered the father of clinical pastoral education.

It is impossible to recount the fascinating and strange process through which this new concept of education and ministry itself grew.[8] Out of the clinical setting there developed a new pastoral theology, which came to most of the seminaries after 1945. Its principal mentor, Seward Hiltner, was inspired in his undergraduate days by the empirical study of religions. In seminary he studied under Boisen, and underwent clinical training in a number of centers. After qualifying for the Ph.D. in theology, he did not go into a parish, but was executive secretary from 1935 to 1938 of the Council for Clinical Training of Theological Students. There Helen Flanders Dunbar, M.D., was in command—a remarkable woman, thoroughly committed to a psychoanalytical model of training. During Hiltner's stay with the CCT he developed the two cardinal principles of his approach: (1) a professional model for theological education, and (2) a dialogical relationship between theological presuppositions and the behavioral sciences. The first is defined by the second. As I have already implied, there was and is little *content* in Hiltner's "theological presuppositions" prior to the behavioral analysis of the human condition. For Hiltner still appears to me remarkably untouched by the currents of American theology that evolved in the 1930s and '40s in clear opposition to the "non-theology" of the 1920s, and he has always maintained a theology that Thomas Oden aptly calls "liberal pietism." [9]

Hiltner's presence at the Divinity School of the University of Chicago (1950–61)—after ten years as executive secretary of the Commission on Religion and Health of the Federal Council of the Churches of Christ in America (1938–48), and two years finishing his Ph.D.—and now his post at Princeton Theological Seminary (1961–   ) has made him in many ways the predominant influence in pastoral care today. His work has been closely allied to the whole program of developing clinical pastoral education for clergy, although perhaps he has come to appear too academic for some in the field. For from the start clinical training has to one degree or another been a reaction to the traditional forms of the institutional Church and established theological education. It has had something of a messianic vision, embracing psychology as the solution to the ministerial dilemma. It is only fair to say that there has always been some tension within the clinical training movement against a too enthusiastic endorsement of psychology, and there is now a move away from this endorsement. The Institute of Pastoral Care, founded in 1944 by Paul E. Johnson and Rollin Fairbanks, claimed that it favored general hospitals as centers for training as opposed to the Council for Clinical Training's fondness for mental institutions. Whether true or not, the emphasis upon the clinical dimension of education, as opposed to the academic, and the commitment to a theology in dialogue with the behavioral sciences, offer good reason for the observed lack of communication for some years between men excited by clinical pastoral education and those in the parish ministry, and between the movement and the seminaries.

As the matter stands at present, most interdenominational seminaries or those representing the major Protestant churches require or strongly urge that students working for their first degree take clinical pastoral education. It is a growing movement in Roman Catholic seminaries. In 1967 the supervision of this program came under one agency, the Association of Clinical Pastoral Education, created by the merger of the Council for Clinical Training, the Institute of Pastoral Care, and several denominational accrediting groups. Consequently the philosophy and methods of this movement, beginning with Boisen, and strongly influenced by the writings and students of Hiltner, has had a great impact on a growing number of American clergy. There is considerable point, therefore, in seeing how the movement describes its own method.

Clinical Pastoral Education is a method of theological education whereby a student learns pastoral skills within a context of responsible relationship to people and under the direct supervision of a trained clergyman. It provides a learning situation for a theological student and continuing education for a clergyman in which they may develop awareness of the theological and psychosocial concerns of persons in crisis. Clinical Pastoral Education also confronts the student with the human predicament. It supplies the nurturing milieu for him to understand himself as a person, to know himself as a pastor, to integrate his theology more meaningfully with life, and to become aware of human worth and potential.[10]

This program is frequently criticized in that it trains men to minister to abnormal people or people in abnormal situations, and consequently does not prepare them to counsel people who are not psychotic in a normal setting. The criticism is backed up by the findings of a survey of counseling in the United States in which "in-practice clergy" reported just this problem.[11] Aside from the fact that general hospitals are now used as training centers as much or more than mental hospitals and prisons are, I suspect that part of the problem lies in the question of whether the student is there to learn about the person (including himself) or skills in counseling. People in stress situations are not radically different from people in general, only their needs are more apparent and accessible. There is no doubt, however, that there is probably more transferable knowledge acquired in a clinical setting in a parish or a general hospital than in a prison or mental hospital.

What most clinical pastoral education has done, however, is reinforce the prevailing image of the clergyman as committed first and foremost to pastoral care, sharpening the image to the point of making everyone want to function as a pastoral counselor. In such settings the significant models for ministry are generally sensitive doctors, psychiatrists, psychologists, psychiatric social workers, and clergy whose specialty is counseling. The orientation is psychological. In the early days of clinical training there was much bitter complaint about seminaries producing amateur psychiatrists. Certainly this has never been the intention, and there is constant affir-

mation of the shepherding model over against the psychotherapeutic; but it would be less than honest to claim that the
distinction between the two is clear, or to say that psychotherapy itself is not in a state of flux that leads it frequently
into the midst of the territory claimed by pastoral counseling.

In 1949 Hiltner wrote that "the generic aim of counseling is new insight, with proof in action." [12] The primary
method of pastoral counseling, based upon this definition, was
derived from the work of the psychologist Carl Rogers (himself a sometime student at Union Theological Seminary) and
his "client-centered therapy." The clergyman learned to listen,
empathize, and reflect. It had the great value of being safe
(it was not psychoanalysis), if relatively ineffective and misunderstood. The swing in psychotherapeutic circles in the past
ten years has been away from the passive therapist (be he
Rogerian or Freudian); and in existential psychology, though
not exclusively, there is much talk about the therapist bringing his own person, with his own particular meanings and
values, to the therapy room. I suspect in light of this that
Hiltner would want to modify his definition of counseling
somewhat. But the point is that this new ideal is being held
before the clergyman not because pastoral counseling has
developed some new role for itself, but because practically all
counseling has.

Hiltner, together with Lowell Colston, published in 1961
a comparative study of counseling in and out of a pastoral
context which hypothesized "that people who seek help from
a pastor in a pastoral setting may make more, or more rapid,
progress than if they seek another type of counselor." In a
very guarded way they concluded that there was some validity
to their hypothesis.[13] It was related, they said, to the positive
regard held for the Church and its representatives, a certain
level of expectancy, and a familiarity that permits a deeper
form of engagement to occur more quickly. It is interesting
that in the several efforts to define the difference between
pastoral counseling and other forms of counseling it is the

context of the Church and the representative function of the counselor that is mentioned, which in effect says that it is *the meaning and value of Christian theology* as opposed to some other point of view that makes the difference. It is somewhat ironic and a little frightening that it is precisely here that the contemporary pastoral care movement is weakest!

In attempting to evaluate the pastoral care movement, with its strong inclination to make pastoral counselors of clergy, I would have to say initially that its call for a dialogic relationship between theology and psychology is absolutely necessary. We can no more ignore today the insights of the various schools of psychology and psychiatry than the Scholastics could have passed over Aristotelianism in the high Middle Ages. Even today I hear psychology dismissed as "pseudoscientific" by otherwise intelligent clerics, and this is sheer folly. We must be grateful to the pioneers in this field and travel their road with them; but we must go further.

My criticisms of the "psychological model" of ministry—and obviously I do not think Hiltner has escaped them by talking about "shepherding"—are four. They are interrelated, but there is a certain logic to their sequence.

First, in its theoretical and emotional formulation, the psychological model has an inadequate anthropology. Gibson Winter is supposed to have said (I cannot locate the remark) that pastoral counseling was "the last form of pietism." There is truth in this quip, for with its fondness for one-to-one and one-to-small-group relations, and a tradition of homeostasis as preferable to conflict, the pastoral care movement has found it difficult to understand those who advocate change, revolution, and even violence. I well recall hearing an after-dinner speech by Don Browning before several hundred CPE supervisors on the need for a prophetic dimension in clinical pastoral education. His audience could be roughly classified as one-third asleep, one-third drunk, and one-third angrily muttering to one another. It was an incredibly insensitive response to what was a very appropriate challenge.

The contemporary pastoral care movement has not grasped the social dimension of human personality. It is well versed in the *vocabulary* of Freud and his interpreters, and Buber is someone it admires, but some critics would complain that it has not even understood and accepted a thorough-going psychological description of man. It hangs between its inherited Christian anthropology and that of the behavioral sciences. Certainly sociology is not given a proper place. The emphasis upon social ethics and prophetic zeal apparent in men like Keller, Fletcher, and Boisen himself has been lost somewhere.

Second, it is persistently anti-intellectual. Here again the charge of pietism is accurate, even though in a very different form. Where Aquinas said the highest element in man is intellect and Bonaventura said will, I get the distinct impression that in clinical pastoral education it is axiomatic that *feelings*, by which is meant *emotions*, are central.[13-a] Certainly the insight into the power of feelings is essential, and no clergyman can be exempt today from an exploration of his own feelings and their relationship to those of other people. My objection is, however, that clinical pastoral education, in its reaction to purely academic training, has not yet worked through its own feelings to where it can accept the role of theoretical constructs and the need for hard thinking. Hiltner argued correctly, in *Preface to Pastoral Theology*, that it is quite possible to undertake theological reflection on a base of operational experience. In a collection of essays honoring Hiltner, entitled *The New Shape of Pastoral Theology* (my feeling is that it is already showing its age a bit), James E. Spicer outlines an educational model for doing this which I find very helpful *on paper*.[14] But who is doing it? I have previously referred to the great difficulty found in "doing theology" and certainly Hiltner's own somewhat elusive discussion of "shepherding" does not qualify as "hardnosed theology" as I understand it.

Third, the psychological model is poorly equipped theologically. This obviously follows from its anti-intellectual bias and is an inherited problem. The men who are producing the theoretical material in the dialogue between theology and psychology—Homans, Stinnette, Outler, Roberts, Oden, Browning, etc.—are generally not leaders in clinical pastoral education. They are not read widely within the movement, nor on works in pure systematic and historical theology. Consequently, students report at least a theological lacuna in training sessions and often a real hostility toward theology.

This raises several interesting questions. Why do supervisors become supervisors? Are they feeling the necessity to work through the theological meaning of their ministry in a manner that demands its constant intellectual articulation? Is it a matter of avoiding for one reason or another a very important task in the Church's contemporary agenda rather than, in fact, entering into a dialogue? My impression is that the fundamental identity of many supervisors is psychological and not theological.

Fourth, we cannot justify *on theological grounds* the prominent position and reinterpretation of pastoral care amid ministerial functions. James Hillman, a past director at the Jung Institute, has said of this movement that because the Church has lost its understanding of "soul," it has retreated upstairs to deal with the mind (if, in fact, it has done even this in a systematic manner). Like many Jungian authors, his definition of "soul" is lost in some rather murky prose; but he suggests with some logic that the clinical setting may not be the best place to learn the art of ministry. "Let the clergy follow the *imitatio Christi* rather than imitate psychotherapy." [15] I have no doubt that this is a very hard thing for clinical pastoral education to encourage, because in meeting people's needs it has lost hold of transcendence (be it in the depths or the heights, or, as we shall see, the future). [16]

If pastoral care is primarily pastoral counseling today— and I suspect that it largely is in one form or another[17]— another problem is that by the admission of its own leaders one summer of clinical pastoral education, such as most sem-inarians get, is hardly adequate training for what they con-sider a qualified counselor.[18] Pastoral counseling requires the kind of training that necessarily forces a man to neglect other dimensions of ministry and supportive theory. This implies that the model is not universal, granting that it is the business of the Church in the first place (which I think it is).

I offer these criticisms not because I think clinical pas-toral education is not a profound help in the preparation of men for ministry. There is no better means at hand either for promoting greater self-awareness and interpersonal sensitivity in all, or in training some in the skills of pastoral counseling. I do *not* think it is *the* answer to ministry today, nor do I believe that it can justify its claim to as large a share of the clergyman's thought and time as it does on the basis of its own model. Pastoral care remains one ministerial function, albeit a very important one today in our keenly psychological age, of the Church. Furthermore, it does not require ordina-tion to the presbyterate for its effectiveness. I am suggesting that if we thought of a Christian layman, who is a psychiatrist, doing pastoral counseling, we might be able to get away from this need to distinguish "shepherding" from "therapy."

Moving now from a psychological model to one drawn from social psychology, there is related to clinical pastoral education, but distinct in origin and methodology, the con-troversial sensitivity training. This has been described recently by the extreme right as "communist brainwashing," aimed at the destruction of the morals of our people and intended to turn us into mindless tools of collectivism. Actually its roots lie in the theories of Kurt Lewin, a social psychologist who came to this country when exiled from Germany, and whose work is based upon *Gestalt* psychology. Lewin describes his own research as field theory: the study of man's behavior as a function of all that is related to him (within his horizon), externally and internally. Obviously, this leads to a concern for the transactions between persons in groups as a clue to their behavior and consequently to themselves as effective people.

Lewin's research during World War II led to the establishment in 1945 at the Massachusetts Institute of Technology of an institute for the study of group dynamics. In 1947 Lewin was instrumental in beginning the National Training Laboratories (NTL), a division of the National Education Association, with headquarters at Bethel, Maine. There originated the development of sensitivity training and the laboratory method. Put simply, this means learning through group experience (called "T [for training] groups," "encounter groups," or "awareness groups") how others perceive you, how you function in a group, and how you might perform in a more productive manner. It requires a great measure of honesty and strength to face the ways we have of avoiding real encounter; consequently it can be a very frightening experience.

From its inception the NTL made a great impact. In 1948 the YMCA sent people to Bethel for training, and in 1949 Theodore Wedel, a leading scholar from the Episcopal Church, attended a laboratory. Wedel's article describing this experience, "The Group Dynamics Movement and the Church," published in *Theology Today*, might be described as the Church's opening gambit in this model of ministry.[19] In the Episcopal Church there followed a period of Group Life Labs, two weeks of sensitivity training combined with training in leadership skills and theory, and Parish Life Conferences. The latter was a weekend experience, designed to bring laymen face-to-face with the purposelessness of a great deal that goes on in our parishes. These various programs were actively promoted from 1954 to 1960.

Meanwhile, practically everyone was getting in on these methods of training, including industry and business. The theory is that the better a person understands himself in interaction with others, the "freer" he is, the better he and others can plan and work together, and the better this is for business. Sensitivity training for industry is a profitable enterprise now, and not a few of its practitioners became acquainted with the process through the Church.

From 1960 to 1968 the Episcopal Church employed an altered model of sensitivity training, called Leadership Training, that was divided into three sessions: one dealing with sensitivity, one with skills, and one with practice. This was a more sophisticated attempt to get the experience of the laboratory, which had originally been run as a "stranger lab" (a person attends a session far from home, with no one he or she has ever met before), into the church setting at home. The principal problem discovered with the original Group Life Labs was that the learning was not transferable. The people who went had a "great experience," and perhaps even formed a sort of "gnostic group" within the Church; but it proved very difficult to share this reawakening to self with others back home. The new method worked better than the old, and although since 1968 the Episcopal Church has ceased to run its own labs, it does support the participation of its leaders in ecumenical and secular training sessions.

Obviously this is the adoption of a model of learning that has no roots in historic Christian ministry. It is to all intents and purposes post-1945, and based upon a particular theory of how to effect learning and change. It is a very powerful instrument. Any theological reflection upon its meaning, which is purely after the fact, would probably move in the direction of alienation as sin, faith as the risk of openness to the other (ultimately God as found in the other), and redemption as the victory found on the other side of honesty and trust. There has been a good bit of effort to work out the implications of the sensitivity model, often in a form that is not quite so "sensitive," in various forms within parish life. Clyde Reid, in *Groups Alive—Church Alive*, describes in a rather cute, sometimes sarcastic manner how to use small groups in the local church. John L. Casteel has edited a selection of somewhat more sophisticated essays, *The Creative Role of Interpersonal Groups in the Church Today*.[20] As these books state, there are all kinds of groups derivative of this model: study, prayer, preaching, social, counseling, action, etc. The degree to which they "sensitize" the individual depends on their emphasis upon *task* as opposed to the immediate *process* within the group. But they all share to a degree a concern for explicit observation of the process as an aid to learning.

Perhaps one kind of evolving sub-model of the sensitivity movement that has made considerable headlines (it received much publicity in the movie *Bob & Carol & Ted & Alice*) is the nonverbal laboratory. This method, which depends on touch, taste, sight, and smell (as well as hearing), receives its most dramatic notoriety from the use of nudity in training. Whereas no church-sponsored program has advertised nude sessions, certainly churchmen have been actively involved in such as at the Esalen Institute in California. The general use of nonverbal forms of communication and exploration of feeling, which offers an even more highly charged and consequently potentially more productive (as well as dangerous) method, is now quite common in the forms of ministry (teaching, caring, even evangelizing, and, as shall be seen, ritualizing). A theological foundation for such ministerial methods is readily found in the Christian's understanding of *himself as body*, and is beautifully explicated in Norman Brown's *Love's Body* and in the chapter "Touch and Feel" in Marianne Micks' delightful book, *The Future Present*.[21] A helpful introduction to the theory and technique of nonverbal sensitivity training is William Schutz's *Joy: Expanding Human Awareness*, where the relationship between the physical and emotional tone of the "fully realized man" is discussed.[22]

My reason for underlining the possible theological defense of the investigation of nonverbal communication has a specific purpose. I am not at all hesitant to criticize sensitivity training as a model for ministry, nor would I deny that often it is used by some as a gimmick to make money or acquire a sense of power; for others it is a way of "getting their kicks," and for still others it is an attempt to receive quick or cheap therapy. Yet I think much of the attack leveled at all forms of sensitivity training, and particularly its nonverbal dimensions, is the hysterical reaction of frightened people. The theory behind this whole model, as originating in Lewin, is a reputable social psychology. There is absolutely no doubt that better communication between persons will open up richer possibilities for a creative life. The well-known Christian adaptation of the Jewish saying, "For where two or three have met together in my name, I am there among them" (Matt. 18:20), is among other things an ancient acknowledgment of the sense of a power found in the group process that transcends the sum of the contributions of the individual members. Body contact, even nudity, is not *in itself* immoral in the Christian view, but can be a means of achieving an awareness and compassion that has escaped us all our lives.

Certainly this has been the goal in the use of the small group and its process in worship. Beginning with Frank Buchman and his "spiritual house parties," characteristic of the Moral Re-Armament Movement which he began after World War I, interpersonal dynamics have been employed to encourage confession, forgiveness, and love. Today the reinstitution of the liturgical "kiss of peace," be it only a handshake, is one very small attempt to awaken a feeling of community in the liturgy—one which has caused much anxiety on the part of many people. Another testimony to the power of touch! The possibilities of verbal and nonverbal communication in small groups has been further explored in experiments in worship that involve group confession, holding hands, hugging, dancing, and even some of the exercises out of Schutz's book. Group meditation, which is hardly a contemporary discovery, has enjoyed a renewal in the Roman Catholic Church. Fr. John Gooch, chaplain at Johns Hopkins Medical Institutions, for one reports he uses it to good effect after the sermon at Mass.[23]

Perhaps the most impassioned attack upon sensitivity

training in recent time was an article by the Roman Catholic sociologist, Andrew Greeley, in the *National Catholic Reporter*.[24] Greeley argues that it is an extremely dangerous procedure, attractive to people with acute pathological problems, which encourages collective regression and destroys the dignity of the individual. Aside from the fact that Greeley's language tends to be rather emotional, which would seem to imply that he has more than an intellectual investment in his position, his data is rather selective. Richard Batchelder and James Hardy, in studying the use of sensitivity training by the YMCA, report on the basis of extensive data that the results for them have been positive, when it is understood that it is not a "panacea" and that the number profiting from it is determined in part by their back-home situation.[25] In an article, "Emotional Stress and Laboratory Training," in the *News and Reports* of the NTL Institute, it is reported that from 1947 to 1968 there have been 14,200 participants in their programs, and only thirty-three (.2 percent) have had to leave the program prior to completion.[26] Many rumors are circulated about bizarre behavior and psychotic breaks associated with this program. Attempts to trace down the actual circumstances prove very difficult. Since 1954, when the Episcopal Church initiated its interest in this field, authoritative sources report that occurrence of this kind of problem has been far less than is commonly reported.[27]

Indeed, before any critic of sensitivity training and the small-group movement becomes too zealous, he needs to be aware of the real effort found here to develop a practical method from contemporary theories of knowledge. I have spoken of the collapse of the Cartesian subject-object model of knowledge in favor of a participatory model, involving the whole person. This is an attempt, an often only modestly successful attempt, to explicate its meaning. On the other hand, I would offer four criticisms of the method and its application to ministry.

Aside from some of the criticisms of the pastoral care

movement which are equally applicable to this model, I would say, first, that the entire small-group movement in general does not provide a universally valid shape for ministry. For several years I have been priest-in-charge of a small mission of some twenty families, where almost everything is done on a small-group model. Some of its successes have been deeply gratifying and have made it possible for this little community to grow despite the priest's fifty-mile distance from the mission. But it has also been more and more taxing to continue to employ this model. Imagine what it would be like in a parish twenty times that size! It would provoke an exhausting fragmentation of the entire congregation (granted that a case could be made for forbidding parishes to reach such a size). But with the continuing projections of population growth, the model becomes even more impossible.

In a number of writings John Dittes has argued a thesis that conflict within the parish, by which he means a difference in agenda between the pastor and his lay leaders, can be treated as one would treat resistance in psychoanalytic theory. Resistance in the analytic process is a phenomenon in which the client unconsciously protects his inner feelings from the awareness of the analyst. The therapeutic method requires that the resistance be met and worked through.[28] Dittes has experimented with this theory, and claims that through a small-group method he has been able to reduce conflict and harness creative energy in the parish.[29] The criticism of the practicality of all this is cogent to my point. Aside from the question of how many clergy possess the skill to do what amounts to group therapy, in how many parishes is there the time and the willingness to engage in this kind of exercise?

Another point that must be faced in this regard is that not every person is capable of functioning successfully in a small group. Therefore, not everyone can be expected to respond to this shape of ministry.

Second, there has been a good bit of irresponsible leadership in the field. Batchelder and Hardy have emphasized the need for "qualified leaders" only to conduct anything resembling sensitivity training, but this has not been enforced. Max Birnbaum, in an excellent article in the *Saturday Review*, made the same plea.[30] Eager disciples, people suffering from sadistic needs, and those looking for a "quick buck" have entered the field, which has lacked proper standards and has failed to require proper credentials. It has been my experience that some clinical pastoral education supervisors, who do not have this particular kind of training, have felt free to employ its methods with highly detrimental results.

It has to be understood that sensitivity training exists for educational and not psychotherapeutic purposes. Group therapy requires years of extensive training. Even with this qualification, it must be expected that trainers meet some universally acceptable standard. Some resolution of the problem is to be found in the organization of the Association for Religion and the Behavioral Sciences which is implementing just such standards.

Third, sensitivity training and also clinical pastoral education has set an unrealistic goal for itself in the training of the clergy. One of the very encouraging signs of the psychological and social psychological model has been an understanding of the vital role of the *person* of the clergyman. It has been an attempt to restore in some ways the image of the "parson"; but it has attempted to do in a matter of weeks and months what takes a lifetime and more. Being a parson—that is, the sacramental person—in a community requires more than being sensitive to the feelings of others. It requires being a part of their world, their *Weltbild*, both in temporal and spatial meanings. Sensitivity training is not going to enable a white, upper-middle-class man of twenty-five out of a suburban parish to be an effective parson in the black ghetto or the rural church; no more than it will enable the son of a black, Mississippi tenant farmer to serve effectively in a North Shore Chicago parish. We have no right to expect these kinds of miracles, as apparently some do.

As a Southerner who has moved into the northern Midwest to teach seminarians, it has been all too apparent to me that there are vast reaches of my "homeland" to which I could never send most of my students. It would require not only a redoing of their secondary socialization—which is possible with effort and time, but not easy; but it would also demand the restructuring of their primary socialization, which is next to impossible and certainly not accessible to any program of group dynamics. I am confident this is true elsewhere, and requires an honest evaluation of the problems of clergy recruitment and deployment.

Fourth, the social psychological model of the small group developed by Lewin into the laboratory method does not, strangely enough, lead to a social ethic. It tends to promote introversive interests rather than a prophetic concern for those outside the group. Quentin Hand, writing about his work with small church groups says,

Only three participants showed changes in their social values. For 90 percent of the group their views on social justice, racial relations, war and peace, production and distribution of wealth remained constant. In the light of the improved interpersonal relationships reported, the lack of change in social viewpoint is striking.[31]

Edward Thornton states: "The besetting sin of people in the small group is self-righteousness and loss of nerve for social action." [32] I have already mentioned this characteristic in the Neo-Pentecostal movement, which, I think, is an unconscious adoption of this social psychological model. The Christian Family Movement in the Roman Catholic and Episcopal churches is a form of the small-group movement, which is ostensibly committed to an action orientation. My impression is that generally their forms of action are far removed from the kind of thing advocated by the "new breed," and that the great benefit derived in what they do is mutual support *within* the group. They then would be a case in point.

The third and last new model of ministry characteristic of the "new breed" to which I shall devote some space is the sociological. As with the previous two, the psychological and social psychological, I cannot begin in this survey to give it the treatment it deserves.

As a generalization it may be said that the antecedents of the sociological model rest in a still different source than Anton Boisen and his associates or Kurt Lewin and his work on group dynamics. Curiously enough, they are to be found in the reaction to the Social Gospel, Reinhold Niebuhr, Neo-Orthodoxy, and "Christian realism." The Social Gospel was an attempt to commit ministry to a building of the Kingdom of God here and now. Reinhold Niebuhr's theological anthropology, based upon a doctrine of the sovereign God and man's essential sinfulness (which he reinforced through psychoanalytic insights), taught that any such optimistic ambition was utterly unrealistic. Jesus' ethic of perfect love lay in the unforeseeable future, and now we must concern ourselves with a social ethic that seeks a *just society* through a balance of power. Therefore Niebuhr expected Christian ministry to emphasize social prophecy and to function as a responsible agent.

Howard M. Mills makes the point that in 1954 at the Evans-Assembly of the World Council of Churches the statement issued concerning the Church's ministry to the world was based upon Niebuhr's "Christian realism." The fact that it provoked no effective response by Christians as a whole is a witness to the dated nature of his social ethic.[33] It presumed an identification between Western Christianity, Western democracy, and God's will that we now understand to be highly problematical. The Evanston Assembly came, ironically enough, the same year as the ruling of the Supreme Court on school desegregation, which can be considered in many ways the pinnacle achievement of Niebuhr's theory of social ethics and the beginning of its decline. For the principle of justice stated in that ruling have never become operative in our society, and those who have been committed to them have come to believe less and less in the possibility of justice through "due process."

There are other criticisms of Niebuhr's social ethic. It lacked a certain Christocentricity and biblical base, though he sought to make up for this in later writings. Perhaps more to our concern was that it was individualistic (as evidenced in its dependence upon psychoanalytic theory), and therefore of less and less value for churchmen alarmed by the cruelty of social structures. Consequently, as the fifties passed into the sixties, Christian social critics moved away from Niebuhr, *but found no Christian theology or ethical theory to support their ideological pilgrimage.* They became committed more and more to various sociological theories and less and less capable of articulating any specific Christian contribution to their desire for justice. In 1968 Richard Shaull could say with Paul Lehman that we must shift from Niebuhr's metaphysical-ontological imagery to the historical-eschatological imagery of Moltmann, Pannenberg, Metz, Cox, etc.;[34] and I rather agree. But who ever heard of these men and the "theology of hope" ten years ago?

Consequently the minister as "change agent" was a concept of action, based upon sociological theory, in search of a theology. One practical route taken by some churchmen was to become involved in community organization, as formulated by Saul Alinsky's theories, consisting of the seizure of the power base in one's own community and the creative use of conflict. This was reinforced by the popularity of C. Wright Mills' studies on the military-industrial basis of power in the United States. It was fed by the "black power" movement (originating really in 1964) and the growing knowledge of the "ghetto"; the new awareness of extensive poverty in the country (Michael Harrington estimated 40,000,000 living in poverty); the disillusionment of the young with the American "dream," particularly in relation to our foreign policy in Southeast Asia; and the ecological crisis. It is a familiar story.

The training of clergy directed itself in the sixties more

and more to enable them *to enter society and to effect change.* It was obvious that change was needed, and many people looking for an ideological base from which to operate sought the ministry. The Urban Training Center in Chicago and the Metropolitan Intern Program are examples of action training centers that were established to expose clergy to the problems of the inner city and to provide them with the desired skills in the transformation of structures. As the polarity of the American society has grown and the necessity for choosing sides becomes more evident, those committed to this understanding of ministry have found themselves advocating confrontation, violence, and revolution in chorus with many who do not share the same ultimate commitment. Marxist and Christian together have already "manned the barricades."

I can see little question but that this movement, just as the previous two, has perceived a prominent truth about humanity and has diagnosed a real sickness within our society. The arguments against that view are very weak. Man is in part a social person, a function of his social structures as well as a creator of those structures. Therefore, when there is suffering, as there undoubtedly is, the social structures must bear a good share of the blame. The question is whether in the resolution of this suffering the structures have the vitality to correct themselves or whether they must be destroyed so that new structures can replace them. It should be said that this is not the kind of question that the Church could ever ask itself before 1914, a question that it was not sensitive enough to ask itself until after 1954, and a question that other models ("psychological" and "social psychological") are even now able to ask only very timidly. It is obvious that those who have much invested in the status quo cannot even allow themselves to entertain the question. They have instead to plead that the business of the Church is the salvation of the individual—a claim that had much precedent and real viability two hundred years ago, but is very remote from the world of today.

In criticizing the sociological model for ministry—which

is a very cold way of describing a very impassioned vocation—
I would offer one general observation and then make three
secondary points. As with the other models, it is not my intention to give any comfort to those who would avoid its truth
and implications for involvement. I would say, however, that
it does not encompass the sole purpose of Christian ministry.

My major criticism lies in the failure of this model to
define its function in terms of a pastoral and moral theology.
Shaull equates "prophetic insight" and "new radicalism," [35]
and I think there is no question that what we have here is *at
least* a prophetic function. Robert Rodes, in a long and reflective article entitled "The Last Days of Erastianism—Forms
in the American Church-State Nexus," has pointed out that
while "underground churches" and persons such as Fr. Groppi
in Milwaukee seek reform (which is a mild word for it), "their
real significance is in their proclamation of the judgement of
God." [36] This reinforces my interpretation.

The problem here is that prophecy, as St. Paul has said,
is *for the edification of the Christian community* (not the
world at large) (1 Cor. 14:22), and it has always been so used
until now. Prophecy in the ancient Church was ecstatic and
apocalyptic, and in the medieval and modern Church was always directed to Christendom. Since World War II, when we
finally admitted that ours is *not* a "Christian nation," nor is
any other, we have still not faced the implications of the prophetic function. Why should we expect the government, for
example, to pay heed to our Christian proclamation? Irrespective of any theory of civil religion and what the government
says in its coinage, it does not function out of a Christian
context.

The answer to this has been to say that our common basis
is simply our concern for humanity. Mills says that the Christian input is to reform humanity and not to serve the
Church.[37] It is interesting that the Uppsala Assembly of the
World Council of Churches in 1968 was soundly criticized by
the evangelicals for such "vacuous humanism." Whereas I

cannot agree with the quaint anthropology of the evangelicals, I must agree that this charge is well made, and Uppsala is no advance over Evanston and Niebuhr's "Christian realism." It is fine to want to reform humanity, but to what pattern? This is the whole problem with Marxism, the "New Left," and Maoism. Without any better ideal of humanity than the one already current, they end up wanting to substitute their exploitation for the current model. (It is remarkable how much the far Right and far Left have in common.) *The task of the Church is to provide a transcendent image of man!*

Therefore, it is not enough to be a prophet. Evangelism is the first requirement, no matter how distasteful this may seem to those who equate "mission" with "colonialism" (and with good historical reason). The Church *qua* Church has only one thing to give the world: an image of God's purpose in creating man and the means of attaining it—namely, Christ. People who call themselves "Christians" may do other things, but it is not Christian ministry. Prophecy requires as its *major premise* that God has revealed the true *humanum* in Christ. This lies at the heart of Ivan Illich's repeated axiom: "The task of the Church is not to 'socialize' but to 'evangelize.' "

This is not to argue that evangelism cannot be carried out on the basis of society rather than individuals. We have, in fact, already seen that it was. It is not even to suggest that conversion by the sword is unprecedented. Nor is there necessarily anything wrong with the sociological model of this movement. What is naïve sometimes is its theological model. It is perhaps possible, however, that if we clarify our theology we will be more selective in sociology. Illich is one who calls for change, but who seems to have done some theological thinking. He writes:

The less efficient she [the Church] is as a power the more effective she can be as a celebrant of the mystery. This statement, if understood, is resented equally by the hierarch who wants to justify collections by increasing his service to the poor, and by the rebel-priest who wants to use his collar as an attractive banner in agitation. Both make a living of the social service the Church renders. In my mind both symbolize obstacles to the specific function of the Church: the communication of the Gospel. . . .

Thus the Church does not orient change, or teach how to react to it. It opens new dimensions of specific faith to an ecumenical experience of transcendent humanism. All men experience; the Church knows what it means. What the Church contributes through evangelism is like the laughter in the joke. Two hear the same story—but one gets the point. . . .

We will need ideological rationalizations for a long time to achieve purposefully planned inventive solutions to social problems. Let a consciously secular ideology assume this task. I want to celebrate my faith for no purpose at all.[38]

This is the most refreshing series of statements I have read amid all the sociology and rhetoric in years.

To these criticisms I would add three additional minor criticisms, all of which may appear to be carping and unfair. Certainly they are undocumented—for they are not capable of documentation—and perhaps represent feelings more than anything else.

First, I sense a use of the sociological model for an escape from the psychological and social psychological. There is not a little pathology in some social activists: unresolved hostility, which is expressed in antisocial behavior with peer approval. The hostility may have a rational cause, but also it would be foolish to dismiss some of its irrational roots. Therefore, in all the explanation of the violence, obscenity, and offensive nonconformity, one gets the feeling that we are not dealing with the whole picture and that the adherents of the movement are not entirely honest with themselves.

Second, there is an oversimplified rejection of the ambiguity of life. This becomes very clear to me in the Vietnam debate. It is no more true to say that Americans are malevolent and Communists righteous than to turn it the other way around. Both are living in sin, both have selfish aims, and both are destroying the world (or, at least, a part of it) in the name of ideals to which neither is really committed. Therefore, we must choose between two evils, and that is always a difficult choice. Perhaps the evil "on the other side of the fence" seems less so; but intelligent men, schooled in the history of Christian thought, ought to know better.

Third, as Jeffrey K. Hadden has pointed out, many who subscribe to the sociological model—I suspect the "followers" more than the "leaders"—are very naïve about institutions. It is popular to damn the "institutional Church." Some years back a member of the "new breed" described himself as "the Lone Ranger, riding the frontier of Christianity." My question would be: "What is he using to feed his horse and where does it come from?" If someone is going to live in a commune in Arizona, he must be willing to farm, paint houses, shoe horses, or something; and even that requires society, and society is made up of its institutions. There has always been an institutional Church because it is made up of "political men" (if I may translate Aristotle literally). There is no doubt that institutions beget problems. We lived through the Crusades, the Inquisition, and the burning of witches; and we shall have to live a while with the "teahouse." But who would know about Jesus if it were not for the ongoing institutional life of the Church?

The effort I have described in this chapter to reconstitute our understanding of Christian ministry around a model other than theological has had one great virtue. It has taken seriously many of the cognitive structures that are changing our reality in this contemporary period. Therefore, it is enabling the Church to be in touch with the life of Rieff's "psychological man," Marcuse's "one-dimensional man," and even those who would break out of these stereotypes. There is little question in my mind that if the ministry had not moved into these areas it would be so far out of touch that it would be difficult to foresee how it could recover a demand upon people's loyalties.

As pastoral theology has passed from psychology to social psychology and now to sociology, I would hope that it would not stop there, but move on to anthropology.[39] This social science, particularly reputed to be populated with "God-haters," offers to the Church some insight into comparative religion that can awaken us to some things we have been missing in all our desire for "relevance." I will elaborate upon them in Part III, and only now refer to them in order to introduce the possibility in the context of a consideration of the behavioral and social sciences in dialogue with theology.

In making the suggestion that anthropology has an additional model to offer us, I must hasten to add that I am not suggesting that it provides *the* answer, not to be found in the previous three. All four models have their values—which are that they bring to bear an *external* organization of ideas, laws, or relationships upon our theology, which is primary. I am indebted to Charles Goldsmith for this point, who also reminds us that the purpose of a model is fourfold: representational, inferential, interpretational, and pictorial. It never serves as *the* final answer.

If the great virtue of the Church's adoption of these models just discussed, or the one to follow, is its serious consideration of contemporary cognitive structures, one further thing revealed in this discussion has been the Church's failure to restructure its own theological understanding of ministry. One prevailing criticism of all options for ministerial models has clearly been this lack. There have been efforts. Eduard Thurneysen's strongly Barthian theory of pastoral care, Reinhold Niebuhr's "Christian realism," and Buber's "I-thou" have all attracted our interest by their perceptions; but none has won the day. We need such a theology in any attempt to work through psychology, social psychology, sociology, or anthropology to some kind of overarching, all-inclusive doctrine of ministry.

## chapter 10

# THE
# PROBLEM
# OF
# PROFESSIONALISM

In the introduction to this part of the study I suggested that contemporary efforts to work out a *modus operandi* for ministerial function in this era that is true to its purpose has largely failed. I attributed this to a lack of imagination and courage, and a succumbing to the age-old temptation of idolatry. The time has come to support this rhetoric.

The effort at a solution can best be summed up by saying that we are attempting to make of ministry a profession (not *several* professions, but *one* profession). This is consistent with the whole concept of professionalism that became prominent in this country at the end of the nineteenth century. The clearest exposition of the effort as it relates to ministry is found in James D. Glasse's *Profession: Minister*. Glasse defines a professional as someone who is (1) educated in some body of knowledge, (2) possesses a cluster of skills, (3) has an institutional commitment, (4) is responsible to a set of standards, and (5) is dedicated.[1] He believes that the clergyman does or should fit these qualifications. In developing this conviction he is obviously very dependent upon the distinguished Roman Catholic sociologist, Joseph H. Fichter, the author of *Religion as an Occupation: a Study in the Sociology of Professions*.[2] I would agree, however, with Murray and Westhues that Glasse does not always share Fichter's scholarly perspective, and suffers from an overt need to "sell" his readers on the role of the minister as professional.[3]

The notion of the "professional" is a relatively modern idea. It focuses around the concept of *technical competence*, and partakes of the modern period with its practical concerns, its Cartesian theory of knowledge ("It is not what I am but what I have and what I do with it that counts"), and its middle-class commitment to work and duty. In education for medicine and law, and later in such fields as engineering and teaching, the intention was to achieve a competence that lay somewhere between the skill of the artisan and the traditional education of a gentleman. The attempt of sociology and psychology to devise an objective body of scientific knowledge that would in turn be a resource for techniques in working with people has led to the adoption of the professional model in these areas which deal with the cognitive-affective structures people's lives. Many in the Church, perceiving that the old understanding of ministry was less and less demanded, decided at a rather late date to cast their lot with this same model. I would describe the rather unreflective adoption of the professional concept as an almost idolatrous acceptance of a cultural phenomenon as comprehending the totality of ministry.

Certainly it would be wrong to say that it was altogether a horrible mistake. Yet as we have seen already, it has created problems in such areas as training; and although without question there is a place for professionalism in the Church, I do not think it makes a good theological "fit" consistent with the contemporary reality. It seems possible to me that the professional model of ministry is more congruent with the world of pre-1850 than it is today. Several reflections upon this model appear to me to suggest just this.

First, the professional model confirms the whole tendency of the modern period. It equates ministerial function with one profession and one role. This is a disaster! The clergyman (by whom I mean the presbyter/priest/pastor/parson) is considered the one man who possesses the techniques, which he in turn applies to his people, who on their part passively accept his ministrations (as long as they like them!). If we compare, as Glasse does, the clergyman to the doctor, lawyer, and teacher, there is no question but that this reinforces such an image. If our claim to our position, our salary, and our status is that we possess this body of skills, based upon our professional education and training, which is called "ministry," and we alone possess them, how could it be otherwise?

It is also common to speak of the role of the "generalist." The clergyman's profession is that of a "generalist," which is to say that he is expected whoever he may be to do everything (well?). He must possess all the skills: counseling, change agent, sensitivity trainer, etc. How many clergy are willing to refer counselees, for example, to other clergy? Very few, because the implication is that the person doing the referring is an "incompetent professional." The strain this places on the man of one or two talents is notorious, not to mention what it does for those to whom he ministers. If we identify ministry with a professional possession of a body of technical skills, the extent of these skills as currently described makes it impossible for any one man to do them all well; and yet this is exactly what we seem to expect.

Related to this is my second reflection. There are certain ministerial functions that are not subject to inclusion under a professional model. Glasse's effort to describe preaching and ritualizing (using Blizzard's word, he describes it as being a "priest"), as "professional" is unconvincing. These are charismatic qualities, with which as a teacher in this field I am more and more convinced a man is either endowed by heredity and environment or "catches." What can be taught is peripheral. Good preaching today, as much as it ever was, is "personal witness" far more than "skillful exegesis" or "knowledgeable theological exposition." A "liturgical presence" is a gift that some have and some regretfully do not. If the "minister of the Word and Sacrament" has a central role today—and despite everything to the contrary, I would agree with Hans Küng that he does[4]—it is not one that is exhausted by a professional model.

These are two functions peculiarly related to the sacramental person, as is discipline, and the very nature of that depends upon one's self-awareness as well as the awareness of others to the self.

There seems to me to be a tendency in the professional model to emphasize skills that depend on a subject/object dichotomy; and the importance of the person or the professional is frequently lost and is at best secondary. Without doubt, recent psychotherapeutic theory has been trying to break away from this tendency, but as it does, the field becomes less "professional" and more obviously "charismatic" (which it really has always been all along). Ministry at this point in the life of the Church cannot afford the risk of divorcing the sacramental person any further from a model of what the function of the Church is all about. We must take seriously the opportunity offered us by the new unity of knowledge (as described by Polanyi), and therefore need to beware of anything that would separate ministry from its source in the person.

It is in this area that Murray and Westhues offer their most severe and effective criticism of Glasse.

Had Glasse read such sociologists of religion as Weber and O'Dea he would have known that the charismatic prophet relies not on divinity school credentials but on the power of the person, not on systematic theology but on the mystery of his message, not on legalistic codes of the route to heaven but on the creative and poetic energies of himself and his followers.[5]

They go on to point out that Glasse is attempting to use sociology to describe what the ministry is and ought to be, and quite rightly state that theology, not sociology, must do this.

Then, third, a review of Glasse's book by Edgar Mills points out quite rightly that Glasse does not grasp the depth of the clergyman's plight today.[6] Fichter, in describing the nature of a profession, states that its skills are something that are highly desired in the culture.[7] There is much evidence to indicate that for the pastor this is no longer so. Glasse does not want to tie the definition of a profession to remuneration, but certainly a professional expects to be able to earn a living commensurate with his state in life and anticipates that what he receives gives an indication of the value placed upon his services. The vast majority of clergy do not earn a living anywhere comparable to "other professionals," and part of the morale problem is that this reflects just what value is placed upon their services.

Glasse's answer is that a professional organization or union is needed that can begin to demand adequate compensation. This answer has not been tried yet in a forceful way, and I wonder if it is whether or not we will price ourselves right out of a job. The problem is one of conversion, and certainly pressure has "converted" people before. But I question whether or not "union professional skills" are an answer to evangelism. Is not the problem more how men of deep spirituality can call others to this same perspective? How can man be free, unless he meets free men and "catches" this freedom from them? Paul van Buren made the point some years ago, and Ernst Käsemann said the same thing more recently (in what was apparently as controversial a book in Germany as van Buren's was in America). Jesus and his Church exist to make us free.[8] It would appear to me that as technology has offered us a release from the burden of just staying alive, we are more open than ever not only to the possibility of greater technical competence but *to the art of being a person in Christ*, possessing a contagious freedom. Contemporary technology frees us from an obsession with professionalism.

This leads to my fourth and final reflection upon the role of the minister as professional, which is the most damning of all. Professionalism tends to focus on the "here and now" to the exclusion of transcendence. The quality of life that projects a strong feeling of that which is apart from the immediate and the known is a sense of the numinous, an aura of mystery, what I shall call in the next part "liminality." Although some professionals are given to projecting this image to their clients, no one wants the doctor, the lawyer, or the teacher to view his object of technical competence as something of a mystery. "I'm sorry that the roof fell in, but you know mathematics of stress has a certain 'numinous' quality to it," would not protect the engineer from a malpractice suit. He and all other professionals are expected to be *in control* of their area of competence.

Is the pastor? One real possibility of our age is that as all the old cosmological structures of our own making have been crushed, now perhaps there is room for God. The value systems we have hypostasized and called "God" are indeed dead! Our coherent world is gone; and as man has no final answers for the present, he may just be open to the future. The professional model could possibly thwart a great opportunity for a renewed sense of transcendence, if we assured ourselves that we are trained professionals *in control* of a body of skills called ministry, *and that is all.*

The only thing that can save us from this is *not* to ignore our psychology, social psychology, sociology, and anthropology. Much is to be learned in those fields—some in this and some in that—and yet all the while informed by a viable theology. The theology is not the result of our scientific investigation, but stands over and against it. Only then can we transcend our culture and at the same time embrace its possibilities for the life in Christ, the whole life of the free man.

# PART III

## THE
## FUTURE
## OF
## MINISTERIAL
## FUNCTION

## chapter 11

# A THEOLOGY
# FOR THE
# FUTURE

It has been my claim from the start
that the task of ministry is to serve
the purpose of the Church in every age. Whereas some dis-
agree, there is wide and sound precedent for my belief that the
purpose of the Church is to serve as the *Ursakrament*, the
primal means of encounter with Christ. If the "quest of the
historical Jesus" has taught us anything, it is that the knowledge
of Christ cannot transcend the fact of the Christian community. In so doing I have focused the Christian experience of
God in the person of Jesus as made known to his disciples
and in the Church, and thereby made Christology the key to
all theology. Christ is "the way . . . the truth and . . . life"
(John 14:6), and if it were not for him you and I would be
pagans!

Christ is both transcultural (i.e. transcendent) and immanent (i.e. incarnated). In keeping with this conviction, it
has been my purpose to demonstrate both the truth of Durkheim's "collective representation"—the belief that man's
knowledge of his reality and hence reality itself is shaped by
the society in which he lives—in terms of the evolving patterns
of ministry, and yet to claim that there is an essential meaning
to this ministry that is eternal and absolute. (Durkheim by
himself cannot explain why men will suffer even death at the
hands of society for their religious convictions.) Effective ministry requires an allegiance to both truths. Until the contemporary period such a loyalty is to be found, as I believe I showed
in chapters 2 through 5. It is the fundamental contention of

chapters 6 through 10 that ministry today has failed in this regard. It has not freed itself from the past sufficiently to grasp fully the reality that is emerging in our own culture, and it has not been sensitive to its own Lord and to the dimensions of contemporary life that afford opportunities to express a sense of transcendence.

It becomes my rather incredible task to offer some indications as to how this problem might be remedied in the future. How can ministerial function in the contemporary period so shape itself as to become an effective instrument of the *Ursakrament*? Since I have asserted on several occasions that we have allowed ourselves to be misled to date because of a theological timidity, obviously I must answer from a theological premise. Part I of this book is rooted in social history. Part II speaks to the social (including behavioral) sciences. Part III is based upon what is sometimes called social theology.

In this chapter I want to address the question of the *communication* between God and man, as expressed in Christ through his Church. This is to speak of Christian *revelation*, and it is one way of thinking of ministry as the service of God's self-revelation to man. This is to say, just as St. Paul did, "We must be regarded as Christ's subordinates and as stewards of the secrets [*or* mysteries] of God" (1 Cor. 4:1). In so doing I will center my discussion about four points. First, man is essentially religious; he has an openness, as Karl Rahner says repeatedly, to God. Second, he has no knowledge of God not given to him in parables that speak to each age. Third, the temporal dimension, growing out of the spatial, perhaps offers the most effective images for contemporary man of the transcendent God. Fourth, these images speak to him in his imagination, in the unstructured, liminal dimensions of his life.

Yet first of all, I shall begin with something of an anthropological analysis of man's need for God. For while, during the past decade, much theology has enthusiastically embraced Bonhoeffer's dictum that "the Christian is not a *homo religiosus*, but simply a man, as Jesus was a man," [1] sociologists and anthropologists have bided their time, unbelieving that man's observable behavior over millions of years could change that radically.[2] Man is to their minds incurably religious. It is a universal response, be he primitive savage or sophisticated theologian, to certain dimensions of the human condition that far exceed some naïve desire to call upon God to fill in the gaps between our experience and our science. Theologians have of late recognized that man's religious reflection does begin with himself, and yet have shown that human nature points to a reality beyond itself.

What it is in man that does this can be variously described. One approach is to show how it is that man does in fact become an object to himself; he transcends himself, and in so doing encounters himself in terms of *meaning and value*. Charles A. Curran defines "meaning" as the *intellectual* understanding of reality and experience, and "value" as expressive of the personal norms, goals, and purposes to which we commit ourselves.[3] I would emphasize the *emotional* element in the pursuit of values; they are those elements of meaning in which we have an emotional investment. Charles Goldsmith has taken this model further to state that meaning and value come together to form *feelings* (notice in this definition that *"feelings" have cognitive content*, which is quite different from the general theory of clinical pastoral education), and so as man perceives himself as object it is in terms of his *feelings about himself*, made up of his understanding of reality (meaning) and his investment in that reality (values).

Clifford Geertz, an anthropologist, has defined religion as "a system of symbols which acts to establish powerful, persuasive and long-lasting moods and motivations in men by formulating conceptions of a general order of existence and clothing these concepts with such an aura of factuality that the moods and motivations seem uniquely realistic." [4] If we equate meaning and conceptions, moods and values, and motivations and feelings, I think we will achieve a reasonable equation between what we have said about meaning, value, and feeling and its context within a phenomenological description of religion. In effect what Geertz has said is the function of religion I have described as the ability of man to transcend himself. Man chooses through religion to cope with the *problem of meaning*, as experienced in his deepest areas of emotion. This includes the bafflement, suffering, and experience of evil which Geertz enumerates; but I think it also includes the equally unfathomable phenomena of love, hope, and sacrifice.

As a "system of symbols" that stands over and against the raw data of life, religion interprets the disparity between what *seems to be* and what in our hope and sense of justice *should be*—between the obvious conflict between the *is* and the *ought* of every man in his better moments—and it provides us with the courage to be something other than a function of the absurd. I choose the words "courage to be" with the obvious intent of linking Geertz's definition of religion and man's self-transcendence to Tillich's exposition of meaning before the threat of meaninglessness in his book, *The Courage to Be*. Tillich closes his book with the apparently cryptic statement: "The courage to be is rooted in the God who appears when God has disappeared in the anxiety of doubts." [5] The very awareness of despair and of the anxiety of death, emptiness, and guilt (Tillich's three types of ontological anxiety) is joined by the perception of its transcendence, that is, meaningfulness.

Gordon Kaufman brought out something of this in an essay in which he describes man's sense of that which transcends himself (is greater than he) in his sense of limit.[6] There is that which is beyond that to which I can move. What lies beyond my limits includes the ability to comprehend meaning in that which, on the basis of my data, looks ultimately meaningless. There is that which transcends man's own self-transcendence. The concept of finitude implies infinitude.

While acknowledging the possible validity of this description, other theologians offer the suggestion that a sense of wonder is a better point of departure for talk about transcendence. Man is struck by the extraordinary in the ordinary, not just by the extraordinary grimness in life's situation, but also by the amazing and unspeakable joy in life (which enlarges the religious experience beyond the theodicy question). I think there is some real promise in this, recalling as it does Rudolph Otto's sense of the numinous, the *mysterium tremendum.*

Otto considered himself an interpreter of Friedrich Schleiermacher (1768–1834), whose seminal role in contemporary theology is beyond dispute. Schleiermacher's teaching is often ambiguously described by friend and foe alike as "the theology of feeling." Religion was for him rooted in a self-awareness of an absolute dependence upon God, which as Richard Niebuhr points out, Otto did not really understand and upon which, despite what he thought, he not only failed to improve but did not equal. I speak of Schleiermacher here because of an intuition (and Part III will be filled with unpursued "intuitions") that in fact he is very important for pastoral theology, if we can ever cut him loose from the polemic of his age and the tendency today to blame him for some of the "fuzziness" of current thought. I find this quote from Niebuhr indicative of his possible value for us. "For insofar as religion is a mode of self-consciousness, it involves the fundamental way in which the self is present to itself; and, again, insofar as this presence of self to the self bespeaks a 'whence' or utter dependence of the self, it symbolizes the relationship of the self to God." [7] This appears to me to be exactly the point I have been arguing from the phenomenon of man's self-transcendence and the function of religion to its pointing to an ultimate transcendence.

Man's ability to transcend himself, to reflect upon his situation ending in death, is the root of the search for meaning in the face of meaninglessness. Man believes there must be meaning, even if he does not believe that there is a personal God. Ernst Bloch, the contemporary Marxist philosopher, in his remarkable chronicle of the persistence of hope for meaning, *Das Prinzip Hoffnung*, speaks of "the sigh of the oppressed which gives form to religion." [8] Bloch is an atheist. Ingmar Bergmann, who can be said to be no more than a pious seeker, once declared, "If God is not there, life is an outrageous terror." [9]

There is no doubt that perhaps the greatest dilemma of the theist is that question which provokes most heartily the feeling that there must be an answer in "God." This is the problem of evil. Some say that contemporary man is no longer interested in the theodicy question, as is Bonhoeffer's judgment about *homo religiosus*. This is simply untrue. What do we think lies behind the campus riots, the drug scene, psychiatrists' profits, and the growth of the occult? Man is inescapably religious, if for no other reason than that he would like to hold "the relatively modest dogma that God is not mad." [10]

Yet, secondly, as I use the term "God" the *problematic nature* of that very symbol forces itself upon me. In much of modern pastoral care there is little detectable awareness that as we drag God into the clinical setting, to prove to ourselves, our colleagues, and our "clients" that we are "different" from the rest of the "healing team," the whole notion is in question. I began this section by affirming my belief that man's demand for meaning and sense of something greater than himself points to that which we call "God." But the pastor cannot be fair to himself and those to whom he ministers if, as he moves from the hard-nosed clinical data to theology, he lapses into some kind of soft-headed "Sunday School piety."

Some years ago, in his book *The Secular Meaning of the Gospel*, Paul van Buren presented the Church with a challenge that cannot be ignored. He believes that the word "God" is meaningless, basing his contention upon the findings of linguistic analysis. [11] For secular man (i.e. man for whom all reality is here and now) it corresponds in his language to no objective reality (e.g. "God is the one who makes it rain," or "God put our astronauts on the moon"—any such remarks are more of the nature of a polite convention than a statement of "fact"), and to speak of God as a "nonobjective reality" is to describe God as a contradiction.

Van Buren's reaction to the description of man as someone who is wrestling with the theodicy problem or who senses
his own dependence upon something that transcends his finitude is not to argue that such a man exists, but to suggest that
he is quite rare. In an essay in response to Kaufman's argument
of limitation as indicative of transcendence, he speaks of "dis-
tinguishing the strange ones from the masses." [12] People who
worry about "limits" or sense the numinous or feel a great
dependence upon God, he says, are a little "strange." This
strikes me as a peculiar way of arguing; as if we had data to support such a quantitative judgment, or as if theological truths
were a matter of a majority opinion.

A very good job of challenging van Buren on his own
ground has been done by Langdon Gilkey, who accepts the
premise of secular man and still demonstrates that talk of God
corresponds to a use of language in man's ordinary life. He
insists that

Within ordinary secular experience, that deeper range, which we
have called that of ultimacy and which religious language seeks to
conceptualize, does appear; that in fact we are aware of it; that
many of our interior feelings and anxieties are concerned with it;
that our public or historical behavior is affected by it; and that
we do talk about it all the time, whatever our explicit conceptual-
izations of experience may say or admit.[13]

Hence, he insists, secular man, unlike van Buren's and Bonhoeffer's analysis, is still "religious."

But this is not to claim anything more than that man expects a meaning to life beyond the limits of his own existence,
that he hopes life is more than an absurd joke, and that he
makes the object of this conviction "God." There is no content
to this concept, there is nothing we can predicate of this
"God" *by power of our natural reason.* We could say that
"God" is a great spider (as some primitive peoples do) or
that "God" is a $5,000 casket (since this is where many Amer-
icans think they shall spend eternity); and there is no way that
we can determine the truth or falsity of either statement. We

cannot on our own describe "God." We have no direct knowledge of "God." Because if we did, God would not be transcendent, and this is the very feature to which we ascribe the name of "God." Therefore, our statements about the nature of that category of ultimate meaning that stands over and against the apparent meaninglessness of our life are problematical, to say the least.

Permit me to illustrate the implications of this statement on the level of pastoral care. Suppose a man in his fifties—intelligent, a lifelong churchman, who throughout his life has conceived of himself as a "successful businessman" and a member of the "landed gentry"—comes to his pastor for counsel. He says, "Everything that has made me happy with myself has collapsed. I have had to sell my business; I have to exist on half of what I once had; and I must cut my scale of living drastically. I really do not know what meaning life now has. I'm not looking for pat answers, *but for some reason for hope.*" What is the pastor to reply? We could begin by answering that the best thing the pastor can do is to share with his parishioner his life, which is to say his feelings. He can say, in one way or another, *"For me,* despite many times that I lose out in life through no fault of my own, God is good." However, what does it mean to say "God is good"?

It can be said that every affirmation about God is in fact no more than a statement of a person's moral intention. To say "God is good" is to say to this man simply that I intend, despite whatever happens, to act in accordance with the concept "good." This is what ultimately counts for me. The usefulness of my statement can be verified on the basis of whether or not I do so behave. So in effect the pastor is sharing with his parishioner his feelings in the form of a moral intention, and whatever help they are depends on whether or not the pastor is the kind of person he wants to be.

But our contention has been that the pastor does not represent only himself, but as a minister (using the term generically) he is a sacramental embodiment of the person of

Christ. It is not just the pastor who says "God is good," but Jesus of Nazareth, who preached and lived this affirmation. There has to be some connection, more than "psychological support," between the historical Jesus and the present situation. For I am saying that the content of "God" is in fact that which is revealed in the life of Jesus of Nazareth, and I am moving beyond the "usefulness" of religious statements as declarations of moral intention to say that this is true—universal and absolute—because it bears the authority of Jesus and was validated in his resurrection.

But a great leap has been made in all this between "God" and "is good." As I. M. Crombie has pointed out, whereas "God" is a concept available to our unaided reason, predications of God (e.g. "is good" or just "is") are *revealed* to us,[14] be it from Mother's knee, the pope, the Delphic oracle, or the Bible. This is to say that *what I believe about* God is what I accept on authority, and authority I trust and test and *feel* is workable in my life. The Church's ministry is at this point only as good as the trust it can command and the form and content it can give to our search for meaning.

But our statements at best are equivocal. They do *not* describe God. They are evocative analogies or parables. "God is good"? Not really, because this *human* word cannot describe what is beyond human limits. But perhaps we can say that God is *something like* good. So to return to our pastor and his despondent parishioner, to say to him "God is good" is to draw on a commonly accepted authority of the content of life's meaning, and to speak from this source *with the hope that the analogy is close enough to evoke a relationship* between the ultimate meaning he seeks (God) and the life he lives, from which the word "good" is drawn.

The whole movement, devoted to what is known as "the new hermeneutic" (i.e. method of interpretation) is based on the theory that the task of the Christian ministry *is to speak as Christ spoke*, for such words when they truly confront man call him to decision about his life and consequently summon him into being (i.e. into a fullness of feeling). This concept has a close parallel in psychotherapeutic theory: namely, that in hearing himself and the therapist, the client is presented with new meanings and opportunities for a more creative investment of himself (values). The problem is finding words that will give content to the quest for ultimate meaning. In what language must our ministry speak today if it is to bridge the gap between the "God" revealed in the Galilean son of a carpenter and "secular man" today?

My third area of concern in this introduction is, then, a response to that question. In what language is God's revelation of himself today to be understood? I would have the reader recall my discussion in chapter 6, where I described contemporary man as having rejected an absolute, predictable cosmology in favor of a personal, anthropocentric, and historical understanding of reality. Leslie Dewart, Jürgen Moltmann, Wolfhart Pannenberg, and Johannes Metz are only among the more notable contemporary theologians who have pointed out that the Greek theistic vocabulary is no longer capable of evoking in contemporary man a deep sense of the reality of God as it did until this century. What was the heart of the patristic and scholastic theology, concepts such as immutability, absolute being, nature, and supernature, now seem to have little ability to grasp our thought. Spatial imagery must give way, they would say, to temporal.

A very clear indication of this has been the struggle to conceive of transcendence. If we conceived of ourselves as situated in space, in our appropriate niche—slightly below the angels, with the animal, vegetable, and mineral kingdoms below us, and neatly divided into body, soul, and spirit—naturally we would think of something transcendent to us *as above us*. As sophisticated a theologian as Tillich in wrestling with this question, and striving to avoid thinking of God as *another* person or being, broke from this traditional picture only to create another *spatial image* just like it. He writes, "As the power of being, God transcends every being and also the

totality of being—the world. Being-itself is beyond finitude
and infinity. . . . *In calling it abysmal* [i.e. of the abyss] we
point to the fact that everything participates in the power of
being in a finite way." [15] This is the concept that J. A. T.
Robinson made popular. The only problem is that it is probably no more helpful to speak of God "down there" as "up
there," for it still leans heavily upon Greek cosmology.

One charge leveled at the nineteenth-century Church,
which as we attempted to say in chapter 4 had some truth to it,
was that God was often invoked as an absolute principle by the
authoritative spokesmen of the Church (officials of Christendom) to justify the oppression of the great majority of people.
It was supposedly said that God ordered the world as it presently exists—because God is both creator and immutable—
and the poor, suffering, and homeless must endure their pain
therefore, only with the knowledge that some day they will
*go up to heaven.* The Marxists made the most of this criticism,
though they certainly had no monopoly on the insight. What
was happening was that the Church was invoking the God
who makes himself known in his absolute perfection. If God
is so known by man, it is an easy step to theocratic tyranny in
the name of the status quo.

When, however, General Motors operates off built-in
obsolescence and the government is utterly dependent upon
the planners and their "think-tanks," not even the most conservative member of contemporary society is in favor of a
*universal status quo.* You cannot have a *half*-absolute God.
Contemporary man inevitably look forward more than anywhere else. As Schillebeeckx writes, "Formerly, man was oriented primarily towards the past, but now he looks resolutely
towards the future." [16] If therefore we are to speak intelligibly
of that which transcends him, it would seem to work best to
relate it to the future and what is beyond him. Contrast, if
you will, Pannenberg's statement that "God is the power of the
future" [17] with Tillich's that God is "the power of being." The
former is more in accord with contemporary man's hopes for

the future than the latter, which really says little to him. Moltmann claims that for man today "theology is eschatology" (i.e. the study of what lies ahead in the future), and no other vocabulary will confront him with the power to give substance to his longing for meaning.[18]

In this view Christ comes out of the future to call us into the future, where he shall be Lord, we shall be free, and all alienation shall cease. The author of the Epistle to the Hebrews made the mission of Christ alive for the readers of his day by picturing him leading the way into the heavenly places above, to the presence of the Father, quite in accord with ancient oriental court procedure and Platonic philosophy. For us Christ still *opens the way*, but it is the way *to a new future and to hope in that future*. The answer to the quest for meaning is so that the present misery is not all there is, for in the future lie infinite possibilities for change. It is this that Christ proclaims, for in his resurrection he has shown that God is true to his promise and yet promises still more for those who would respond. Under such an approach the Church's ministry becomes centered in the task of opening man to his future, of enabling him to enter into new patterns of life that are truly *consistent* with that revealed in Christ. I say "consistent," because the stereotyped and thoughtless imitation of a Galilean peasant makes no sense to a "member of the space age." We are talking of meaning and values, not archeology. We are speaking of possibilities, not prescribed duties. The very thing we must escape, in the name of Christ, is *predictable* behavior; for the God of the future, revealed in Christ, is not predictable but open to infinite possibility.

To grasp what this means it would be helpful to understand Moltmann's distinction between *planning* and *hoping*. Planning can be defined as a disposition toward the future, a judgment of what shall be on the basis of scientific prediction, and a setting of realistic goals in the light of past experience toward which we might work. On the other hand, hoping "refers less to the future which is at one's disposal by virtue of one's own power than it does to that future which another puts at my disposal through promises and in which he puts himself at my disposal." [19] Planning is what you do in a business, hoping is what you do in a marriage. *The Christian does both.* He does not forget the past, for he understands the future out of the past (and if he did not he would fall into an aimless millenarianism); but he never allows himself to become bound only to those possibilities that the past prescribes (for it leads to the conceit that *we* can build the perfect society).

Revelation is God's indirect communication of himself *in history.* God as personal and the infinite value of man as person in relationship to God is a treasure of Christian conviction—recalled to us recently by the existential theologians —that can speak to us today. But beyond this, God's revelation of himself is always in history, in the events of mankind (not just in the inner recesses of the individual conscience), and he is therefore as concerned for the society of man and its future as he is for the immediate state of one person's disposition to holiness. In a time when the Church must speak to vast numbers more and more, and will be able to spend less and less time with the single person, this seems to me to be reality with which we must cope and the value of what Moltmann calls "political theology."

It is, then, in the "theology of hope" that I suggest we might profitably look for the vocabulary and concepts that can be instruments of revelation in man's search for meaning. As we seek to understand transcendence in our age, I would stress the sense of God as the future of mankind. But I would not want to do this in any kind of exclusive way. There seems to me a certain validity to those criticisms of Moltmann and others that in their eschatology they run the great danger of invalidating the present and even spatial experience of God.

It is true that in the development of the human person the sense of space comes far earlier than the sense of time, and that space somehow speaks to his more primal, penumbral being. The sense of the numinous is often experienced first not in the experience of history, but in the *spacious* forest, before the *tall* mountains, or at the edge of the *boundless* sea. The Resurrection is itself *at first* a spatial image. We might be tempted to say that it is spatial as opposed to the Greek, intellectual notion of immortality, which appears to be a temporal image. But in fact immortality is a time*less* notion, and the Resurrection as a witness to the first fruits of those who are asleep is in the last analysis a temporal image. So the temporal follows and grows out of the spatial. "Even for Jesus himself the direct relationship with God, whom he calls his Father, is the basis of his conception of the coming kingdom of God." [20]

I come now to my fourth, final, and most crucial point in this discussion of the theological context for ministry in contemporary society. Another criticism of theology as eschatology is that the future lacks content. If we speak of God as "the power of future," and describe the future as filled with infinite possibilities that arise as he comes to meet us (and *not* as the result of some natural unfolding of creation as found in Teilhard de Chardin), the problem is how to build any kind of program in its light. How do we engage what is first and last "open" to infinite possibility? This is to ask about revelation, because it assumes that, although we must always take into account the tradition of the past, it is never final and will change. As it changes it informs our life in the world.

Perhaps it might be helpful to explain this by posing another pastoral problem. A woman comes to her pastor and explains that her mother has been in the hospital in a terminal illness for several weeks. Her treatment is running to $150.00 a day, the insurance has run out, and she is incurring a debt that will seriously jeopardize the college education of her children. The doctors tell the daughter that her mother has deteriorated to the point that she can never regain consciousness, but that she can be maintained animate, perhaps even for weeks, by a respirator and other procedures. What is she to do? The question being posed is a brand new one, and all the quibbling, pious appeals, and sentiment are not going to gainsay the fact that no precedents in Christian thought speak directly to it. The question is whether *life* and *existence* are the same thing, and if not, how do we determine the end of the former in the face of the latter? The answer for this and countless questions will have to come, in a real sense, out of the future, not primarily out of the past—for we live in a *new* world! Yet the answer asked of us is a theological one, and we cannot slide off into physiology, psychology, or sociology.

*It seems to me that there are many recent indications that the context for struggling with the theological significance of such questions lies in the capacity of man to test behavior and to find the power to change through the stimulation of his imagination.* This is a crucial point, and there are a number of thoughtful and creative scholars in several allied disciplines whose writing is converging on this particular matter. I have the opportunity here only to be suggestive and wait for a more definitive exposition of the pastoral implications of the theology to which I am speaking.

Owen Barfield, to whose book I referred in chapter 1, has shown that as man's consciousness has evolved he has seen the familiar phenomena around him more and more as *objects*. He has lost the power of imagination. He has become literal-minded, which Barfield considers in its extreme form idolatry (making "ends" of means). Phenomena have become ends in themselves; *and we have ceased to participate in them.* If man continues to do this, "he will have done nothing less than to eliminate all meaning and all coherence from the cosmos." [21] Man cannot return to some kind of primitive existence, where he identifies with the created world as one being with another. But Barfield believes that a different kind of participation can be restored to man, and consequently that meaning can be retained, by the use of the imagination.

What Barfield means by imagination is the willful, deliberate, and conscious effort to achieve an immediate experience of phenomena; what he describes as a nourishing of the "tender *receptiveness* of heart." [22] His term for this is "final participation" (as opposed to primitive man's "original participation").

Some of Barfield's development is open to question, such as his dependence upon Levy-Bruhl's theory of primitive man's prelogical thought patterns, now rejected by most anthropologists. His basic thesis, however, is supported by William Lynch's fascinating theory that mental illness is an expression of the loss of hope, and that this loss is effected by a failure of imagination. Particularly helpful to us is his distinction between fantasy, which is to live contrary to fact (common to the mentally ill), and imagination, which first of all discovers the fact. Imagination

must not leave the discovered fact an isolated absolute, but must give it perspective and landscape, a local habitation and a name. There must be no such thing as a pure fragment, a pure fact, untouched by the composing, enlarging spirit of man. It is the fragments, left to themselves and grown into wholes, that make not only the sick but all of us ill.[23]

Elsewhere he says that the sick *absolutize* their fragments of experience, an idea very close to Barfield's notion of idolatry. He also speaks of the relationship between *waiting*, hope, and imagination. He who possesses true humanity is ready to wait, to "image," and then to grow toward the future, into these images that are the gift of God, without being bound in the inflexible and rigid strictures of his mind.

Both Barfield and Lynch are acknowledged to have influenced the profound and very difficult work of Ray L. Hart, *Unfinished Man and the Imagination.* I will make no effort to summarize what is developed in that book, other than to state that Hart sees the imagination as that dimension of man's humanity in which God comes to him. Revelation is more a matter of the given "vision" and "illumination" than our efforts at "comprehension," [24] an idea that catches up Barfield's emphasis upon receptivity or openness, but also stimulates our thinking as to the nature of prayer and meditation.

In the light of this research, the work of the anthropologist Victor W. Turner emerges as extremely suggestive and helpful. Turner, in his studies of the Nbendu tribe of northwestern Zambia, has in a number of publications developed the theory that the function and power of ritual (i.e. religious practices) lie in the fact that the symbols that constitute the rite are multireferent. For example, the color white refers to shrouds, ghosts, death ("pale as death"), as well as joy, pureness, weddings, etc. Consequently, symbols are equivocal and ambiguous. Rites therefore do not "fit" any of the structure of a given society (e.g. male, female, servant, king, hunter, farmer, clean, unclean, etc.). They are "liminal" (from the Latin for "threshold"). They are conducive to a rudimentary, undifferentiated, weak commonality, in which men live together in a state of "humankindedness," which he calls "communitas" (since "community" bespeaks too much structure and differentiation). It is "un-structure" as opposed to "structure." Turner is clearly dependent in many ways and in a very illuminating manner on the French anthropologist Claude Levi-Strauss.[25] But in his own right we ought to be able to make the connections readily between what we have already said about the future, hope, and imagination in such a statement as this:

Communitas breaks in through the interstices of structure, in liminality; at the edges of structure, in marginality; and from beneath structure, in inferiority. . . . Instinctual energies are surely liberated by these processes, but I am now inclined to think that communitas is not solely the product of biologically inherited drives released from cultural restraints. Rather it is the product of peculiarly human faculties, which include rationality, volition, and memory [I would add imagination], and which develop with experience of life in society.[26]

He adds elsewhere that society is a process (a key word in the theology of hope), whose dynamic consists of a dialectic between communitas and structure.

All this is to say that the power of the Church's ministry lies in the fact that it is a little "weird," it does not fit with the expectations of the sociocultural system, nor can it be predictable and conformed to the known. A symbol is not a symbol (but a sign) unless it is ambiguous, and consequently a little threatening, which is to say "numinous."

I hope it has already occurred to the reader that there is a distinct correlation between what Turner describes and the contemporary counter culture; between Barfield's agenda and that of the "hippie movement." The rejection of the industrial technocracy in favor of the commune seems to me an attempt to recover "communitas," an opportunity to fall back into an undifferentiated "humankindedness," wherein alone stands the possibility of reconstituting our life together. How many of the symbols of the counter culture are in fact "liminal"? For the sceptic, a study of the meaning of hair would be enlightening, beginning with the paper on the subject by Edmund Leach.[27] Barfield could just as well have written the real substance of these words of Theodore Roszak in *The Making of a Counter Culture*: "Beyond the tactics of resistance, but shaping them at all times, there must be a stance of life which seeks not simply to muster power against the misdeeds of society, *but to transform the very sense men have of reality*." [28] The sincere churchman of our day has the obligation to ask himself if God does not speak to us out of the future in the imaginative language of the counter culture!

Permit me one more "salvo" of ideas. Harvey Cox has recently written about a "theology of juxtaposition." He like many others sees in the theology of hope a recapturing of our sense of God's transcendence, but wishes to counter it with the theology of presence. Cox recalls my mind to Turner when he writes: "To 'frequent' good society but not to belong to it; to be its 'habitué' and at the same time to observe it from the sidelines—this sounds very much like St. Paul's suggestion that the church should be 'in but not of the world.' " [29] Is this not "communitas" versus structure?

Then Cox goes on to insist that we must recover in the Church the spirit and fact of festival and fantasy. Cox is in complete agreement that contemporary man is deeply aware of history. He also says, however, that he must be aware that history operates in a divine milieu (one way of speaking of God as the power of history, but not as "history"). Festival serves this function. "In festivity, paradoxically, we both heighten our awareness of history and at the same time we take a brief vacation from history-making." [30] Fantasy for Cox is not what Lynch means by it, but is "advanced imagining"; we let ourselves go. Ritual is social and bodily fantasy, of which we have a desperate need (but in living forms), that reconstitutes society.

Cox's reference to "bodily fantasy" recalls a startling statement made by Barfield to the effect that we should not be unsympathetic to phallic cults in primitive religion, for "to be intensely aware of participation is, for man, to feel the centre of energy in himself identified with energy of which external nature is the image." [31] What do we make of this comment by Sam Keen:

Unless we are able to locate the presence of that which heals and saves *in contemporary history* [as opposed to the past], on the soil of what is immediately experienceable, unless we are able to get away from the idea of that obedience (intellectual or moral) to some external authority that testifies to having heard THE WORD as prerequisite for healing, we will not be able to understand that grace which comes from the viscera and which is available wherever beauty or tenderness may be found—in a flower in a crannied wall, or in the morning sun on a California beach.[32]

This needs to be qualified enough to observe that we are not going to recognize God or his grace anywhere—crannied wall or California beach—unless some "external authority" has told us about him. But beyond that, this is all good food for thought.

It also leads to some very provocative notions about the future shape of ministry. It is my intention to develop these now in terms of the context for ministry, persons and ministry, and preparation for ministry. But I would continue by asking first, at the conclusion of this introduction (which in a real sense is the heart of this book), that we consider the possibility that authentic ministry must have at its center the person who, while open to God, is in fact, as a person, above all not a psychologist, change-agent, or teacher—but an *artist*. It should be remembered that it has been said that an artist is one who shows us the future, who is a "priest" calling us to our destiny.

## chapter 12

# SECT
# AND
# CHURCH

There is no question but that the parish church, as well as its denominational establishments—be they on Riverside Drive, in Lambeth Palace, or the Vatican—are as secular as the Kiwanis Club, the Pentagon, or the United Nations. They are expressions of a sociocultural system with which we live every day. They are structures that operate on the same principles as the New York Stock Exchange, Harvard University, or General Motors. I am using the term "secular" here in relation to *secularism*, which as Harvey Cox points out is the term for an ideology, "a closed world-view." [1] Consequently my observation means that the real life of a typical parish church can be easily understood without any appeal to anything outside our society. It lacks a transcendent dimension.

I am not referring here to *secularization*, which can be varyingly defined as the disappearance of religious norms for cultural integration or, perhaps better, as the disenchantment of our world. This in itself we can carry too far very quickly. Certainly the *separation* between the sacred and profane is disappearing in our world (if it was ever more than the imagination of a Puritan conscience), but as Mircea Eliade tells us, there is a sacral dimension to all of life as well as a profane. [2] Be that as it may, the question of secularization needs to be distinguished from secularism in the Church. To illustrate this distinction: it is a *gross inaccuracy* to say that if a priest leaves St. Stanislaus by the Steam Plant to become a probation officer that he is "entering a *secular* ministry." My belief is that more likely he is *leaving* a secular ministry for one that is far more powerful, that is, more open to God's grace, because it is liminal (not of the structures, nonsecular). Think if you will of liminality, communitas, grace-ful, ambiguous, open, imaginative, etc., as opposite to secularism, differentiated (e.g. job descriptions), inept, defined, closed, busy, and something of what I am saying will become apparent. As chapter 7 documented, the very thing that drives men out of the parish is its subjugation to secularism.

The first step in this process was the move from the community of the ancient Church to the *Eigenkirche* of the Middle Ages, a process of about five hundred years, more or less. Because the medieval and early modern world was itself nonsecular (people who burned witches could hardly be considered "secular"), the second step did not take place until the end of the eighteenth century. Secularism arose and cast off the Church, but the Church succumbed about fifty years ago to the same disease.

The original concept of the parish was as a communitas, the product of a liminal existence, the temporary dwelling place, the community that is neither here nor there. It is a great error to filter our understanding of this freedom to be in dialogue with a world but not totally committed to it, which is characteristic of the pilgrim, through a maudlin, nineteenth-century pseudo-piety (which generally is a pale reflection of the fifteenth, sixteenth, and seventeenth century). There was a great strength to the ancient and medieval concept that there was more to life than met the eye, and that what went on in the parish church acquired its true rationale from what went on "beyond."

As I write this I feel a little uneasy, because I am very well aware of what it appears to say. I am not, however, abrogating the social consciousness of the Church. I am saying that it is no better to create a Christian community that is congruent with the black, militant, inner-core community, than it is to create one that is congruent with a North Shore

Chicago suburb. They are both tragically wrong, because it is the very business of the Church to be congruent with *nothing* in the sociocultural system. That is because in so doing we really cease to be open to the future, and we lose that transcendence that is our *raison d'être*.

Several years ago Stephen Rose wrote a book, *The Grass Roots Church*, in which he projected the Church of the future. There is some very wise material in those pages, which has a recognizable influence upon my thinking. But we also differ. Rose described the ministry as chaplaincy, teaching, and abandonment.[3] It may be that he and I simply come out of very different backgrounds, but I find the presuppositions of his choice of the first and third terms most regrettable. "Chaplaincy," to me, describes an attitude of "taking care of the troops"; "abandonment" conjures up images of leaving your aged mother out on the ice to die. First Rose includes the priestly, liturgical, and kerygmatic ministry of the Church, and speaks of them as "resources" for mission.[4] I frankly cannot see the ritual and preaching functions as "resources." Why do they have to be identified with what goes on back at the "central house," and why, in abandoning oneself, which means being active in areas of human need apart from the "building," do we leave these things "back there"? Rose needs to see that the Church is a community devoted to certain symbols, among which lie the power of its imagination and the source of its mission. Its understanding of what it has to give to a changing world, therefore, lies in its ritual life, which is in no sense confined to the corner of Fourth and Elm. If he understood this he would not have so clearly missed Kilmer Myers' point that all we need to proclaim the Gospel is a tent and an altar.[5] The same can be said about preaching the Word. It has nothing to do with pulpits, "introduction, three points, and conclusion," or even necessarily John Wesley. It has to do with who I, as a person in Christ, am. I am my words, and my words should be such that in them the other person perceives a new, transcendent meaning to existence.

This brings in another factor, which Rose very rightly calls to our attention but which is often forgotten. There is no truer Christian teaching than the doctrine of Original Sin. It has nothing to do with St. Augustine's exegesis of the Latin version of Romans 5:12, which was a mistranslation and created the impression that we all suffer from an inherited defect from Adam communicated, according to the Bishop of Hippo, in the sensuous ecstasy of an orgasm. It has to do with the fact that we are situated in an imperfect world, which utterly frustrates our good intentions. Man's "nature" is defective, because his *social* self pertains to his "nature," as does his unconscious where has been stored all the inappropriate behavior he has learned since birth or even conception. The Church's vocation is constantly to call this to our mind, and consequently never to *identify* its ministry with the structure of any group or cause. The Church must remain in the interstices!

It is perfectly possible, for example, for the Christian community to say that America has no place in Vietnam. It is entirely within reason to work to get us out of Vietnam. This is to take a prophetic stance, which we can reasonably expect to be taken seriously by others who share our presuppositions, that is, those who are members of the Christian "communitas." But our cause is not the cause of the Peoples Liberation Front anymore than it is the cause of the Pentagon. This is the point which words like "abandonment" tend to miss, because if we must be "somewhere" and we abandon the Church's position, then we are required to take some other position. Jesus was no more a Zealot than he was a Sadducee. He died for neither cause as far as we can tell (which is no more than what his disciples tell us), but because he was free of all "causes."

Most books that talk about the Church in the world today are not *radical* enough, in the etymological sense that they do not go to the *root* of the matter. The task of the Church is not to "organize for action" per se, but to provide a life where inevitable change can be tolerable for the frightened and tempered for the angry, and where both have the freedom and power to explore and pursue the alternatives. The program of the Church is not to have a "program," in the sense that we have a "plan" or that Karl Marx, Ayn Rand, or COCU "has *the answer*." Cox is right when he suggests that the Church ought to be inalterably opposed to "feasibility studies." [6] What a blessing it would be if the Church were the "place" where people could ask, "What would it be like *if . . . ,*" and experiment with the idea; and no one would put a label on the image or he who images.

It is to be regretted that so many Protestant writers have abandoned their heritage to ignore the centrality of that definition of the Church as being where "the pure Gospel is preached and the sacraments properly administered" (Article VII of the Augsburg Confession). As Hans Küng rightly says, there is nothing "un-Catholic" about this at all, even though some would prefer to add what he calls the "dimensions of the Church"—one, holy, catholic, and apostolic—to distinguish institutional Christianity from an unguarded "enthusiasm." [7] Here the emphasis lies on those functions of ministry that speak most directly to the power of the Church, its liminal, imagining quality.

What in essence this is saying relates directly to Part I, in which I characterized the previous epochs of Church history as emphasizing the person, rite, and word in turn. In their own way, those who have come before us grasped the core of transcendence, the key to the imagining process within the life of the Christian. What is needed is for us to distill from their experience the truth of what they did, without bringing with it the "baggage" of a reality that no longer exists. This is difficult and very readily misunderstood. *I am definitely not advocating an anachronism.* There is nothing liminal about a museum. This is not a plea for reproducing a fourth-century Eucharist in our parish churches, for building a thirteenth-century Gothic cathedral, or for reinstating the

Protestant ethic. I wish to offer no comfort to those who would appear as a model for an Italian holy card. When St. Paul said we should be "fools" for Christ, he was referring to our denial of secularism (1 Cor. 4:10). It has nothing to do with a silly appearance. I suspect symbols of liminality in our times must be more internal than external. What I am saying is that rite and word are intrinsic to the person, and that the Christian religion finds in the interpersonal relation an inclusive analogy to man's position before that which transcends him.

I am sure some would respond to what I have said with the fear that it leads to an ingrown notion of the Church, as opposed to one of service, and continues to promote the clericalism of the modern period. Certainly if we do not realize the implications of secularization (*not* secularism), and hang on to some kind of dual notion of the sacred and the profane, this kind of thinking does encourage the "teahouse" concept of the Church. But if we could embrace secularity and speak the Word and do our ritual in the midst of the marketplace, then we would have the possibility of avoiding part of this risk. Frankly, the alternatives appear to me to be a *disappearance* into irrelevance, on the one hand, or into "current events" on the other; and then the world is closed to a Christian transcendence.

When we talk about ministry as "service" (as we have done) let us make sure what "service" we have to render. I would distinguish between the primary, which has to do with transcendence, and the secondary, which involves meeting the needs of man that can be satisfied nowhere else, such as running a leper colony, counseling college students, or feeding the poor. When Christians are described in their better moments as people of love, it is not because of their philanthropy per se, but because of the awe-inspiring quality of a love that obviously *transcends* just the meeting-the-needs-of-others. I once asked a black community organizer whether or not he thought there was a job for clergy in the inner city. His reply was both negative and open, and he put the question neatly back into my lap. "It depends on what you come to do! We have enough social workers; but maybe you have something else to bring which the black man in the ghetto needs. But I don't know what it is, and you never have been able to show or tell me."

But then I want to go on to say that I do not see the Church as measured by the names of the people on the parish register. I doubt that it ever has been, except in the minds of the clergy. Every Christian community has almost always been identified by its relation to its priest or pastor, and we ought to acknowledge this openly. Much worry has been expended over the "personality cult" in the Church, but in fact this is what makes it all "go." Clergy are not technicians. They must be sacramental persons; people through whom is experienced the person of the Church and of Christ. I have referred to this in chapter 1, and now it needs to be picked up again and emphasized. I am convinced it is what Ignatius meant when he identified the bishop with the Church. This is not an argument for or against Apostolic Succession; and it is certainly not a suggestion that "clergyman" is a word in the active voice and "layman" in the passive voice. It is simply to say that we acknowledge the sacramental person, the *sine qua non* of the cohesive Christian congregation, as the source of ministry. Furthermore, he has the primary responsibility for the two ministerial functions which of the eight are the key instruments to the transcendent and graceful witness of the Church: ritual and preaching.

Discipline, another of the ministerial functions, can also be more readily understood as relating to what goes on between persons rather than following rules and being categorized. If a wife and husband never converse, never touch, and never have intercourse, nothing is happening, the legal contract notwithstanding. When we are "in communion" we are in communion with someone, and that means the sacramental person. As in any relationship, there are certain terms to that rapport. The great strength of the Sacrament of Penance, which we need very much to restore to the full life of the

Church in a non-thirteenth-century shape, lies in its expression of the interpersonal break between the sacramental person and the penitent. It would be much more fruitful to pursue questions such as the effect of divorce on Church standing, the financial support of the Church, and participation in a given congregation on the basis of these terms than by some juridical process. Granted, this is less precise in the sense of being less certain; but though I would argue that we need today the precision we associate with clarity of thought, I am convinced that we need the power that resides in the ambiguity or opacity of existence.

The terms of the relationship of the members of the congregation to the sacramental person define the life of the community far better than the means now used by many parishes, namely, their countless organizations. This is a difficult concept for Americans, in particular, to grasp. I know of a small congregation where the attempt has been made to create a "communitas" whose life could be described in terms much like those found in this chapter. The struggle to live a pretty high ideal is constant, and there is in particular one man who has had the courage to face up to his priest and say, "If we just had better leadership—someone who would serve as a 'clearing house' [what some people mean when they call the pastor an 'enabler'] for our activities, I could feel good about what we're doing. But so far I've just been putting in and getting very little out." The tragedy is that this man has been crushed by the "bookkeeping mentality" of society, and what he needs, and I suspect many others need, is better insight to himself, *a moratorium on results*, and an opportunity to let the power of God reconstitute his life (which is one way of defining *repentance*).

This is to say that we ought not only to move away from a community defined by its records, but also a community defined by its program. Rose speaks of the Church of repose vis-à-vis the Church of action. I am not advocating the former option, but I am rooting action in the ontology of a relationship. Its causality goes much deeper than a general humanistic moral indignation. It springs from our personal knowledge of the Christ who believed that his coming initiated the culmination of God's purpose in creation. We need as his disciples to speak of ourselves in all our actions for justice as St. Paul did of himself: "This is my way of helping to complete, in my poor human flesh, the full tale of Christ's afflictions still to be endured, for the sake of his body which is the church" (Col. 1:24).

If the Church of the future is a communitas focused in a person, what are we to say about its size and composition? Andrew Greeley has pointed out that there is a growing interest in our times in the "sect" as opposed to the "church." [8] By these distinctions he means something different from Ernst Troeltsch's categories by the same name. *By a "sect" Greeley means a "small, personal, intimate religious community of fellowship," and by a "church" he means a "formalized, hierarchial, and juridic social structure with elaborate specialization of roles and institutionalization of behavior."* It is perfectly possible and more frequently the case than not that sects and churches exist within the same framework. The Neo-Pentecostal movement is found in sects, the "underground churches" are sects, and even some expressions of the Liturgical Movement reflect a sect mentality. The word generally conjures up pejorative feelings. This I would have us avoid, since the communitas of which I have been speaking in strong, positive tones would be constituted more commonly in sects, although not exclusively.

The sect has obvious strengths for which our times call. The possibility of intimate, personal relationships, defining our Christian commitment, is one item to which I have already spoken. It should be added that mobility and flexibility of life, the option to move where the Holy Spirit directs unencumbered by various types of ecclesiastical baggage, and a membership in a given group based on a common understanding of the implications of our relationship in Christ all provide an additional source of appeal.

For it is at least *theoretically* possible for such a group to escape the very sobering and often spiritually retarding effect of the church mortgage, the growing burden of the priest's salary, and the time-consuming as well as dollar-consuming problem of maintenance and repair of real property. I say "theoretically," because very few congregations seem to be able to avoid establishing their "place." This seems to be like the basic human need to identify a family with a home, and maybe we would be wiser to talk about the kind of church house that is most flexible and less financially and temporally exhausting than to advocate the abolition of church buildings. Some years ago I heard Peter Hammond, who has done extensive writing in the field of church architecture, suggest that we stop building churches until we decide what the Church is. This struck me as a little unreal, but his alternative was better. If we do not stop building, at least, he said, let us build temporary structures which make as few permanent statements as possible.

Before passing from the matter of church buildings, I would also make two further points. First, Joan Petersen has effectively demolished that "patristic fundamentalism or self-conscious neo-primitivism" which has infected elements of the Liturgical Movement, in which it has been suggested that we, like the people of the ancient Church, should worship in homes in order "to get the Eucharist into the lives of its people where they are." If people in the ancient Church worshiped in houses, she says, it was out of necessity and not for any theological reason. What rooms they used in houses they did their very best to set apart for this special purpose.[9] Second, if we build churches, let us remember that there is ample precedent for employing them for secular use as well. J. G. Davies has gathered a great mass of evidence for this practice from all ages,[10] and in chapter 3 I have called attention to this custom. An interesting illustration of some of the points made in my discussion of the sect is found in a description of a mission in Birmingham, Alabama, by its vicar, Bob Ross. ("Is This Any Way to Run a Church?" *Faith/At/Work*, February, 1971, pp. 5–8.) Fr. Ross outlines how, under the then Bishop of Alabama's instigation, a congregation was organized with no intention of building a building, with a desire to pursue a "group type" worship, and with an insistence on a deep personal commitment upon the part of every member. His analysis of the problems involved and of the possibilities that have emerged is both sobering and encouraging. I was particularly interested to note their resistance to things like Sunday Schools and the difficulties they have met in keeping their experience of worship fresh (with a decision to stick to the Eucharist, in whatever form it may evolve). This article is worth the reading by anyone truly interested in this movement of the Church.

I have spoken exclusively to the value of the sect (after Greeley); but I think we make a mistake if we ignore the great value of the church. It is much more structured but can also have elements of Turner's communitas. The Church speaks to another side of man, but nonetheless one that needs to be addressed. It appeals more to some than to others, but such people witness to a truth in our religion. The sect expresses an intimate, focused, and spontaneous relationship within the Church. The church, still centered in the Sacrament and Word, as I would see it, testifies to the timeless and transcultural dimensions of the Christian experience of God. There is a need for a liturgy that is aesthetically sensitive and emotionally majestic, for a sermon that possesses polished rhetoric, and for great numbers and magnificent pageantry that awakens in us the sense of our catholicity. There is something more to life than the ability to enter into a deep personal relationship. There is no question that we all need to be exposed to assured competence, profound learning, and the dignity that is expressed in an ordered talent. So the sect needs to be balanced by the church, though both in different ways are liminal. The symbols of the church are oriented more toward inspiring awe than love, but they feed the imagination just as well.

What I am suggesting, to take a more practical turn, is that every Christian needs the experience of the intimate community, as well as the great church. The very fact is that with notable exceptions, today we get neither. The average parish church (running from 200 to 1,000 members), is too large for spontaneous intimacy and too small to develop a multistaff ministry of *truly* professional competence (the next chapter discusses what I mean by this) demanded by the life I envision for it. This is to say that the present parish structure, with a pastor and perhaps an assistant (both with no more than three years of undergraduate seminary), a few administrative aids, and a lot of voluntary labor, ministering to more people than any one person can know well, may be financially viable in our present conception of ministry, but it is in fact a *dead end.*

This point is so crucial to what I am proposing that it is important it be made as clear as possible. This is not the popular attack upon the "parish," a plea for an institutionless Christianity, or a proposal for some variety of artificial cross-cultural restructuring of the parish. I am saying that the present structure, which is largely a contemporary phenomenon, is incapable of doing either of two constellations of functions needed today and described under the terms "sect" and "church." There is nothing intimate and spontaneous about the "family Eucharist" at the average parish of 750 members. There is nothing awe-inspiring about it either. In the case of the Episcopal Church, it is more a validation of the socio-cultural subsystem of the local upper middle class than anything else; and consequently it is about as "liminal" (i.e. as transcendent an experience) as a meeting of the Lions Club.

When we discussed in the first chapter of Part II the efforts to reform the Church in terms of the Christian Education, Neo-Pentecostal, Liturgical, Ecumenical, and "underground church" movements, it should have been evident that in part the real creative thrust of these movements has been deflected by the inadequacy of the present parish structure. Some require a freedom and flexibility not possible in the present system, and others demand a professional competence not available in what we now have.

Because the parish falls between two real needs of people and fulfills neither, much of what goes on in it is "made work" or "busy work" (e.g. parish bulletins no one reads, parish calls when only one member of the family is home, endless meetings of organizations whose purpose is to assure the need for endless meetings of organizations, managing a building whose use is limited to a few hours a week, etc., etc.). A good bit of the low morale and misplaced function of the parish—ghetto or teahouse—may be attributed to this failure to do well anything that needs doing.

My proposal would be that we need to move in two directions from our present impasse. We need to reconstitute our Church life into small groups (more than fifty begins to get cumbersome) after the sect model, which in turn are "cells" of a large church (constituting maybe two or three thousand members or more). The sects would meet in some multipurpose building for the liturgy, including preaching, and would identify themselves in terms of the sacramental person who presides at their gatherings. Both the rite and preaching would be of the informal, interpersonal character. Pastoral care and administration would be either of a *very light* variety or simply referred back to the "mother church." Evangelism and prophecy, which I see as uniquely lay functions, I will discuss in the next chapter; however, professionals in the area of urban sociology and social change would be related to the church, or even beyond this to the urban area or diocese. Teaching, both of children and adults, would be done on a *strictly professional basis* in the church. The recent proposals made by John Westerhoff, in *Values for Tomorrow's Children,* for the drastic revision of the Church's educational system set very well with what I am saying here; and I recommend them to the reader.[11] If adopted it would be the first time in centuries that the Church took a positive, creative attitude toward this function, which was not a reaction to an external threat. The sect simply would not do any formal instruction.

The question here might be raised about parochial schools. If we have any, they must be related to the church if they are to be competitive or better. Basically there are probably three reasons why we have parochial schools today. The first and without question the principal reason (though many refuse to admit it) is in order to provide selectivity in the socioeconomic and ethnoracial background of students. Why else have Episcopal Church schools grown so rapidly in the South? The second reason is that we want a better education for our children. If that is the case, and I think it is legitimate, then the financial expenditure demands a large base for such a school. The third is that we want a "Christian education" for our children, though in this setting the possibility is very much open to question. Unless the church backs the school with massive grants, there is an automatic selection process through high tuition, and this may well be "un-Christian." Then, again, there are very few teachers or materials equipped to integrate math, history, English, general science, geography, and so forth with Christian insights. To date we have attempted too much with too little, and the only possible option for a Christian education system is the church concept described above, and even then it is open to serious questions.

It should be evident that all tasks requiring full-time professional competence—counseling, teaching, *formal* preaching, social analysis—as well as those skills requiring particular talents within ministry, would be related to the church or beyond. Those undergirding dimensions of life that call for a special quality of person, a commitment to Christ, and an ability to communicate the vision of transcendence (in the terms we have outlined—in other words, to be "a citizen of the eschaton") would be the special order of business for the sects, not to say that they would be inconsistent with the Church. In this arrangement it would logically follow that the sect would be a minimal source of financial expenditure and all possible resources would be devoted to the church and diocese, where salaries, equipment, facilities, and materials would be competitive. There is no value to be gained in appearing second rate to ourselves and to the world in everything we do.

Without belaboring the point, I would remind the reader of the problems raised by James Lowery (see page 114) about the financial viability of many congregations below the two hundred communicant, $20,000-budget level; as well as the opportunity for experimentation and full program for those above these figures. This proposal would seek to meet that situation head-on, by creating two kinds of congregations. The one that does not attempt anything but minimal funding (enough for altar supplies, coffee hour, rental of space, etc.), and the other that even to open its doors must have responsible funding equivalent to any business norm. It strikes me that in doing this I am also speaking to the objections to Lowery's thesis raised by Mead.

To make this kind of financial arrangement "go" it would be necessary beyond question that a churchman recognize his membership in Christ to be expressed *both* in the sect and the church. There is a certain risk in developing the paranoia common in the Church today, where vestries ask, "What is the diocese doing with *our* [i.e., St. John's] money?" This bifocal ecclesiastical allegiance could be reinforced by gatherings of all the sects at the church on certain festivals, and by the visitation of the church clergy, as well as the interchurch and diocesan clergy (particularly the bishop), to the various small communities.

Some churches I can see approaching the nature of a cathedral (the bishop's church). The context out of which I am speaking is, of course, that of Anglican polity; but this is more a matter of convenience, because I see this as an ecumenical venture and I have no desire to prejudge what the precise vocabulary of any ecumenical Church might be. Having said that, there is real merit, to revert to Anglican terminology, in considering the increase of the number of dioceses and their bishops, and this would mean that more and more churches could, in fact, be cathedrals. But it is also possible to think of the large parish church continuing to function in some ways as it does, for several reasons. One is that not all people can or wish to be part of a sect. There is a demand involved in a sect that is more than many people can bear, whereas in numbers there is a certain support and strength. Second, there is a real place in the Church for a ministry in which, although a degree of intimacy is lacking between pastor and parishioner, the possibility exists of *expert* counsel (which will require specialized training) in areas of family life, that is available nowhere else. I refer particularly to parent-child tensions, marital problems, and grief situations, in which the "I-you" relations, described by Harvey Cox,[12] can be a satisfactory base for a very valuable ministry.

One very ready criticism of my description of the sect, with its nonstipendiary sacramental person at its core, is the conviction of some that no congregation can function effectively without a full-time leader. Peter Winterble, in reporting on his experiences as a seminarian at St. Augustine's Episcopal Church in Washington, D.C., when the parish was without a full-time priest for almost a year, reported that the people of this very venturesome parish experienced exhaustion in running their own show.[13] My reply would be that the sect is smaller by several times than a congregation such as St. Augustine's, and it has no intention of running a multifaceted "program." Its action orientation would profitably consist of one or two concerns that involve the mutual skills and life situations of the entire group. But I would say that this has to be held before the membership constantly, because it becomes very tempting to succumb to the contemporary American idol of success measured by size and by how many things we are doing.

Around what principle would the sects be organized? I am not among those who think of the self *defined in terms of residence* as completely passé. There is no doubt that many people conceive of themselves primarily in terms of their jobs, their opinions, and their economic and social class. I am confident that this has been going on for centuries, the only difference being that before fast transportation and in a less complex society people of the same trade and socioeconomic status tended to live in the same place. Gibson Winter chose to deride the homogeneity of the average suburban congregation, and much of what he has said is important. But Scott Donaldson has a point in replying that, first, the desire for homogeneity is not unique to the suburbs, it is found in rural and urban areas as well; and, second, that we err in interpreting suburban neighborliness in a strictly negative sense as an expression of the worst in racism and class consciousness.[14] Undoubtedly it can be this, but the desire to live in a neighborhood and to enjoy the sense of belonging to such a residential community can be found, with all its problems and apparently some often ignored virtues, in the midst of New York City, Chicago, or Los Angeles. My belief is that as long as this is true—and I suspect it shall be for some time to come—we would do well to use such natural communities as the organizing principle in our "sect."

There has to be some sense of commonality in such a group *before* it ever begins. Ideally, it should be our life together in Christ; but even the "underground" churches are bound together by more than that and sometimes in lieu of that (as witness their now famous "convention" in Boston several years ago, which erupted into a name-calling session). We may share in common our hatred of the "establishment," our belief in the sacramental value of peyote (as in the Native American Church), our Irish heritage, or our jobs at a certain economic and educational level. Before, these things held in common went with residence; but today that is not necessarily so. Still, any of them can constitute the commonality that forms the organizing principle of the sect, without necessarily denying the possibility that we are seeking a oneness in Christ. I would foresee, therefore, small groups centering in a number of different kinds of principles, making up the church.

Does this condone or even promote racism in the churches? It would only if the sacramental person intended that it do so, and that person himself is, with the people in the sect, subject to the informed life of the Church. It could in fact be a way of overcoming racism in a manner that cannot be handled in the average parish church, if the problem was acute enough and the sect could draw on the professional resources of the church. James Dittes' method of meeting resistance within a congregation, which I discussed briefly before (page 184), can be employed in such a context, and change in outlook can take place. It is unreal to pretend that we must expect a freedom from racism before we gather as Christians. We are simply blind if we think the present system is doing much to break through the prejudice of our people. Some sort of opportunity for encounter with the transcendent judgment of God upon racist views must be provided, and it seems to me there is no more ideal setting than that of the sect.

I have already made some distinctions within the function of the church, defining it as anything from a cathedral to a very large, family-oriented parish. Perhaps it would help to consider it as most closely resembling the collegiate church known in seventeenth-century Lutheranism, where there would be a "college of clergy" possessing certain special competences. Other historical precedents for this are obvious and do not have to be pursued. Not all churches would have all the possible professions available within the Church. But if we concentrated the stipendiary functions of ministry within these structures, which would number far less than our present parish churches, and centered the nonstipendiary functions in the sects, we could by judicious arrangement assure a full and as effective as possible ministry to all our people, without losing the intimate and personal touch vital to the Church's life as *Ursakrament.*

It should be obvious that what is suggested here is not a project of the Episcopal Church only nor of any other denomination. One clear thing in the contemporary period, as we move from a simple equation of the nature of ultimate truth to the words we use, is that the propositions that divide many Christians cease to have an absolute, nonnegotiable quality.[15] Life together becomes more possible. This is not to say that linguistic distinctions are unimportant. I would maintain that the future of the Christian religion depended on whether at the Council of Nicea we defined Christ as *homoousion* or *homoiousion* (of the "same substance" or of "like substance" with God the Father). But at the same time, no definition is free from later qualification or modification. Through dialogue, revelation is continuous. Consequently, the verbal distinctions that once separated Christians no longer function in this way, and all other things being equal (and that is a large condition) we are free from a dogmatic literalism in favor of a hermeneutics of dogma.

I would cite as evidence for this the seemingly remarkable (but not really so amazing) accord being found among Roman Catholics, Anglicans, and some Lutherans,[16] and the relative ease of the mergers forming the United Methodist Church and the United Church of Christ. There are elements in the Consultation on Church Unity (COCU) which indicate that if merger fails it is not necessarily because of some inalterable propositional truth that each group holds. Some of the protest from various quarters about the current COCU proposal, in a tacit acknowledgment of the deftness of language, now complains of COCU's concern for bigness, institutionalism, and power politics.[17] Undoubtedly there is truth to these criticisms, though I doubt that we can completely dismiss the possibility that they are pegs upon which we hang our anxieties over the threatened loss of familiar signs of identity.

It also has to be said, however, that a common recognition of the heuristic value of propositional theology over against an absolutizing of the same is not common to all Christians. Rodney Stark and Charles Glock some time ago pointed out that there is within the Christian community an emerging, even deeper fragmentation than that with which we are familiar from the Reformation. They choose to identify it through denominational groupings (e.g. the Congregationalists, Episcopalians, and Methodists are "Liberals," the Disciples of Christ and Presbyterians are "Moderates," etc.), which is a dubious procedure. For example, they suggest that there is no hope to Roman Catholic-Anglican conversations, because of the limitations of their methodology.[18] But what they do rightly document is a difference among Christians in the *basic understanding of reality*, which, in fact, crops up within denominations just as much as between denominations. This would be particularly expected in times of rapid change. Many Episcopalians, for example, have discovered that they find more "compatible Christians" within, say, the Roman Catholic and Presbyterian churches than within their own. So in saying that what I propose in this chapter presumes an ecumenical character, I am suggesting two qualifications. First, the sects can also represent differences within the Church of conceptualizing God's revelation in Christ (much as is found in the Anglican Communion today). Second, although a great simplification in denominational entities would occur if we would "stop beating our ideological drums," there is no reason to expect an end to pluralism within the Church. It is a persistent characteristic of any noncoercive society, and in fact exists "underground" in those that choose to suppress dissent.

Having said this, however, I would want to support the broad outline of Stephen Rose's proposal that the ecumenical movement can better serve as a basis for dialogue and the pooling of resources on the local level than it can reform Chris-

tianity through constitutional negotiation on the national or
international level. Unless we are anti-institutional, it is true
that what happens within the local community must be validated by the hierarchy to become a permanent gain. But this
is different from suggesting that we present to the "grass-
roots" congregation a ready-made plan of a relationship of
which they have no immediate personal knowledge.[19] The
model for this kind of local dialogue is probably best found
on the college and university campuses, where chaplains and
their followers have for years been engaging in an ecumenical
and differentiated ministry up to the permitted limits, and
sometimes quite beyond.

Glock and Stark identify five groups of Christians within
the total professing body. I see no more than three: the "fundamentalists" (people who subscribe to a pre-1914 reality
view), the "immanentists" (people who accept the post-1914
secularism), and those who believe in the *continuing nature
of revelation* (which is the position I take here). This third
group represents the strength of Christianity today, and includes a great number of Roman Catholics, Anglicans, Lutherans, some members of the Methodist Church and United
Church of Christ, Presbyterians, and others.[20] My task is not
to identify some plan of merger. It is illuminating however,
to notice that most existing plans are not unlike what I am
proposing in this scheme, a historically rooted ministry, with
modifications suitable for our time.

Rose sees the local ecumenical movement as an opportunity for pooling resources and talents. His approach is dis-
tinctively Protestant, which I think would be a gross error;
and he really has not worked through the differentiation of
stipendiary versus nonstipendiary ministry, or the need to
provide for distribution of ministerial function throughout
the Body of Christ. This is to say that the equation voluntary
= lay ministry, and paid and profession = ordained ministry
needs to be abolished. Just how this might be done will be
part of the agenda for the next chapter. But aside from criti-

cisms such as these, Rose's proposal needs to be taken seriously by all of us. "Empire building" and clerical illusions of omnipotence are not going to serve the Kingdom of God, but a little planning and hoping will.

My intention in this chapter has been to recover something of the feeling of the lighthearted spirit of the ancient parish, filled with people for whom the measure of their success and the proof of their faith lay more in the consummation of their life together in Christ in the future than in the approval of the present culture. Yet, at the same time, I have wanted to acknowledge the learning of our present age and the justification of the demand for competence in those who minister in areas now requiring technical skill (e.g. counseling, social work, teaching, preaching, etc.). I have accepted these two polarities, and paired them with two moods of the communitas: love and awe, perceiving transcendence within the human situation and recognizing it "out there." The goal has been for balance. This same theme will reoccur in the next chapter, as we move to the discussion of the possible nature of ministry in the future.

## chapter 13

## CHARISMATIC
## AND
## PROFESSIONAL

In a conversation I had with a Lutheran churchman about clergy renewal, I was struck by his succinct analysis of the dilemma of the contemporary pastor. Implicit in his remarks was also a possible approach to new ways of thinking of ministry. He made the point that since World War II more and more clergy have been saying, "Look, I'm just a man like any other man; and I want to be treated this way. I want an adequate salary; I want to pay my way and own my house; and I want to be considered as any other professional man." Then the question is asked, "What is your profession?" The reply is, "Well, I'm something like a 'counselor,' but not really. I'm more a 'teacher,' but not in a formal sense. Maybe you could say that I'm interested in change, but not quite like anyone else." The point is that in pursuit of professional status we have divested ourselves of a different kind of symbolic role, without ever resolving the question as to what precisely our unique professional competence might be. Every time we think we have come up with an answer, someone has been there before us.

Whereas the "symbols" of our past atypical role—such as the rectory or parsonage, the clerical garb, the discount at stores, the deference to clerical ears—are open to some question as to their specific value, they may at least have been expressions of a liminal status in a previous culture. If that is true, in principle they express something that needs to be considered before we endorse too heartily the almost axiomatic plea of the contemporary clergyman: "Look, I'm just like any other man." For perhaps we have dismissed too readily the possibility that the clergyman's status lies not in the fact that he is a professional man like any other professional man, but that he is in fact an *extraordinary man*. This is to say that it is possible that *in a sense*, like the shaman, the healer, the medicine man of primitive religion, the contemporary clergyman ceases to be that which he most effectively is when he is conformed to the social structures. Is it not possible that, if you can completely understand what it is to be a priest or pastor in accordance with univocal cultural norms, then you no longer have an effective ministry?

I imagine that this is a rather alarming suggestion, even when couched in the subjunctive mood. It smacks of superstition, ignorance, and magic. But when we get down to it, I suspect that most laymen would hope for their clergy to be at least a little "apart," even if many pastors themselves find unbearably irritating the clumsy efforts made to characterize this "apartness." Does the man in the pew think of his pastor as a "professional"? Does he not rather expect him to embody some sense of "holiness," which is to say some feeling of a reality and perfection that transcends the present culture?

This expectation finds stronger expression in the counter culture. Theodore Roszak in his book on this subject makes an eloquent plea for us to look again at the meaning of magic. He continues by saying

When we look more closely at the shaman, we discover that the contribution this exotic character has made to human culture is nearly inestimable. Indeed, the shaman might properly lay claim to being the culture hero *par excellence*, for through him creative forces that approach the superhuman seem to have been called into play.[1]

He goes on to explain how the shaman, through the use of magic, opened man's imagination to realms of existence he would never have known otherwise. It is no wonder that a whole segment of our population are out looking for their "guru." As Roszak remarks, this need of people for new images of life confronts our anemic American religion with an undeniable challenge that pure rationalism cannot answer. Without pursuing to absurdity the notion of the shaman and his magic, it seems entirely possible to me that the charismatic quality he possessed, which marked him as a liminal man, is in fact what is needed in our ministry if we are to awaken people's imaginations to the possibilities of the future. I am not suggesting that we place in leadership roles actual or incipient psychotics, and nothing in this chapter should be so interpreted. But it is possible that we have made a fetish out of "normalcy."

Andrew Greeley, in describing the clergy of the future, talks about the ambivalences of the clerical role. Being a person apart has both privileges and burdens, both advantages and disadvantages. There is always, he says, a dialectic element in the clerical vocation, which he describes as being between the "monastic" and "secular" or between a detachment from the present world and being a man of the people. If in the latter polarity, we cannot forget the validity of the other pole.[2]

It is very easy for this image of the pastor as a man apart to be corrupted into a demand that the clergyman serve as a sop for a guilty conscience, an escape for the Christian unwilling to face the reality of his and his fellowman's sins within the present society. Racism, economic exploitation, and failures of justice are often covered by mysticism and religious privatism. But it is no answer to this great risk to insist that somehow we define ministry solely in terms of the culture and its integral needs. What we need to do is see clearly from the start that there are *two dimensions to the Church's ministry: the charismatic and the professional.* I am surprised that John Harris, in what is in many ways an excellent article in the July 1969 *Anglican Theological Review*, "The Clergy and Their Work: Some Observations and Recommendations," fails to make this distinction and speaks specifically of ministry as synonymous with a profession.[3] His is the common error of many pastoral theologians who fail to temper sufficiently their sociology with theology.

I would define the charismatic person as someone to whom is given a quality of character that is contagious, spontaneous, mysterious, and essentially eschatological. When one comes into relation with a charismatic person there is communicated a sense of greater wholeness, purpose, and self-worth. The imagination is charged! We are confronted by an artist who lays the future before us. The professional person I would define as someone who on the basis of a body of acquired knowledge has developed skills to achieve in his relations with others a predictable end. He is his profession as a result of his training, and we go to him for reasonably well-defined purposes. Examples would be the counselor, the community organizer, the teacher, and the administrator.

The heart of the Christian ministry is its charismatic, liminal quality. Without question there is a place for professional capacities in ministry, but it is the charismatic character of the Church that lends a strength to professions such as counseling, teaching, and community organization that they cannot possess otherwise. Colston and Hiltner made a case for this in their research reported in *The Context of Pastoral Counseling*.[4] Ten years ago Lewis Whittemore argued for its truth in education.[5] George Crowell, in *Society Against Itself*, pleaded for a professionalism in social action, which more by implication than express statement derives its strength from Christian moral teaching.[6] But the power of Christian ministry lies in the sacramental person, who possesses the capacity to communicate the love of Christ not by virtue of training but through the transcendent dimension of God's love that exhibits itself in his life.

This leads me to a crucial point. It is possible to take a young man out of college, send him to medical school, put him through internship and residency, and produce a *technically competent* surgeon. He can repair hernias, take out appendixes, patch up hearts, and cut out cancer. The same thing is true of an engineer, a research sociologist, or an airplane pilot: training makes for competence. It does not, however, produce a sacramental person; and in fact it can sometimes inhibit his effectiveness.

Perhaps one of the books most worthy of our study is the work of an Anglican priest and one-time missionary, Roland Allen, which was first published in 1912. Allen argues in *Missionary Methods: St. Paul's or Ours?* that contrary to the Apostle we are overly concerned with being assured of the intellectual understanding of the clergy and converts in our missions to the detriment of endorsing their enthusiastic repentance and faith. We fail to see what St. Paul saw so clearly that if we lay the emphasis in our churches upon Baptism and the Eucharist, entrust the Gospel with simple, brief teaching, and ordain within a community the indigenous, natural leaders, then we will have in the end a far stronger and more imaginative community than we attain by our compulsive stipulations for baptism and ordination.[7] One thing should be clear from chapter 11: the difficulty of making meaningful statements about God when working within the culture. The problem is immensely magnified and of highly questionable value when we demand of someone foreign to our tradition an understanding of two thousand years of Western cultural baggage.

The sacramental person, the natural leader, the charismatic pastor is someone who is found within the community and who is an integral part of that community. This is to say that the capacity of person he possesses is both his and the community's of which he is a part. The point Allen made is that St. Paul ordained men as elders *of* the community. They were chosen because of their moral qualities, not necessarily their intellectual capacity. Their task was to see that the sacraments, the *sine qua non* of every Christian community, were performed.[8] There is ample precedent for this in the ancient Church. The practice of raising up priests and pastors within the local community for that community is common in the medieval period and even the modern. But as education became the compellingly felt need of the Church, there was a tendency to encourage the bright individual, not necessarily the charismatic person, to seek ordination. He was removed from the local situation and trained to a deep awareness of the profound truths of the universal Church. Yet if he returned to a local parish, only the grace of God saved him from a ministry lacking in that natural rapport so essential to a charismatic ministry and yet so difficult to possess unless it be truly indigenous.

As I have suggested, the move away from a charismatic, indigenous ministry reached its apex in the nineteenth century when the clergy were largely drawn from the middle classes, educated in the cloistered atmosphere of the universities and seminaries, and then sent out to live among a people with whom they had no natural bond and who had no knowledge of the academic world from which they came. Allen laments the effect of this mentality upon the foreign missions. We need only expand the principle to suggest its equally deleterious impact upon the working classes, the rural missions, and ultimately the new middle class.

In the previous chapter I advanced the value of the sect, gathered about the sacramental person. I am now prepared to carry this notion further and state that this person is probably not the young man who has chosen a ministerial career, passed through three or more years of seminary training after college, and then been sent to be the shepherd of people whom he little knows and of whom he is probably considerably afraid. Rather the Church looks at a given Christian community and finds there the natural leader, the charismatic Christian, and gives him—or her—the training necessary to sharpen the gift of grace already evident in his life, and authorizes him through ordination to function as the presbyter, the *sacerdos*, of that community. He is *not* a "professional"; he is not paid for this, just as the presbyters may not have been paid in the ancient Church. This person works alongside his people, as priests have done in many ways for much longer than they have not, and in this way shares even better with them the liminal quality of his life.

The point to be inferred here is that while the Church must affirm its universal quality, it also must recognize the reality of the distinct community. We acknowledge that man must have a life shared within a natural group, which may be residential in character or centered in some other dimension of existence. *But the unique nature of a given community demands a match with its sacramental person.* No one can minister effectively "just anywhere." It is time that we recognized this, honored the peculiarities of given communities, and ceased confusing commitment to the Lord of all with the assumption of a "clerical ideology" that is unrelated to anything but the clerical fraternity. As in the ancient Church, a man is ordained to the cure of which he is already a part, and the assumption is that he remains with that community. If he moves to another community, he must be acknowledged by that group as the sacramental person before he so functions. Clearly this foresees men entering the priesthood as a rule at a later age than twenty-four or twenty-five, and abolishes the accustomed notions of the "clerical career" (which is a term John Harris uses a little too loosely in his article on this subject). It also plays down the notion of "character" in Holy Orders, and emphasizes the communal nature of the priestly office.

I do not wish to imply, however, that the selection for ordination to the priesthood of the natural, charismatic leader of a community is the only possible route to assumption of the role of sacramental person within a community. It would probably be the normative method. But it is entirely possible that persons who have sought to achieve some professional competence within Christian ministry might also be priests (this distinction is something very often dismissed), become identified with a community of Christians, and have a priestly ministry within it.

In the series of essays edited by William Cleary, *Hyphenated Priests: The Ministry of the Future*, we read the testimony of a journalist, a sociologist, a poet, a lawyer, a physician, an aerospace engineer, and others, all of whom share in common the fact that they are priests and yet spend most of their time doing "non-priestly things." In different ways it is important for these men that in their professional communities (e.g. medicine), or with a congregation that they serve on Sundays, they preach the Word and share in offering the Eucharist. Ned Cassem reports how, during one summer he spent as a doctor in Vietnam, he found the opportunity at the end of a hard day to join with his co-workers in celebrating the Holy Communion, which was a means of making their union as a healing community more perfect.[9] But the interesting thing is that it also works the other way. As Charles Whelan reports, his competence in law lends credence to his priestly ministry, which he sees extending beyond Word and Sacrament into the sacramental effect of being who he is in a world apart from vestments, dim light, and dream music.[10] It is clear that these men believe this is the direction in which the priestly ministry must move; that the power of the priest will lie more and more in his sharing this capacity with areas of so-called secular competence.

I must testify that this has been true for me as well. For over five of the ten years I was a university chaplain I was also a lecturer in Greek (classical as well as New Testament). Upon reflection I would say that the effectiveness of my priestly ministry was in proportion far greater among those whom I also knew as "instructor" than among those who knew me only as "chaplain." I believe that this has something to do with the liminal quality of someone who is neither "here nor there," but always "in between." There is a possibility of engaging such a person and sharing with him a life in a way that does not require a prior acceptance of specific conditions for a relationship.

So I am suggesting that in the future we need to embrace a concept of relatively nonstipendiary, frequently indigenous priestly ministry not as a "stop-gap measure" of an economically floundering Church, but as a tested method of effective service. It should be made clear once again that the priesthood or presbyterate is defined here, somewhat in accord with Vatican II, as essentially that office of sacramental person, possessing the responsibility to preach the Word and minister the Sacraments (in particular, the Eucharist). I do not see it as *necessarily* related to administration, teaching, evangelism, prophecy, or care. In the realm of preaching, it is probably advisable to distinguish between the more or less informal communication of "What Jesus Christ has meant to me," and a formal, authoritative sermon. The function of the priest relates more immediately to the former than to the latter, and what we need is more of personal witness and less of attempts at authority. Discipline, inasmuch as it partakes of the relationship of persons to the sacramental person, inevitably falls within the priest's natural concern.

If, then, only three of the eight ministerial functions are essential to the priest, what of the other five? It would appear that they were lay functions; but I am not prepared to concede this too easily. It is possible to divide these five into professional and nonprofessional ministerial functions. I would want prophecy and evangelism to be understood as the responsible nonprofessional function of all Christians; but among the former I would include administration, teaching, caring (including counseling and community organization). I have already suggested that as functions specifically related to the Church they acquire a particular strength, and it is important that we define them as such. This could be done effectively by restoring the diaconate to *the order of those with professional tasks* such as administration, pastoral counseling, social action, education, and music. It would both define their vital place within the ministry of the Church and yet spare us this confusion of vocation to a charismatic ministry as opposed to a professional ministry.

For it has been my experience that among the many motivations for men coming to seminary, there are two almost entirely different sets of expectations between those who are seeking to exercise a charismatic ministry and those who desire professional training. Among the former may be found particularly older men who have sensed a real conversion to Christ in their adult lives, and want in fact to share with others what this knowledge is doing for them. The latter group, although I suspect it is initially much smaller, consists usually of younger men who have always been attracted to the Church and who are really in seminary to find a way of serving it. These include men who in fact are not especially excited about leading the worship of the congregation, but do indeed want to identify their vocation with the Church's witness. This would mean that those entering the professional ministry would have the option of ordination to the priesthood or diaconate.

If we then clearly defined the priesthood as the order of those who wish to assume the role of the sacramental person, and remain responsible for the cultic life of the community (including preaching) and then defined the diaconate as the order of those possessing a professional competence, it would be clear that we would do best to undo the fourth century and abolish the hierarchial ordering of deacon, priest, and bishop. There is no demanding theological reason for requiring a man seeking the priesthood to be first made a deacon, and the diaconate will never be understood as a significant order until it ceases to be a stepping-stone to "higher things." Despite the Book of Common Prayer, it is only a late medieval notion at best that the diaconate is an inferior office. It is encouraging to note that in its proposed revisions of the Ordinal of the Book of Common Prayer, the Standing Liturgical Commission of the Episcopal Church has made a step in the right direction by making the three orders of deacon, priest, and bishop distinctive in their own right.

I am not saying that one cannot occupy a professional role in ministry and be a priest. That view is precluded in my discussion of the hyphenated priest, and is obviously not the case in certain areas of competence that require in addition a priestly ministry. It is to say that one does not *require* the other, and it is behind my suggestion now that we need to introduce more universally the concept of "faculties" (the authority or licensing to exercise certain ministries requiring a level of competence not presumed in ordination). Roman Catholic canon law, as we have already mentioned, requires faculties in performing marriages, preaching, and hearing confessions. I would want to continue these (with the possible exception of performing marriages), and add areas such as counseling (broken down into various types), teaching, administration, and even social action (which requires as much skill as any of the others).

A good example of how faculties might work can be found in the role of the stipendiary parish priest, a man in charge of a church (as described in the previous chapter). His is a charismatic ministry, but it also requires professional competence specifically in the area of family, marital, and grief counseling. It might also demand an administrative ability that cannot be assumed in the average ordained person, and he would have to hear confessions. All of these require competent professional training, which exceeds what is generally found in the average three-year seminary curriculum and in the person of the parish priest exercising these functions today.

John Glasse, in his book *Profession: Minister*, presents a thesis from which I radically depart in various ways. It is really a tract providing a rationale for an accrediting organization called the American Academy of Parish Clergy. As we have seen, Murray and Westhaus, in their review of this book, give a devastating analysis of the plea for a sociological model of the professional role of the clergyman, and affirm the essentially charismatic character of the Christian ministry.[11] My feeling, however, is that in offering a proper corrective to what Glasse writes, they miss the need of the Church to take greater responsibility for those dimensions of ministry that require professional competence. Since I agree with John C. Harris that we must get over the notion that the parish priest is a "generalist," and recognize that his ministry requires certain special skills,[12] it appears to me that such an institution as the American Academy of Parish Clergy could serve a much greater value than giving, as Murray and Westhaus predict it will, mediocre clergymen a dubious status. It could be the source of "faculties" required of a man before assuming leadership of what I have described as the "church."

Other specialties are also developing their professional standards and accrediting organizations. The American Association of Pastoral Counselors, once they clarify the precise nature of pastoral counseling, needs to receive wider recognition in the Church as a whole; so does the Association for Clinical Pastoral Education as the accrediting organization for chaplains of hospitals, correctional institutions, and other allied facilities. The Church has been very slow to recognize, first of all, the great amount of counseling done by clergy; and, second, to acknowledge that, although much good has been done by this ministry, much harm has also been accomplished by ill-equipped though well-meaning pastors. Other counseling professions are not going to take us seriously until our standards are equivalent to theirs.

When the Church's ministry to higher education began, largely in the thirties, it was considered a good place for an attractive but still immature young man to work until he was ready for the "active ministry." As the campus ministry reached adolescence, it became the place for the rebel, the malcontent, the restless cleric. There is still an element of that, but one hopes organizations of chaplains such as the Episcopal Society for Ministry in Higher Education can address themselves not only to issues for which they wish to lobby, but also to the question of standards for college and university chaplains. I am personally convinced that they should include the credentials to teach on the college level, and am unimpressed by the arguments I hear that this identifies a person too closely with the faculty.

No accrediting organization has yet come out of the action training centers, such as the Urban Training Center in Chicago. If Crowell is right, however, and "engaging in social action, and especially initiating social action, demands as much talent, skill, and drive as the sort of work that is done in professional and managerial positions in our society," [13] then such must follow.

One very interesting development lately has been that of clerical "unions," like the National Association of Episcopal Clergy. This organization is interested in standards, although being an all-inclusive body it is questionable how specific these can be. Obviously the immediate value of such an association is in the protection of the clergyman from exploitation, and the possible demand for more adequate means of placement and remuneration. Those who believe such protection unnecessary are simply naïve. Any move, in my mind, to recognize the professional, stipendiary dimensions of ministry will require the kind of pressure a labor union can provide.

There is absolutely no doubt to me that where a man is paid a stipend for ministry, it must be commensurate with salaries in other professions and it must be out of the control of the local congregation. This is a contention also made by John Harris.[14] We will not get quality ministry until this happens. Local remuneration as well as the haphazard method of selecting local clerical leadership encourages the worst kind of congregationalism and defeats the best qualities of the clergy. Yet the pastor who expects an adequate salary, paid from a supracongregational agency, must also be willing to be evaluated and to surrender some freedom in his choice of particular positions. It is interesting that there is a great fear among some clergy of a deployment agency within the Church, largely because they do not trust the hierarchy. My suspicion is that with years of debit financing and of tenure at the whim of our congregations, many clergymen have developed a paranoia about their work that is truly frightening. We must move to overcome this, even if the first action is painful.

Another very happy sign for the men committed to a professional ministry is the development of church-related career counseling centers, such as the Northeast Career Center in Princeton, New Jersey. These offer an opportunity for a man to evaluate himself and his work in mid-career and to make an informed choice of different forms of ministry or even to leave the stipendiary ministry itself. The point being that it takes the concept of "profession" completely seriously, and therefore allows for evaluation, leaving untouched the whole question of charismatic ministry, which is not open to such appraisal.

Perhaps the strongest argument in John Harris' article, to which I have referred several times previously, is his review of the need for clerical evaluation. He illustrates beyond any doubt the fact that we need (1) an understanding of the qualifications desired in a given position before we fill it; (2) an appropriate brokerage for clergy seeking a change; and (3) a national information center for responsible administrators such as bishops. He believes these would go a long way toward improving the morale of the average pastor today, since much of his problem involves the feeling of being trapped in situations that in effect destroy his integrity as a person.[15]

Clearly the polity from which I write involves a threefold ministry of bishops, priests, and deacons, and from this position I have already spoken to the function of priests and deacons. If now I speak of bishops, the non-Episcopal reader will have to make his own translation.

It seems to me that the function of the bishop is to represent the universal Church, and to cut through the strong tendency in all Christian communities to congregationalism. Whether or not a given bishop is elected from the charismatic ministry (I think we must include the possibility of a layman elected directly to the episcopate) or, as is more likely, he is drawn from the professional, stipendiary ranks, I should think his task would be that of authoritative teacher and preacher. This would require considerable imaginative powers and theological acumen, more than administrative skill (which can be performed by a deacon). It would call for the selection of a man who commands wide respect, whether he was considered "safe" or not. It would mean that there would need to be more bishops and smaller dioceses, so that there could be close enough contact between the teacher and his people for solid learning to take place. His cathedral would be a familiar place for all sects and churches within his jurisdiction. He would have ample time, once divested of impossible confirmation schedules, countless and often superfluous board meetings, and astronomical distances to travel, to read and to write. This I hope would give a note of priority to reflection within the life of the Church, placing at its head those who possess the temperament to live as thoughtful charismatics and not as politicians or financiers.

Of course, reform of the membership of the episcopate is difficult to obtain, because the ecclesiastical power structure tends to be self-perpetuating. The traditional anti-intellectual bias of the American political system extends to the Church, and there is a grave suspicion of people who appear a little esoteric. It is very difficult for theologians or saints to achieve high office, when the matter is subject to popular vote. I am loath to suggest that the Church may have to sink into even lower repute than today for a "revolution" of this kind to succeed, but it is hard to imagine how anything else will break through the safe, dull, unimaginative character of so much of our leadership.

I hope that some distinct impression of the future shape of ministry as I would have it has now emerged. There are several reflections upon this image that need to be made, some of them the results of "trial balloons" raised in the process of testing my theories with various audiences.

First of all, there is the question of the ability of many congregations to respond to the liminal model of ministry and the notion of communitas as the norm of the Christian community. A young graduate of Nashotah House dropped in to see me one day. It took a good hard look and an educated guess to recognize who was behind the shoulder-length hair, full flowing beard (long hair and beard are highly liminal!), and metal-rimmed, octagonal glasses. We talked about what ministry was today, and the liminal role of the priest. He told me of a wedding at which he had officiated down on someone's farm, where for vestments he wore an Arabian burnoose and beads. It impressed him that the bride and groom remarked with enthusiasm on how he "looked like a priest ought to look —weird." But he added that in contrast the last thing the people in the suburbs, who pay the church's bills, want is for their pastor to appear "weird." Others have said the same thing to me. The new middle class, the people between thirty-five and fifty-five, do not want their imaginations stirred by off-beat clergy.

My response is to quote a hard saying, with which I think the Church in the latter part of the twentieth century must reckon. " 'He has blinded their eyes and dulled their minds, lest they should see with their eyes, and perceive with their minds, and turn to me to heal them' " (John 12:40). The perversity that refuses to open the imagination to new possibilities has effectively shut itself to God's revelation. It is difficult to see how we can help such people be open to God's Word and if we cannot by God's help awaken them, and they insist on living with a closed mind, I know no way that we can force them to hear. We simply have to acknowledge that we are not omnipotent, which is hard at times for clergy to accept.

Second, it may have been noted that I have spoken of ministry in the masculine gender throughout. This is not to imply that women do not exercise ministerial function. They always have. The question today is whether *all* ministerial functions, including ritualizing and preaching, are open to them. More and more denominations are accepting this position or speaking in favor of it, and even some Roman Catholic theologians have entertained the notion.[16] Will the ministry of the future disregard gender?

I myself do not subscribe to the Idealism of the Women's Liberation Movement. We are our bodies, and men and women have different bodies. This necessarily means that men and women are different (though not that one is "superior" to the other). Difference is no more slavery than our need for sleep, food, shelter. The question is whether the still nearly universal practice of the Church to deny the priesthood and the episcopate to women is simply an expression of a historical cultural phenomenon, or whether something in our sexual differentiation inhibits a woman from fulfilling a priestly ministry. Could the creative role of human sexuality be thwarted by women assuming a ritual function? In Christianity does the role of sacramental person demand similarity of sex between the *person* of Christ and the *person* of the priest? Emotionally the idea of women as priests is repulsive to many of us ("Mother cannot say Mass this week, she's about to have a baby."), but intellectually it is very difficult to defend the relationship between sexual differentiation and prohibition to the priesthood. I suspect, with Hans Küng, that the prohibition is a cultural phenomenon, and if the present changes to our culture continue, we may expect women to fulfill all ministerial functions.[17]

Third, there is a tendency to equate the concept of liminality, of creative weirdness, with the desire of some clergy to identify with the customs, thought patterns, and appearance of past centuries. I know priests who profess a belief in the "divine right of kings," who would wear a cassock and a curé's hat on the streets, or who attempt a strictly scholastic worldview, and defend all this in the name of liminality. There is no necessary equation, however, between the known behavior of a bygone age and living in the interstices of our present social structures. A museum is not a communitas, and there is nothing liminal about an anachronism. We cannot withdraw into the past in order to open ourselves for the future. This is not to turn our backs on the past, nor even to suggest that necessarily traditional symbols do not have liminal value. They may well.

For example, one possible liminal symbol would be the ancient custom of *voluntary* celibacy. Obligatory celibacy loses its mystery, but the man who chooses of his own will to live apart from a wife very definitely lives outside the social structure of the family. There has always been power in such a choice, and it is only to be regretted that the Roman Catholic Church, by institutionalizing it, weakened its effect appreciably. Even Hollywood, with Bing Crosby in "Going My Way," perceived the certain charisma in the virile man who renounces coital behavior.

On the other hand, in an affluent society, where easy credit and the wide distribution of wealth has made the possession of money meaningless, I doubt that poverty has the same liminal power it once had. It is more likely to be interpreted as bad luck, a lack of industry, a sign of oppression, or any combination of the three.

The possibility has occurred to me that a source for both the understanding and shaping of liminality would lie in Jung's analytical psychology and the study of archetypes. Certainly Jung did much research on the meaning of symbols and of the collective unconscious that in some sense embodies the common human communitas. One of the things that bothers people about Jung is his ambiguity and murky conceptualization. In our view of the meaning of symbol and the roots of its power, this could be his greatest strength. We need further work by theologians, particularly those with a pastoral concern, in this area.

Fourth, it is important that we divorce artistic sense and aesthetic perception from notions of homosexuality in order to free the conditioned male to express the artistic creativity that so many possess and an almost equal number are afraid to cultivate. (This is not the place to explore the role of the homosexual in ministry. I am not so sure but that a revised expectation of the clerical role might inhibit their creative functioning as much as present concepts do.) But certainly the liminal and charismatic quality of the model I am suggesting in this study must rely heavily upon the arts to awaken the imagination. Music, poetry, painting, sculpture, architecture are not luxuries for the indolent wealthy, but disciplines employing the equivocal symbols that live in the "cracks" of our social structures and create images of the future for us. Life without the arts is doomed to the hell of the positivist, untouched by the possibility of a new order. We in the Church are salesmen for a new order.

Finally, clericalism dies with this form of ministry. There is no equation between active, paid, and ordained, any more than there is between passive, voluntary, and lay. Ordination is the bestowal of the authority to exercise ministerial functions that, for the reason of good order, is reserved to certain persons. Stipends are paid for those ministerial functions that require a full-time activity. There is a focusing of the community's life upon the sacramental person, but there is no necessary difference between that person's charisma and the holiness of the whole membership. The double standard ought to vanish.

In chapter 8 I spoke of the crisis of the contemporary clergyman as centered in problems of (1) identity, (2) theological education, (3) support system, and (4) theological ambiguity. It might be well now to review my attempt to respond to these.

In the first place, I think the liminal identity of ministry is both a viable model for our time, as witness the quest of the counter culture, and theologically more appropriate than any other. We can take the professional model seriously, while recognizing its need to be related to the charismatic. None of this is easy to adopt, but with persistence it promises to provide an identity with which I think we can live better.

The second item, training, I shall discuss in the next chapter, but the third concern, the support system, I want either to remove from the local situation (as in the case of stipend), or to develop by shared leadership, or to reconcile to a degree by matching the sacramental person to the community. I would hope the resulting reduction of tension would not remove all conflict, for tension has its very creative side. The aim is simply to reduce it below the level of paralysis.

I have also sought at least to offer an alternative to the leadership vacuum. It is here I feel the greatest frustration, for if what I write is a serious proposal, at least for our conversations, it poses an immediate challenge to many vested interests. Once we acquire power, we do not anticipate with ease the alteration of the system that bestowed the power.

Fourth, these last few chapters are an effort at a clearer theological expression of the meaning of ministry. I believe very much in the possibility that the central fact of ministry is its instrumentality in God's communication (i.e. revelation) of himself to man. This is what the whole emphasis upon imagination and liminality attempts to conceptualize.

At a conference where I was presenting much of this material someone asked me what I thought was its possibility of acceptance. My answer was that it depended on whether the proposals coincided with whatever creative change could be found in our society. If this change is represented by the counter culture, and I think it may well be, then a clarification of ministerial function, in which the transcendent God can take on a comprehensible incarnate form, something like that which I suggest here, is a possibility. But the problem lies with vision, the willingness to take a risk, and therefore, finally, with leadership. My experience is that many of us in positions of responsibility tend to misjudge the feelings and pressures of the subjects of our policy decisions; and this can be fatal. Ours is the time for reflective change, and it is in that spirit that I offer this model.

## *chapter 14*

# *FORMATION*
# *OR EDUCATION*
# *OR TRAINING*

It has been said that the first task of a seminary is to disabuse its entering students of their reasons for being there. There is a certain truth to this; for a degree of romanticism prevails among many who apply to a theological school. The idealism of the young, the unqualified enthusiasm of the convert, and the eager anticipation of the older man changing vocations in mid-life all challenge a faculty too much aware of the frustrations of the calling and the limited possibilities of three short years in seminary. Yet we cannot despise the somewhat unrealistic motivations of many candidates for the ministry. If they were as cynical as many of us become, would they ever apply in the first place? Furthermore, we must be patient. We did not reach our own degree of "sophistication" overnight, and maybe if we do a better job they will not lose the flush of enthusiasm as readily as many of us did.

But there is also a certain irony about such a statement. It assumes that the Church and its seminaries know what a theological school should be doing. As I engage in the continuing debate within the Church over the education of its clergy, I find that we do not know, and that some very distinct disagreements exist. Roughly, opinion falls into three categories. Historically speaking, the prevailing purpose of a seminary since its recent evolution as a post-B.A. curriculum in theology (in the broad sense of the word) is *graduate education*. Since most theology faculties are trained in research, they tend to-

ward this point of view. However, with the rise of professionalism among clergymen, under the leadership of those committed to pastoral care and clinical exerience, there has
emerged most recently the theory that a seminary is a place
for *professional training*. Largely I think this is the feeling of
the faculty in the practical areas and the majority of the clergy
in the field. But in its original Tridentine and Reformation development, a seminary was conceived primarily as a place for
the *formation of priestly character* through discipline, prayer,
and indoctrination. I suspect—and there is no way of verifying
this feeling—that this is how most of the laity, as well as a substantial minority of the clergy, view theological education.

Obviously, if we committed ourselves as a Church to any
one of these three general purposes, there would still be some
overlapping. No seminary is without an element of all three,
and the general practice in recent years has been at least to
acknowledge each as important. But if we attempt to give every
one equal place, the troika involves us in an impossible situation. For each demands a different methodology, ecology, and
personality of leadership; and consequently, if we are to avoid
a debilitating schizoid climate of education, one must prevail
in any given institution.

It seems clear to me that the current dominating spirit
among theological educators, as represented in the American
Association of Theological Schools (AATS), the national accrediting organization, is professional education. This is represented very clearly in Charles Feilding's "Education for Ministry," an issue of *Theological Education* published by the
AATS. There Feilding chooses professional training over graduate education, though at the same time recognizing formation as a part of such training.[1] Certainly the emphasis placed
on field education, learning by reflecting upon actual pastoral
experiences, is an expression of the current demand that every
student pastor develop the skills that are at the heart of his
profession. There remains the problem, however, of distin-
guishing those skills which, although different from the act of

simply relating to another as an open human being, are still distinct from other professions.

It is largely in the spirit of developing better professional education, with a desire for a more deeply learned clergy only a secondary consideration,[2] that the AATS and groups such as the Board for Theological Education in the Episcopal Church have pushed for urban, ecumenical, and university related seminaries.[3] It is felt that much of the problem in theological education stems from seminaries that are too small, socially isolated, and short on resources. It is also with the intent of encouraging professional recognition of the pastor that a switch from the degree of Bachelor of Divinity to Master of Divinity or Doctor of Ministry is being urged, much as the law schools have recently moved from a Bachelor of Law to a Doctor of Jurisprudence in accordance with the medical model of the degree of Doctor of Medicine.

In response to these charges, I think if we take the professional model seriously, it is going to require more than just moving seminaries into ecumenical clusters in big cities, near large universities. My own feeling about the urban question is that it demands, like any community, an indigenous ministry. Sending the son of a suburban banker to seminary for three years in the slums will not make an inner-city pastor out of any but the barest fraction of such people. Furthermore, it ignores the critical problems of the suburbs, where Episcopalians at least have a much greater chance of operating as sacramental persons. The "urban mystique" needs a more radical relating to the nature of Christian ministry before we start investing in depressed property. There is no doubt that professional training must be related to universities. The only problem is that it is very difficult to do. There is some justifiable suspicion on the part of secular faculties and administrations of downgrading their standards if they cooperate with theological schools, as well as a great deal of ignorance of one another on both sides. These drawbacks can be overcome, but it will take an almost heroic willingness to cope with academic red tape and the university establishment. The call for ecumenical involvement has probably met the happiest response, and we may rejoice that in almost every institution the denominational barriers are falling. As for the change in degree nomenclature, it is part of the academic game, and when you "get on to the playing field, you have got to play by the same rules if you hope to win."

But when we have said all this, it is still evident that we have not dealt radically enough with the theological institution itself. Obviously, if we divide ministry into two kinds, charismatic and professional, it might well follow that they require two different kinds of preparation. Furthermore, there is an interest in theology that is not ministry, but pure research (like the difference between the physician practicing internal medicine and the biochemist). This requires even a third form of preparation, which concerns us only as it becomes confused (as it frequently has) with the development of the first two. Charismatic or liminal figures cannot be created by any school, although their gifts can be sharpened and made more available. Professionals are in fact created by their training, but it is by the acquisition of certain skills and not a concern for theory as found in graduate education that creates them.

Focusing once more on the professional himself, it is my conviction, as repeatedly expressed in this study, that there is not one profession *of* ministry but a number of professions *within* ministry. To think you can train a pastor counselor, a social actionist, a catechist or educator, a parish pastor, and a church administrator in the same three-year curriculum makes no more sense than it does to think you can train a clinical psychologist, a case worker, a high-school principal, a marriage counselor, and a personnel manager in the same school of a university. Yet we attempt it every day. It is no wonder that the secular professions question the credentials of their clerical counterparts.

My plea is then, *first of all*, that we recognize that many seeking to fulfill a ministry in the Church are in fact persons with a charismatic gift, capable of functioning creatively as liminal figures, and that we design for them an education that particularly meets their needs and makes no pretense at being professional training. These people will fulfill a nonstipendiary ministry, and in this regard are of two kinds: those already possessing a means of earning a living and those who also need to acquire a proficiency in a secular field.

What would be the purpose of seminary for them? Formation seems to be the obvious answer. A B.A. degree would only be required of those who upon entrance wanted to combine Christian formation with training in some profession such as social work, library science, graduate study in education, etc. The seminary curriculum would be designed to last only nine to eighteen months, and it would consist largely of courses intended to give understanding of the commitment the candidates already felt. Training in spirituality (the prayer life, patterns of Christian discipline, the writings of the mystics, etc.) would necessarily lie at the heart of what I am suggesting here. For if the role of the sacramental person and the concept of liminality is to have any reality, it depends upon the development and practice of a truly contemporary spirituality.

With the stress upon professional training, urban and university involvement, and increased size, the contemporary seminary has allowed its chapel life and training in spirituality to slip further and further out to the periphery. The Pusey Committee had some very incisive things to say about this.[4] Walter Wagoner as well needs to be taken seriously when he writes, "But the time has now come to recognize as sub-Christian any theological position which (in the name of demythologization, or existentialism, or linguistic analysis) effectively undercuts the personal obedience to God and consequent response to Him of person-in-community." [5] I can sympathize, if not agree, with a faculty that wishes to make chapel attendance optional, and provides a "cafeteria of services." Their motives are of the highest. I think it is absolutely necessary that experimentation in liturgy and prayer be encouraged and practiced. Would that all seminary chapels, built in previous generations in the romantic hope of creating a thirteenth-century monastic community, would crumble to dust tomorrow! But we must learn the lesson psychology did a generation before us. Man needs a disciplined community for creative living. We are free in Christ, but not all of us know the difference between that and irresponsibility or just "muddling through." You do not teach someone to drive by having him start out alone on the Los Angeles freeways. We need to show by example and expectancy of our students the nature of Christian spirituality and restore it to the central place in the life of our seminaries. Whereas we are all members of many communities or subsystems (family, social circle, outside parish, educational institutions, as well as Church), we accomplish nothing if we do not encourage the gathering of the seminary community in the worship of our Lord. It is inconceivable to me how, if our purpose is the spiritual formation of the student, we can create so many distractions from this end.

Of course the question persists as to what the nature of the spirituality that is developed in our clergy must be. There has been a tendency for leaders in theological education to leave this decision to the very few scholars who maintain an interest often identified with the antiquarian. Therefore the impression is gained that Christian spirituality requires living in the fourteenth or fifteenth centuries. This is most regrettable. I personally have been very much helped in this area by the writings, of John Coburn, and by my conversations with a close friend, Robert Cooper, both of whom are convinced and have led me to see that there can be a contemporary spirituality. Coburn for one, in writing of contemporary man's incredible struggle to conceptualize God (as described here in chapter 11) and the need to develop an individual as opposed to a regimented life of prayer, says, "To say Yes to Someone—or Something; to be certain that existence is meaningful; to know that the goal of life is in self-surrender. That is the new spirituality, as new as Dag Hammarskjöld—and as old as Abraham." [6] I am also impressed by the plea of John Townroe that

we recognize that in the entire history of Christian spirituality
the main thing is to be open to the work of God in even the
most desperate situation, and to let the form of our spirituality
follow from this. For our contemporary times he believes the
best form, as I do, is the life of prayer within the small group.[7]

To return to the nonprofessional, nonstipendiary candidate: aside from a regular pattern of chapel attendance, instruction in prayer, and meditation, I would see much emphasis
upon ascetical theology as well as forms of encouragement in
artistic and imaginative expression. The last mentioned may
well surprise the reader, because the Church has never really
set out systematically to encourage artistic perceptions in its
clergy. We have been remiss. There would also be instruction
in practical liturgics and pastoral resoures. The latter would
seek to aid the priest in an informed referral of those in emotional and spiritual distress, not to equip them as a psycho-
therapist. The study of the Bible would be restricted to an
understanding of its contents, and theology would be of the
catechetical kind as found, say, in *The Dutch Catechism*.

I also think that there is a great necessity for training such
candidates in greater self-awareness. It is very easy to confuse
somebody who is creatively weird with someone who is de-
structively crazy. I shall say something more about that when
I speak of the seminary and the screening process. The charismatic person needs not only to be in touch with himself spiritually, but also emotionally, for his stock in trade will be his
ability to communicate to others his experience of the person
of Christ. By undergoing extensive and responsible group training, we can hope to develop such self-awareness without creating a half-baked therapist, and we will also have an opportunity to catch up with those who, undetected by the screening
process, are in fact more mentally ill than liminal.

Obviously what I have pictured here is approximately half-
way between what the canons foresee for a licensed lay reader
and what we presently do in some of our diocesan evening and
weekend training schools. My opinion is that the concept of lay

readers, as foreseen in Title III, Canon 25 of the Episcopal Church, is a mistake. They encourage the absurdity of the daily monastic offices (i.e., Morning and Evening Prayer) as the principal service on Sunday—one of the more indefensible positions the Anglican Communion has slipped into—because men with a pastoral charge are not equipped with the very thing they need: the authority to preside at the Eucharist. The requirements of Title III, Canon 25 regarding the instruction of lay readers assigned pastoral or administrative charges suffers from the common ambiguity of not asking ourselves, What is this man to do? If it is a little bit of everything, as the prescriptions seem to imply, then once more we are in the same old trap. There is a certain reasonableness to such bodies as the Methodist Church that authorize people they call "lay preachers" to preside at the Eucharist where there is no "minister." My only caveat is to ask why not go ahead and ordain them and stop calling them "lay preachers." Is it not the same modern problem of equating education and ordination?

As for the diocesan schools, I think they are probably a very good thing, only they tend to borrow from the professional and graduate models. My hope would be that they become more specifically institutions for the formation of non-professional, nonstipendiary, charismatic priests. If they did so, they would have to find some way of developing a keener sense of community than is possible in the "commuter college."

If a man came to an institution of formation with the intention of learning a secular occupation as well, it would be necessary for that school to have a relationship with a nearby university. This would not be the same thing as the relationship required for training in professional ministry; it would simply be important for the purpose of convenience in travel and economy of time. His total time spent at the institution would be longer, of course, than nine to eighteen months.

A *second* form of seminary would be that which provided an introduction to professional, stipendiary ministry. It would then be related in turn to the various specialized professional schools, granting men the credentials for exercising various forms of ministry. A bachelor's degree would be required for admission, and a master's degree would be granted at the completion of the two-year introductory course. Further specialized training would earn a doctorate. A person could enter with the option of remaining a layman, or seeking ordination to the diaconate or the priesthood. Those who chose the latter would also undergo formation.

These first two years could also serve as a trial period, and anyone who decided not to pursue a professional career in ministry could stop at this point with some academic accomplishment to his credit. Also if one chose a career in academic theology, he would at the end of the two-year master's program move into a graduate (rather than professional) school and earn his Ph.D. Obviously my intention is to provide as great a flexibility and freedom of vocational decision as possible, since this accords with the need for various kinds of competence in ministry and the apparent desire of many students to make a trial of theological studies.

The two-year master's course would be a basic, largely academic curriculum (with possibly one summer of field experience). Philosophy, Systematic Theology, Apologetics, Biblical Exegesis, and Church History—the traditional subjects—would provide a basis for a further career decision, with perhaps some survey of the nature of the Church's mission and ministry added. There might well be training in Christian spirituality for all students, but not with the emphasis found in the formation of the charismatic ministry (with the exception of those who seek ordination to the priesthood).

It would be of little practical worth to attempt to project in detail the various possible specialized doctoral curricula beyond the master's program. What I foresee would be an additional one to three years of study in areas such as counseling and chaplaincy, ethics and social action, church administration, education, and the parish ministry. With the exception of the last named, I imagine that what was studied would conform in most ways to the standards of a similar secular pursuit, though perhaps with some special orientation (particularly in thesis research). It should therefore be related very closely to a secular university, and would be completely ecumenical.

Lest what I suggest here seem too utterly fantastic, I would call the reader's attention to Roman Catholic seminaries such as St. Francis' Seminary, Milwaukee, which has developed a two-track program. The student there decides whether he is interested in a psychological or a sociological orientation, and during his last years of study pursues one to the exclusion of the other. It seems to me an easy step to add an educational track, and then recognize the distinctive roles of the parish priest and the pastoral counselor. I think that church administration will be the last of those categories of ministry I have named to be granted a separate status. It is probably one that dioceses need to adopt most quickly.

Readers of the AATS publication *Theological Education* will recognize that this plan has close affinities to the proposal of the Resources Planning Commission in 1968. There three levels of theological education are outlined in detail. Level I is undergraduate college or university. Level II is a basic theological curriculum lasting approximately two years. Level IIIa is professional training, and Level IIIb is graduate education.[8] Aside from differences in detail, my radical departure from this plan results from its failure to see that, as important as professional ministry is, as vital as solid scholarship is, neither can replace the charismatic, liminal ministry of those who may have no desire or talent to be professionals or scholars. The Church must use them as well, for their ministry lies at the heart of the Christian experience.

One of the benefits that could very readily accrue from a diversified system of theological education such as this is the possibility of persons of widely varied talents and strengths finding their place in the Church's ministry. Since the modern period, as we have seen, the tendency has been for all ministry to focus on the priest or pastor, who is subjected to one system of education. Quite different from distinct major and minor orders of the late ancient and early medieval Church, it has increasingly stereotyped the character of Holy Orders. The Roman Catholic Church has escaped this limitation to a degree, with the widely differing spirits of its religious orders. But even then there has been a suspicion since Trent of anything other than a celibate, priestly ministry.

This leads to the question of screening candidates for the ministry, a matter being increasingly debated throughout the Church. Largely what we mean by "screening" is the discouragement of those seeking ordination who are judged to be so emotionally unstable as to run the risk of doing damage to themselves or the people to whom they might minister. In most cases those with insufficient academic qualifications never get into a screening process. Matters of deficient moral or spiritual character rarely are raised.

It can be fairly said that the main burden of screening falls upon the seminaries. This is apparently intentional in some denominations; in the Episcopal Church screening by the seminaries occurs more by default. The canonical provisions require an initial screening by the parish priest and the bishop of the applicant's diocese. The tendency of diocesan authorities is, with notable exceptions, to give the man a chance at least to try things out in seminary. Objectivity is very hard for the local pastor to obtain because he understandably looks on the prospect as a protégé, a "feather in his cap." The Canons call for a physical examination that includes the candidate's "mental and nervous condition." Daniel Stevick in an understatement describes this as a not very fortunate expression,[9] and its use is frequently even less happy. My experience as a parish priest, university chaplain, and now as a seminary professor is that not infrequently the psychiatric examination employed in fulfillment of the canon would be lucky if it detected active psychotic behavior.

The next screening process comes when a man applies

to seminary. Since many seminaries are actually competing for students and most are marginal financial operations, the procedure has from the start a very questionable motivation. It would be interesting to poll seminaries to discover how many applicants they turned down, compared to how many in all honesty they would *like* to have refused. But even then it is very hard to tell whom you are admitting. In the Episcopal Church the same psychiatric examination obtained by the bishop is used by the seminary, and it is frequently worthless. Recommendations of laymen and clergy often imply that the applicant has achieved sainthood, and leave the reader wondering why he was not assumed into heaven long before now. Bishops, I find, are generally very taciturn in such applications, which is certainly the better part of valor. The tendency is therefore for seminaries to admit men whom they suspect are poor risks, with the feeling that when they know them better they can make a decision.

The problem is that when you come to know someone better your feelings of affection for him as a person conflict with your judgment as to his potential capabilities in the ministry. The seminary faculty procrastinates until faced with the possibility of telling a man a month before his ordination, after years of study, that they just do not think they can recommend him. This is very hard to do.

This third screening process is probably the crucial one, partly because of the tendency for all of us to engage in a well-meaning "passing of the buck." Also because more and more, if the seminary does *not* recommend a man for ordination, his own diocese will not ordain him. There are two reasons for this. First, we do not have a great need for more clergymen. Second, often all of us are just waiting for someone to have the courage to say, "We cannot recommend this man," in order to make an explicit refusal. This is not his "court of last resort," but it is certainly a traumatic challenge to his sense of vocation.

Why do we not do a more efficient and fairer job of

screening? Several things make it very difficult. In the first place, there is no objective criterion for judging how a man will perform in the ministry. There are a great number of studies in this area, and all testify to the uncertainty of psychological testing and psychiatric evaluations.[10] Second, a priestly vocation is a very personal thing, and we are all aware of our own shortcomings; so we hesitate to stand in judgment of God's will for another human being. We are troubled by the responsibility the Church has laid upon us and know the great damage done by a well-meaning but inept or disturbed ministry. We hope, then, that maybe there is someone else better qualified to judge who may act in our stead. Third, there are enough loopholes in our system and enough bishops who either desperately need men or who let sentiment get ahead of realism, so that if someone really wants to be ordained and has tried hard enough he can be. Before long the men we have discouraged return from these remote spots as full-fledged priests, and all the anguish is for naught. One is inclined to ask, "What's the use?"

Once again my conviction is that much of this problem could be solved if we did not ordain men *to do everything*. There are some fine people I could see as very effective ritualizers, although they cannot preach, or those whose understanding of theology is next to nothing, or those who should never counsel. Then there are the revolutionaries, those who have a real mission for social change but who would destroy a parish overnight. If we had some control over what a person did once he was out as a deacon, priest, or layman, then the screening process would be far fairer, we could sleep at night, and a place in ministry could be found for men longing to serve their Lord and yet constitutionally incapable of doing some of the things that we fear might be required of them under the present system. This is one reason why I have pleaded so strongly for the employment of faculties. It at least acknowledges what St. Paul knew long before, that there are a variety of gifts.

It also speaks to the question of "national exams," which is being debated presently by the Episcopal Church. Up to the present the custom has been for every diocese to examine its men on their knowledge and skill before ordaining them deacon or priest. The feeling is that this is too haphazard a system, which ultimately is unfair to the Church because of the widely different standards that have developed. My argument would be not against national exams, but against one set of exams for everyone. It would simply promote the horror of the monochrome professionalism we have now. There needs to be provision for special exams for particular callings within ministry.

Once a man is out of seminary and ordained at least a deacon, he becomes quickly aware under the present system that he probably emphasized the wrong things in seminary, and he starts looking for help. This is the "feedback" one gets as a seminary professor, and it is certainly the testimony of all the surveys of clergymen and the impression one gathers from the flood of men seeking additional specialized education. It is the reason why continuing education has become so important in the Church today.

In the survey of Episcopal clergy of the upper Midwest it was found that all but 8 percent of those questioned and answering had had "growth-producing experiences" over the past few years.[11] This indicates an unquestioned interest in continued development. Thirty-eight percent reported sensitivity training, 31 percent psychotherapy, 30 percent spoke of seminars sponsored by universities, mental health centers, and community agencies, and 35 percent expressed gratitude for vacations. Study leaves, church-sponsored seminars, and professional conventions ranked far below other items. *"Dismay was expressed that the church itself had not generated sophisticated seminars in order to support continuing education."* [12]

In this survey it is clear that the personal growth of the priest (and, very important, that of his wife and their marriage) is more or less combined with the narrower understanding of continuing education as professional development. I perceive a rationale behind this in that both relate to a more effective ministry. The first pertains, however, to the charismatic, liminal dimension of ministry, and the latter to the professional. Since I separate these two, I want to say a word about both.

The Midwest survey emphasizes the great stress that the Episcopal priest, in response to the questions asked, placed upon his marital and personal health "and its relation to his effectiveness in the interpersonal aspects of professional work." [13] It also notes that clergy do not feel comfortable availing themselves of public mental health resources, which are relatively inexpensive but lack a sense of confidentiality and personal concern. They prefer to consult private psychiatrists and psychologists, who are more expensive but more conducive of trust. Almost half are willing, however, to seek the services of fellow clergy and pastoral counselors as well.[14] Of the clergy responding, 85 percent had sought some kind of help in time of need.[15] My point is very simple. An interpersonal ministry creates stress and demands sensitivity and strength in family and personal life that are extraordinary. The clergyman and his wife often, therefore, require help in maintaining these qualities.

The problem is financial and to some extent one of image. Some diocesan hospitalization plans pay a large portion of the cost of psychotherapy. I am personally familiar with situations where diocesan funds have provided a portion of the expense utterly impossible for the priest to manage. What we need, however, is a universal policy, with competent, sympathetic psychiatric and psychological help made readily available, and financial assistance openly offered. This would include the services of pastoral counselors, since in fact they are practicing the same profession as other psychotherapists. It would also involve the open acknowledgment that the use of such professionals by clergymen is a normal and natural part of their equipping themselves to serve their people more effectively. Statistically it is clear that clergy are now using psychotherapy as a means of personal growth, and in the future it should be explicitly stated that it is available and recommended.

Of course, we are dealing with a society in which education in mental health still lags far behind other areas of knowledge. My feeling is that church authorities are largely very sympathetic to the values of psychotherapy for clergy, be it therapeutic or training. Few hold this against a man, at least consciously. The average churchman is probably not as well informed, and something must be done to assist the image of the priest who is known by his people to have sought emotional aid. They must be led to see that in all probability psychotherapy will make him a more effective sacramental person, instead of being an indication of his impending collapse.

The charismatic ministry today requires some kind of directed introspection into the emotional life of the priest, an understanding that needs to be repeated from time to time. Current psychotherapeutic theory would encourage the involvement of a man's family as well. If what we need is competence not only in professional, but all ministry, then the Church will have to see that the means are provided.

Turning to continuing education as professional development, we must admit that most of what we are doing is "mickey mouse," despite a few great exceptions. Seminary summer graduate schools, such as those at Sewanee and Nashotah in the Episcopal Church, are solid programs, but they offer graduate education, not professional training. The same can be said for some of the very worthwhile fellowships such as at the College of Preachers in the Washington Cathedral and at some seminaries. Virginia Theological Seminary at Alexandria is attempting, however, to break out of the traditional academic mold in its program. The involvement of ordained men and professional women in clinical pastoral education and the various action training centers provide a substantial professional training that should not be overlooked.

But these programs and the others like them do not reach the great majority of stipendiary clergy, crying for a professional competence they are all too aware they lack. They want something more than two weeks here, a weekend there, and two hours a month at the local hospital.

My contention is that what they really need should be provided before they ever are made to minister on a full-time basis: thorough professional training, which requires not a "short course," but years. This calls for the selection of a speciality, but so does law, medicine, and engineering. Ministry is no more exempt from the knowledge explosion than is any other field. Continuing education cannot take the educated gentleman and turn him into a professional. It can only bring up to date the man already well grounded in his speciality. This is its task, and this we could do well.

In the meanwhile we "muddle through." We must certainly honor the sanctity of those who struggle on in their parish with the meager resources we provide them, and respect the men who are attempting, through continuing education, to make up for the lack that without doubt is felt almost to the man.

I have said nothing yet about the prevailing opinion among many theological educators that the future requires fewer and bigger institutions. The AATS has suggested that the minimal operational size of a school at Level II, which as I have noted corresponds roughly to the basic two years of professional or graduate instruction, is 29 faculty and 290 students. The "Modular Nucleus" is 53 faculty and 540 students.[16] Speaking for the Episcopalians, no seminary at the present time meets the minimal standard. The Board of Theological Education states that in 1969–70 the average enrollment in an Episcopal seminary, including those enrolled part time, was 97 (out of 7 seminaries). In the Lutheran Church of America it was 169 (out of 7 seminaries), and in the United Presbyterian Church it was 295 (out of 6 seminaries). As seminaries get smaller, the cost per student for equivalent quality education grows. So small seminaries are caught in the increasing cost factor and are faced with the demand to expand and deepen the quality of their instruction and learning opportunities.

It is this pursuit of greater competence at a reasonable cost that has motivated the move to merge seminaries within denominations. Usually this step has been conceived without any radical revision of the three-year seminary program, save for the addition of a fourth intern year between the second and third year in residence at the seminary. In the Episcopal Church, at least if we acted on Almus Thorp's report of the opinion of the Board of Theological Education as of January 1970 and considered "five centers for theological education in the continental United States is an ample number," [17] we would still not measure up on the average to the ideal minimum suggested by the Resources Planning Commission of the AATS in 1968. We had 1,066 students, full and part time, in 1969–70. It is doubtful that the Episcopal Church on its own could create the kind of ideal theological schools foreseen by the AATS. The United Presbyterian Church apparently can, and undoubtedly others like the United Methodist, the Southern Baptists, and obviously the Roman Catholics do.

For those who cannot make the ideal on their own, the answer of the AATS is the "cluster" concept, where a number of seminaries of different denominations gather in relation to a university and centers of clinical training to share faculties and library, as well as refectory, classrooms, and possibly a chapel.[18] This has been tried at such places as the Boston Theological Institute, Colgate-Rochester/Bexley Hall, and the Graduate Theological Union in Berkeley, California. Others are exploring the possibility. Although the final report is not in, if it ever will be, there is evidence that this is a good solution for at least some institutions.

However, the revision of theological education into Levels I, II, IIIa, and IIIb by the AATS differs from my own proposal in that apparently it foresees that it is preferable for Level II to be carried out in relation to the same institution as Levels IIIa or, at least, IIIb. That is, the basic two-year curriculum would be provided in association with professional training and graduate education. It appears to me that this is a possibility, but not a necessity, and that perhaps it is not even desirable. My experience is that for many students not oriented toward research, a solid basic curriculum for professional training can be provided in an institution with a relatively small faculty and library. Furthermore, if formation is desired—as it would be in my scheme for those also seeking the priesthood—it can better be undertaken in a setting where a community life and intimate relationship with individual faculty members have the opportunity to develop. Then again, education carried out in different settings can in fact be stronger than one received in one place. This would be particularly true if the Ecumenical Movement does not accomplish its goal completely in the next few decades and our desire continues for denominational grounding in the first two years and a completely ecumenical setting for professional or graduate education.

This is to say, then, that I am not at all sure the seminary that does not meet the minimal standards of the Resources Planning Commission of the AATS has no future, if it recognizes what it can and cannot do. Obviously, it can also offer the shorter curriculum aimed at developing the nonprofessional, nonstipendiary ministry, which I believe is so very important for the future of the Church.

My concern is, then, that before we act on a plan for the revision of theological education, we explore the nature of ministry in a manner more radical than we have done to date. The reflections in this chapter are based upon a desire to undo the clericalism of the post-Reformation, to avoid the crass professionalism that clericalism tends to attract, while capturing the strength of both a charismatic and a professional ministry. I have deep respect for the apparent differences of temperament and goal in those seeking to serve in the ministry, and believe that we make a mistake in setting our hopes on too narrow a model. At the same time, we must recognize that the present state of theological education cannot provide the competence and quality we must have. What is suggested here is one attempt at dialogue from one who does not necessarily accept completely the current evolution of ministry.

## chapter 15

# AN EXERCISE
# IN IMAGINATION

It is my intention that the reader understand chapters 12 through 14 to be an exercise in imagination, but not in fantasy. The definition of imagination as creative speculation rooted in reality should be recalled, as opposed to fantasy, which has no such roots. In concluding this study, it is important that I support this contention.

Generally speaking, ministry in the history of the Church has moved from function to ontology. This is to say that whereas we begin by seeking to create structures to meet needs, we have continually hypostatized these structures so that they endure as some sort of expressions of the will of God, or at least the *sine qua non* of the Church, long after the needs have changed. The ever-evolving nature of reality means that inevitably the manner in which the transcendence of God will be incarnated in the sociocultural system must change to perform the essential mission of the Church as *Ursakrament*. But we have resisted this, particularly in our time, or have so muddled our theology that we forget the transcendent prerequisite of ministry.

The effect, first of all, has been the distortion of the role of ministry. We have moved from a personal and charismatic basis, with a subsequent loss of the numinous, to a strong emphasis upon education and professional skill. We have not been very clear about the eight discrete kinds of ministerial function. This has made ministry the function of one type of minister (the priest/presbyter/parson/pastor), and has created multiple problems. My response has been to reinstate the personal and charismatic character of the priest (we do not lack for candidates) and free him to operate within structures that encourage a contemporary sense of dependence upon the mysterious. We must free man to live in liminality. In our professional roles, let us recognize the diversified nature of professional ministries, and develop them accordingly. We must also take seriously the lay participation in functions of ministry.

A second effect has been the blind acceptance of the inevitable development of the self-supporting (but barely so) parish, headed by a pastor who has received a gentleman's education and little more. If the residential notion is largely theoretical in fact, it still persists enough to bind the Church from opening up in an aggressive manner numerous possible principles of organization (while still retaining the residential as one option). I have suggested that we quit falling between two stools, and develop the sect and the church; that is, the small group and the complex, large structure. Furthermore. that we educate our clergy with this in mind.

Then I would call attention to a third effect, namely, the constant confusion between commitment to Christ and his Church and what we think is loyalty to tradition, but is in fact a loss of theological nerve. A great deal of unnecessary impedimenta is associated with ministry today, both in Catholic and Protestant circles, which only someone who thinks theologically can have the courage and the insight to clear out without wrecking the Church. Therefore, I am urging that we move back into the discipline of pastoral *theology* in a serious way, while acknowledging the concern for pastoral care (the applied end of the discipline). Those heading up our training of professionals need no less psychology, sociology, and anthropology, but a good bit more theology. They need to have a much stronger influence upon Church leaders, who find the "safe" route the best because in many ways they lack the information to feel secure in seeking alternatives.

If we were to recover the theological fundament of ministry, I think we would be free to read our times more clearly and find the courage to move to meet them unencumbered by various shibboleths such as congregationalism, professionalism, liturgical, ecclesiastical, or biblical fundamentalism, historicism, and social and behavioral scientism. When St. Augustine suggested that if we loved God we could do as we please, the loving of which he spoke was not merely some kindly feeling, a warm glow in the area of heart. It meant living in the context of a thinking, theologizing community of faith; it meant beginning with a living spirituality that let Christ reign in our lives. Yet once that was a reality, and *only* when it was, we could move in an instinctively appropriate manner to manifest his presence in the world in which we lived. We could be liminal and yet not absurd; men of our times, but not secular.

My hope here has been that by taking a first step in this kind of imaginative process, I could initiate some kind of dialogue where all the hallowed, traditional structures are left "up for grabs" and yet the absolute necessity of the community and its life of reason and spirituality is recognized. Such a conversation would be on a much deeper basis than I think has gone on before where the broad view or long perspective has been lacking. It would begin with as few essentials as possible and build in rapport with our times.

It should then be clear that I have sought to secure the exercise of the Christian imagination in a functional understanding of ministry, as opposed to some developed ontological notion. But unlike many other functionalists, I would protect our reflections from an aimless and sentimental liberalism by insisting that we take seriously a theological understanding of the Church and ministry as the servant of its purpose as *Ursakrament*. I would insist that an incarnational or sacramental view of the nature of our life with God is essential to the development of a function of ministry that is consistent with the New Testament and the continued revelation of God's will for humankind. This needs to be developed in a pattern outlined by the eight ministerial functions that prevail in all eras of Church history.

Obviously, this is not something that one person, even with the help of his associates, can accomplish. What is desired then from the reader of this study is not simple agreement or disagreement, but a response in the spirit of the same concern and hope that I have sought to express. The imagination of every person is built with the symbols shared with others. This is the meaning of liturgy, and it is the desire of any creative community. But its effect for the good of the Church depends on our explicit recognition that this is what we should be doing: reaching into the future through a corporate imagination open to God's will. If we begin with the premise that anything for the sake of Christ is possible, we may then proceed to test the symbols of our faith against one another and the reality that is ours today.

# NOTES

## Chapter 1

1. The terms for the clergyman heading a local congregation are a source of confusion. Most people probably speak of their "minister," which refers to one who ministers and consequently is a very broad and meaningless term. In the Episcopal Church others refer to their "rector" (meaning originally "ruler") or "vicar," both of which are administrative titles. Still a few use the term "parson," which has its own peculiar history that we shall discuss. "Pastor" is a common Lutheran expression, and is also widely employed in other denominations, including the Roman Catholic. "Preacher" is heard in rural America, and has a certain dignity and status to it. Many people dislike the term "priest"—it smacks of medieval priestcraft to them—and still others use it as a battlecry. A point that we shall make is that "priest," or *sacerdos*, is really a descriptive term in itself. The title in longest historical use is "presbyter," and it has the broadest application. It therefore will be employed widely in this study.

2. Vatican II, *Dogmatic Constitution on the Church*, Chapter III.

3. J. Robert Nelson, "Styles of Service in the New Testament and Now," *Theology Today*, XXII (1965), 90–94.

4. Owen Barfield, *Saving the Appearances* (New York: Harcourt, Brace and World, n.d.), pp. 28ff. Barfield's unqualified acceptance of Lévy-Bruhl's theory of the prelogical nature of primitive man is unfortunate, but it does not affect the basic thesis concerning man's "collective representations," a term he gets from Emile Durkheim.

5. Peter L. Berger and Thomas Luckmann, *The Social Construction of Reality* (Garden City, N.Y., Doubleday Anchor, 1967).

## Chapter 2

1. Gregory Dix, "The Ministry in the Early Church," *The Apostolic Ministry*, ed. K. E. Kirk (London: Houghton & Stoughton, 1946), p. 228.

2. Kilian McDonnell, "Ways of Validating Ministry," *Journal of Ecumenical Studies*, VII (1970), 221.

3. Walter Schmithals, *The Office of the Apostle in the Early Church*, trans. John E. Stelly (Nashville: Abingdon Press, 1969), pp. 72–73.

4. *Ibid.*, pp. 249–50.

5. Dix, "Ministry in the Early Church," p. 228.

6. Schmithals, *Office of the Apostle*, pp. 114–92.

7. William Telfer, *The Office of Bishop* (London: Darton, Longmans and Todd, 1962), p. 20.

8. Rudolf Bultmann, *The History of the Synoptic Tradition*, trans. John Marsh (rev. ed. New York: Harper & Row, 1968), p. 141.

9. This is a pivotal concept in the theological school of Wolfhart Pannenberg.

10. Günther Bornkamm, *Jesus of Nazareth*, trans. Irene and Fraser McLuskey with James M. Robinson (New York: Harper & Brothers, 1960), p. 160.

11. Massey Shepherd, "Ministry, Christian," *Interpreter's Dictionary of the Bible* (Nashville: Abingdon Press, 1962), III, 387.

12. H. Richard Niebuhr and David D. Williams, *The Ministry in Historical Perspective* (New York: Harper & Brothers, 1956), p. 10.

13. Kenneth M. Carey, ed., *The Historic Episcopate* (Westminster: Dacre Press, 1954), pp. 24–25.

14. Eusebius, *Ecclesiastical History*, III, 11.

15. Telfer, *The Office of Bishop*, pp. 1–23.

16. Edward Hardy, "Deacons in History and Practice," *The Diaconate Now*, ed. Richard Nolan (Washington, D.C.,: Corpus Press, 1968), p. 12.

17. Dix, "Ministry in the Early Church," p. 244.

18. *Ibid.*

19. McDonnell, "Validating Ministry," p. 219.

20. Ernst Käsemann, *New Testament Questions Today*, trans. W. J. Montague (2nd ed. London: SCM, 1967), pp. 236–51.

21. Anyone wishing to enter the insoluble debate concerning the meaning of *I Clement* 44:1–2 should begin by referring to Kirk, *Apostolic Ministry*, pp. 253–66, and Carey, *Historic Episcopate*, pp. 41–47.

22. Dix, "Ministry in the Early Church," p. 246.

23. Gerhard Friederich, "Prophet, *etc.*," *Theological Dictionary of the New Testament*, trans. and ed. Geoffrey W. Bromiley (Grand Rapids: Wm. B. Eerdmans, 1968), VI, 859.

24. Massey Shepherd, "Smyrna in the Ignatian Letters: A Study in Church Order," *Journal of Religion*, XX (1940), 152–53.

25. *Ibid.*, p. 143.

26. Dix, "Ministry in the Early Church," p. 226.

27. Hardy, "Deacons," p. 15.

28. Willi Marxen, *Der "Frühkatholizismus" in Neuen Testament* (Frankfurt, 1958), pp. 8–10.

29. Telfer, *The Office of Bishop*, pp. 43–63.

30. Dix, "Ministry in the Early Church," p. 218.

31. Johannes Quasten, *Patrology* (Westminster, Md.: Newman Press, 1953), II, 341.

32. Bernard Dupuy, "Is There a Dogmatic Distinction between the Function of Priests and the Function of Bishops?" *Apostolic Succession: Rethinking a Barrier to Unity*, ed. Hans Küng (New York: Paulist Press, 1968), p. 83.

33. J. Tixeront, *L'Ordre et Les Ordinations* (Paris: Librairie Victor Lecoffre, 1925), p. 92.

## Chapter 3

1. It has been popularly thought that the term "pagan" is derived from the Latin *paganus*, meaning "rustic," since it has been generally believed that in the ancient Church Christianity was an urban religion and the

heathen were concentrated in the rural areas. However, Henry Cadwick, *The Early Church* (Baltimore: Penguin Books, 1967), p. 152, n. 1, argues convincingly that the term "pagan" is first used in the West in the fourth century, and by 300 there were as many Christians proportionally in the rural as urban areas. The word *paganus* also means "civilian," and he believes that it was coined to describe those who had not become "soldiers of Christ."

2. Clemence Dupont, "Les Privileges des Clercs Sous Constantin," *Revue D'histoire Ecclesiastique*, LXII (1967), 729–52, discusses the rise of clerical privilege at length.

3. Jean Décarreaux, *Monks and Civilization*, trans. Charlotte Haldane (London: George Allen & Unwin Ltd., 1964), p. 100.

4. Eusebius, *Ecclesiastical History*, V, 24, 4; V, 18, 8.

5. In Greek *dioikesis* meant "management," and the first-century pagan philosopher, Epictetus, used it to mean "God's rule." In Latin *dioecesu* appears in the first century before Christ in the works of Cicero, but its common use is found in the late Empire.

6. A "glossary" is a book containing interpretations of the law. In the Medieval Renaissance (i.e. twelfth century) it was important to clarify the inherited code, such as that of Justinian, and this was done by the glossators, beginning in Tuscany.

7. Colin Williams, *Where in the World?* (New York: National Council of the Churches of Christ, 1963), pp. 6–8.

8. William A. Clebsch and Charles R. Jaekle, *Pastoral Care in Historical Perspective* (New York: Harper Torchbooks, 1967), pp. 21–22.

9. J. B. Russell, *A History of Medieval Christianity: Prophecy and Order* (New York: Crowell, 1968), p. 89.

10. A "canon regular" was a priest who lived in the cathedral community under a rule, but was not a member of a religious order.

11. Alcuin's palace school made a premature attempt to revive the classical learning, which had to wait until the eleventh and twelfth centuries and the Medieval Renaissance to regain importance.

12. Tixeront, *L'Ordre et Les Ordinations*, p. 100, points out that the tonsure made a man a clerk, a member of the clerical order, but was not the rite of any specific order. It is interesting to speculate on the possibility that it was in fact a surrogate castration. Cf. Edmund R. Leach, "Magical Hair," *The Journal of the Royal Anthropological Institute*, LXXXVIII (1958), 147–64.

13. J. R. H. Moorman, *Church Life in England in the 13th Century* (Cambridge: University Press, 1945), pp. 24–27, describes in detail how the office of rector in the thirteenth century was still filled by two kinds of men: (1) devout priests in residence, and (2) avaricious individuals, often not ordained, and never in residence.

14. Margaret Deansely, *Sidelights on the Anglo-Saxon Church* (London: A. & C. Black, 1962), p. 154.

15. This seems as good a place as any to offer some guidance on the matter of clerical attire through the centuries. As early as Charlemagne clergy are admonished to dress in somber colors, expressive of their renunciation of the world. This, together with the *corona* of the tonsure, marked their place in Holy Orders. Apparently the *style* of dress was originally no different from the layman's. Monastic habits, for example, which look strange to us today, are in fact the simple attire of the medieval peasant at the time the order was founded. The Fourth Lateran Council (1215) ruled against clergy

wearing red or green stockings, and we get this kind of legislation in later synods; so there is continuing evidence that men in orders were expected to dress in dark colors and that there was some resistance to this. There is some indication that clergy also wore their clothing long, as with other "serious people" of the day. This is not always true, as the clergy in the funeral procession of Edward the Confessor on the Bayeux Tapestry are wearing short garments. But in the twelfth-century picture of the first autopsy, the doctors are in long garments. When in 1300 the overgarment began to be generally worn short by the important people, the long style was retained by the men of the universities, which would include the educated clergy. It seems that clerical styles then *become* different because clergy resist adopting the latest fashion.

During the Reformation Protestant clergy rejected the customary dress of the secular priest—an embroidered garment with fairly tight sleeves, reaching to the feet—for the academic gown, which was dark, loose, and open in the front. We are all familiar with pictures of Martin Luther so attired. The cassock, correctly associated with clergy attire (at least in choir, if not as street dress), was originally a male or female overcoat, worn in the sixteenth century for horse riding. It was also the uniform of cavalrymen. In the seventeenth century it was adopted by the Church. Samuel Pepys mentions acquiring a cassock for a clerical friend. However, many clerics simply employed the gentleman's dress of the day, and in the eighteenth century, except in Roman Catholic countries where the cassock or soutane was customary, it was normal to see the parson or preacher in black knee britches (of which the gaiters of contemporary English bishops are reminiscent, though they were originally part of a nineteenth-century gentleman's dress for riding or walking in the country) and coat, with white bands attached at the collar. A tight-fitting collar, called a stock, was used from 1700 from which to attach a piece of black silk, worn over the chest. It is the ancestor of the clerical linen—now plastic—collar, which came to be accepted in the nineteenth century and worn with the customary gentleman's dress of somber color. Hence we see something of the evolution of contemporary "clericals," actually more properly called "canonicals." It might also be said that there is tendency throughout Christian history for clerical street dress to become church vestments (e.g. the chasuble, the cassock, and even the formal suit).

16. Moorman, *Church Life*, p. 185–94.

17. Russell, *Medieval Christianity*, p. 104.

18. I have made an arbitrary choice of dates the first of which marks the accession of Leo IX, the first of the great reforming popes, and the second the death of Boniface VIII, the last great upholder of the absolute sovereignty of the papacy.

19. Russell, *Medieval Christianity*, p. 123; R. W. Southern, *The Making of the Middle Ages* (New Haven: Yale University Press, 1953), p. 141.

20. Theoretically a man was ordained priest only when he had a title, as is implied in Canon 35 of the Episcopal Church today. But this was no more strictly followed then than it is now.

21. Clebsch and Jaekle, *Historical Perspective*, pp. 23–26. The Seven Sacraments are not formally defined until the Council of Florence (1439).

22. Every priest had a page or clerk to look after his needs.

23. This is illustrated by a comparison of Anselm's (1033–1109) governmental theory of the Atonement with Irenaeus's (c. 130–200) theory of recapitulation. They illustrate the fundamental difference in the thinking of the two cultures.

24. McDonnell, "Validating Ministry," p. 235.
25. Hardy, "Deacons," p. 25; cf. Trent, 23rd Session, chapter II.
26. Dix, "Ministry in the Early Church," p. 286.
27. *S.T.*, III, lxiii.
28. Trent, 23rd Session, chapter IV (1563).
29. E. Schillebeeckx, "The Catholic Understanding of Office in the Church," *Theological Studies*, XXX (1969), 567–87, does the best possible job of defending the continued use of this term. Although it strikes me that the word "character" really does not convey the meaning Schillebeeckx claims for it: the setting apart of the pastor to function under apostolic authority.

## Chapter 4

1. Marshall McLuhan, *The Gutenberg Galaxy: The Making of Typographic Man* (Toronto: University of Toronto Press, 1965), pp. 162, 164, 181. Indicative of the new spirit in the sixteenth century is the publication, in Dutch alone, of two hundred works in that period on bookkeeping. The new demand for precision in commercial enterprise required that for the first time we add and subtract from right to left, rather than from left to right.
2. *Ibid.*, p. 170.
3. I am indebted to my colleague, James Patrick, for this observation.
4. Quirinus Breen, *Christianity and Humanism* (Grand Rapids: Wm. B. Eerdmans, 1968), pp. 107–29.
5. McLuhan, *Gutenberg Galaxy*, p. 220.
6. Stephan C. Neill and H.-R. Weber, eds., *The Layman in Christian History* (Philadelphia: Westminster Press, 1963), p. 117.
7. Stanislau Woywod, *A Practical Commentary on Canon Law* (2nd ed. rev. New York: Joseph Wagner, 1926), I, 506.
8. Vatican II, "Decree on the Ministry and Life of Priests," chapter 2; cf. William H. Cleary, ed., *Hyphenated Priests: The Ministry of the Future* (Washington, D.C.: Corpus Books, 1969), pp. 15ff.
9. John T. McNeill, *The History and Character of Calvinism* (New York: Oxford, 1954), p. 161. For Calvin, unlike Luther, it is clear that the "ministry was a permanently ordained office." A man would present himself to the other pastors for election, if he believed himself called, and they would ordain him. The people, however, were given a veto. John R. Crawford, "Calvin and the Priesthood of All Believers," *Scottish Journal of Theology*, XXI (1968), 153. However, before the revocation of the Edict of Nantes (1685) the French Calvinists Claude and Juneu declared that the election of a pastor by the people constituted his authorization, and that ordination was "simply a ceremony of human institution." Eloi Leugrand, "Le Probleme de la Legitimité des Pasteurs," *Revue D'Histoire Ecclesiastique*, LXIV (1969), 401. This is indicative of the development of Calvinism (as opposed to Calvin himself) over those hundred years.
10. A. G. Dickens and Dorothy Carr, *The Reformation in England* (New York: St. Martin's Press, 1968), p. 163.
11. *Ibid.*, p. 145.
12. Richard Burn, *The Ecclesiastical Law* (9th ed. London: Sweet, Stevens & Norton, 1842), III, 442.
13. Roman canons 872, 1109, 1338.
14. Roland G. Usher, *The Reconstruction of the English Church* (New York: D. Appleton and Company, 1910), I, 207.
15. W. Roland Foster, "A Constant Platt Achieved: Provision for the

Ministry, 1600–38," *Reformation and Revolution*, ed. Duncan Shaw (Edinburgh: The Saint Andrew Press, 1967), p. 130; W. Roland Foster, "Ecclesiastical Administration in Scotland: 1600–1638 (unpublished Ph.D. thesis, the University of Edinburgh, 1963), pp. 265–66. "By 1600 most of the ministers of Scotland were men who had completed their degrees. . . . By 1638 ministers who had no degrees had virtually disappeared."

16. Pierre Janelle, *The Catholic Reformation* (Milwaukee: Bruce, 1963), pp. 115–20.

17. Henry Daniel-Rops, *The Church in the Seventeenth Century*, trans. J. J. Buckingham (New York: Dutton, 1963), p. 257.

18. *Ibid.*, p. 275.

19. The "House Prayer" at Nashotah House, an Episcopal seminary in Wisconsin traditionally maintaining Anglo-Catholic principles, illustrates this point as well as anything I know. "Give Thy grace and wisdom to all the *authorities*, that they may exercise *holy discipline*, and be themselves *patterns of holiness*, *simplicity*, and *self-denial*. Bless all who may be *trained* here; *take from them* all pride, vanity and self-conceit, and give them *true humility* and *self-abasement*. Enlighten their minds, *subdue their wills*, *purify their hearts*. . . ." The words I have emphasized are part of the classic vocabulary of seventeenth-century Roman Catholic clerical piety, picked up by nineteenth-century Anglo-Catholicism.

20. R. Frick, "Pfarrervorbildung und -weiterbildung," *Die Religion in Geschichte und Gegenwort*, V (1961), 297.

21. Thomas Wood, ed., *Five Pastorals* (London: SPCK, 1961), pp. 231–32; cf. pp. 115, 161. Richard Baxter's work was the classic Protestant text in pastoral care, even two hundred years after its initial publication.

22. *Ibid.*, pp. 113–14.

23. Raymond J. Cunningham, "From Preacher of the Word to Physician of the Soul: The Protestant Pastor in Nineteenth Century America," *Journal of Religious History*, III (1965), 327ff.

24. *Ibid.*, 327.

25. Wood, *Five Pastorals*, p. 127.

26. Jeremy Taylor, *Rule and Exercises of Holy Dying* (London: Bell and Daldy, 1857), p. vii.

27. J. A. H. Murray, ed., *A New English Dictionary on Historical Principles* (Oxford: Clarendon Press, 1905), VII, 496.

28. The concept of the "person" as "the actual unique reality of a spiritual being, an individual whole existing independently and not interchangeable with any other" is derived from Christian speculation concerning the Godhead, though rooted in a Jewish-Christian "metaphysics of the exodus." Max Muller and Alois Halder, "Person," *Sacramentum Mundi*, IV (1969), 404–05.

29. Murray, *New English Dictionary*, VII, 496.

30. Ronald Knox, *Enthusiasm* (Oxford: Clarendon Press, 1950), p. 398.

31. Yngve Brilioth, *The Anglican Revival* (London: Longmans, Green & Co., 1925), p. 257, speaks of "the trait of Puritanical severity which at times seems to form the fundamental tone of the Tractarian temper." This atavism persists. It is noteworthy that Reformed publishers in this country reprint the works of nineteenth-century Anglo-Catholic authors. There is often a common political, economic, and social philosophy in pockets both of the Reformed and Anglo-Catholic traditions, which seems to grow out of a common understanding of man akin to the Synod of Dort (1618–19). It is a subject worthy of a doctoral thesis.

32. Cit. Altman K. Swihart, *Luther and the Lutheran Church: 1483–1960* (New York: Philosophical Library, 1960), pp. 193–94.

33. Andrien Dansette, *Religious History of Modern France*, trans. John Dingle (New York: Herder and Herder, 1961), I, 13.

34. Norman Sykes, *Church and State in England in the XVIIIth Century* (Hamden, Conn.: Archon Books, 1962), p. 217.

35. *Ibid.*, p. 270.

36. *Ibid.*, p. 272.

37. Cit. Bernard A. Weisberger, *They Gathered at the River* (Boston: Little, Brown & Co., 1958), p. 8.

38. *Ibid.*, p. 5.

38-a. John X. Jobson, "The Tridentine Seminary Decree: Some Aspects of Its Formation." *Nashotah Review*, XI, 2 (March 1971), argues persuasively that the Tridentine seminary is a development out of the writings of the Protestant Johann Bullinger (1504–75) (as well as influenced by Ignatius Loyola), through Thomas Cranmer (1489–1556), Peter Martyr (1500–62), and Reginald Pole (1500–58). It is significant that Protestant and Anglican humanists, as well as the Roman Catholic Pole, contributed to this effort to create a more moral and better educated priesthood in the interests of more effective preaching and teaching. Once again Jobson has documented the common roots of both the Reformation and the Counter-Reformation in the new spirit of learning that pervaded the modern period.

39. H. Richard Niebuhr, Daniel Day Williams, James M. Gustafson, *The Advancement of Theological Education* (New York: Harper & Brothers, 1957), p. 7.

40. Stephan Neill, *A History of Christian Missions* (Baltimore: Pelican Books, 1964), p. 222.

41. *Ibid.*, p. 254.

42. Dansette, *Modern France*, I, 82.

43. Brilioth, *Anglican Revival*, pp. 94–95.

44. Owen Chadwick, *The Victorian Church* (New York: Oxford University Press, 1966), p. 127.

45. *Ibid.*, p. 518.

46. Dietrich Bonhoeffer, *Letters and Papers from Prison*, ed. Eberhard Bethge, trans. Reginald Fuller et al. (rev. ed.; New York: Macmillan Co., 1967), p. 196. What Bonhoeffer is saying here is very much connected to a basic theme of this study: culture constructs reality.

47. Martin E. Marty, *The Modern Schism: Three Steps to the Secular* (New York: Harper & Row, 1969).

48. Cunningham, p. 327.

## Chapter 5

1. "Valid ministry is attached to the meaning and nature of the church." McDonnell, "Validating Ministry," p. 258.

2. *Ibid.*, p. 212. "At least up until very recently Roman Catholics have not really had a doctrine of ministry. All we have had is a doctrine of priesthood, and ministry was tied in a rather restrictive way to the theology of priesthood."

3. *Ibid.*, pp. 239–44, brings the status of the debate right up to the present.

4. *Ibid.*, p. 260.

5. In Cleary, *Hyphenated Priests*, p. 17.
6. Cf. *ibid.*, pp. 23–32; McDonnell, "Validating Ministry," p. 260.
7. In Cleary, *Hyphenated Priests*, p. 23.

## Chapter 6

1. Ernst Bloch, *Man On His Own: Essays on the Philosophy of Religion*, trans. E. B. Ashton (New York: Herder and Herder, 1970), p. 216.
2. Langdon Gilkey, *Religion and the Scientific Future* (New York: Harper & Row, 1970), p. 19.
3. Iwao M. Moriyama, "Mortality," *International Encyclopedia for the Social Sciences*, X (1968), 501.
4. Paul R. Ehrlich, *The Population Bomb* (New York: Ballantine Books, 1968), p. 18.
5. Langdon Gilkey, *Naming the Whirlwind* (Indianapolis: Bobbs-Merrill, 1969), pp. 40–57.
6. Hans Urs von Balthasar, *The God Question and Modern Man*, trans. Hilda Graef (New York: Seabury Press, 1967), pp. 12–90.
7. Herbert Marcuse, *One-Dimensional Man* (Boston: Beacon Press, 1964), p. 57.
8. Philip Rieff, *The Triumph of the Therapeutic* (New York: Harper & Row, 1966), pp. 58, 59, 60, 61.
9. *Ibid.*, p. 251.
10. *Ibid.*, p. 252.
11. Jürgen Moltmann, *Religion, Revolution and the Future*, trans. M. Douglas Meeks (New York: Charles Scribner's Sons, 1969), pp. 55–56.
12. Peter Homans, *Theology after Freud* (Indianapolis: Bobbs-Merrill, 1970), pp. 152–53.
13. Marjorie Grene and Michael Polanyi, *Knowing and Being* (Chicago: University of Chicago Press, 1969), p. xi.
14. Thomas S. Kuhn, *The Structure of Scientific Revolutions* (2nd ed. Chicago: University of Chicago Press, 1970), p. 191; cf. Grene and Polanyi, *Knowing and Being*, pp. 183–207. Knowing, according to Polanyi, is a process involving two forms: *focal* (that toward which we direct ourselves) and *subsidiary* (subliminal and marginal). We know particulars in terms of wholes, after Gestalt psychology, even though they are not the object of our focal awareness. Knowledge is achieved, however, in terms of these particulars, which help form the whole. Hence tacit knowledge is "our subsidiary awareness of particulars in terms of a comprehensive entity" (p. 133). It is knowledge of that of which we cannot now tell.
15. Digital language is univocal, precise, logical; analogic language is equivocal, ambiguous, and descriptive of relationships.
16. Michael Novak, *A Theology for Radical Politics* (New York: Herder and Herder, 1969), pp. 92–121.
17. Gilkey, *Naming the Whirlwind*, p. 367, n. 2.
18. *Ibid.*, pp. 57–61.
19. Rieff, *Triumph of the Therapeutic*, p. 27.
20. Ernest Becher, *The Structure of Evil* (New York: George Braziller, 1968), p. 381.
21. Herman Kuhn and Anthony J. Wiener, *The Year 2000* (New York: Macmillan, 1967), p. xxv.
22. Ehrlich, *The Population Bomb*, p. 18.

23. Paul Elmen, *The Restoration of Meaning to Contemporary Life* (Garden City, N.Y.: Doubleday & Company, 1958), pp. 49–74.

24. Marshall McLuhan, *Understanding Media: The Extensions of Man* (New York: McGraw-Hill, 1965), pp. 62ff.

25. Abraham Maslow, *Toward a Psychology of Being* (2nd ed. Princeton: Van Nostrand, 1968), p. 143.

26. Rieff, *Triumph of the Therapeutic*, p. 258.

27. For theological commentary cf. Hugo Rahner, *Man at Play*, trans. Brian Battershaw and Edward Quinn (New York: Herder and Herder, 1967).

## Chapter 7

1. "Report on Congregations," *Top Priority Empirical Research Program on the Clergy*, a mimeographed publication of the Strategic Research Services Group of the Executive Council of the Episcopal Church, 1969–70 (hereafter referred to as TPERPC), p. 23. Of the men studied, 25% desired small parishes, 22% suburban, 20% big city, and 8% missions. In the Report of the Temporary Commission on Continuing Education of the United Presbyterian Church, entitled *Blue Book: Part III* (General Assembly of the United Presbyterian Church in the United States of America, 1969) (hereafter referred to as *Blue Book, Part III*), para. 70: 75% of the men surveyed stated that before seminary they sought a "pastoral ministry," and after seminary 85% so intended.

2. "Report on Congregations," TPERPC, p. 4.

3. "Distribution and Deployment of Clergy in the Episcopal Church, 1966–1968," a mimeographed report distributed by the Executive Council of the Episcopal Church, 1969 (hereafter referred to as DDCEC), pp. 6–7.

4. James L. Lowery, Jr., "Small Congregations and Their Clergy" (an unpublished paper), p. 13.

5. *Ibid.*, pp. 3–4. The average pledge per unit in the Episcopal Church in 1967 was $208.66. Loren Mead, "What Kind of Parish Really Makes It," *The Episcopalian*, CXXXV, 9 (September 1970), 8–9, argues against Lowery's definition of "viability." Mead's article is unclear as to the practical alternative to the present canonical parish structure, upon which Lowery builds his definition. If he intends to say that the costly items of clergy salary, house, travel, pension, etc., church buildings, and diocesan allotments are unnecessary to the existence of a thriving Christian community, I agree with him, as the reader will discover in chapter 12.

6. Lowery, "Small Congregations," p. 13.

7. All information concerning Mrs. Master's thesis, soon to be completed at Michigan State University, was obtained in a personal interview with the author in June 1970.

8. Neill, *Missions*, p. 322.

9. *National Catholic Reporter*, VI, 35 (June 5, 1970), 7.

10. J. R. Seeley, R. A. Sim, and E. W. Loosley, *Crestwood Heights* (New York: John Wiley & Sons, 1956), pp. 212–16.

11. Gibson Winter, *The Suburban Captivity of the Churches* (New York: Macmillan, 1962), p. 79.

12. *Ibid.*, p. 87. Charles Y. Glock, Benjamin B. Ringer, and Earl R. Babbie, *To Comfort and to Challenge* (Berkeley: University of California Press, 1967), p. 82. The authors challenge this *simple* identity of parishes and social class.

13. Winter, *Suburban Captivity*, p. 113.

14. *Ibid.*, p. 119.

15. *Ibid.*, p. 120. Another heated but less well documented discussion of this is to be found in Pierre Berton, *The Comfortable Pew* (Toronto: McClelland and Stewart, 1965).

16. Robert M. Bellah, "Civil Religion in America" *The Religious Situation: 1968*, ed. Donald R. Cutler (Boston: Beacon Press, 1968), pp. 346, 350–51.

17. Joshua 24:15: "Choose here and now whom you will worship: the gods whom your forefathers worshipped beside the Euphrates, or the gods of the Amorites in whose land you are living. But I [Joshua] and my family, we will worship the LORD."

18. Glock, *Comfort and Challenge*, pp. 99–109. This book is based on a nationwide survey of Episcopalians in 1952.

19. Earl D. Main, "Participation in Protestant Churches," *Review of Religious Research*, VIII (1967), 176–86. The article is based on a pan-Protestant survey in Illinois.

20. Jeffrey K. Hadden, *The Gathering Storm in the Churches* (Garden City, N.Y.: Doubleday & Co., 1969), pp. 3–33.

21. The percentage of baptized members attending church on an average Sunday in the Episcopal Church dropped from 48.6% in 1963 to 41.7% in 1968, according to figures released by the Strategic Research Services Group of the Executive Council of the Episcopal Church. Cf. Hadden, *Gathering Storm*, p. 22.

22. *Ibid.*, p. 25.

23. Total pledge payments in the Episcopal Church have grown unabated from 1963 to 1968, according to figures released by the Strategic Research Services Group of the Executive Council. But more and more is kept at home: 72% in 1920, 75% in 1952, and 83% in 1967. Also see Lowery, "Small Congregations," p. 14, n. 10.

24. This has been principally documented in Rodney Stark and Charles Y. Glock, *American Piety: The Nature of Religious Commitment* (Berkeley: University of California Press, 1968). In summary they state: "The religious beliefs which have been bedrocks of Christian faith for nearly two millennia are on their way out; this may well be the dawn of a post-Christian era," p. 205.

25. Hadden, *Gathering Storm*, pp. 68, 98–99. B. F. Lonergan, *Insight: A Study of Human Understanding* (3rd ed.; New York: Philosophical Library, 1970), argues that knowledge is the result of a process of experience, understanding, and reflection, and that the real is not therefore "out there," but within the cognitive process. Ethics (presumably including social ethics) is the result of the same process, and action *follows* reflection. What I mean here by "faith" is basically the intentionality of the conscious individual, which includes all that insight or understanding and reflection implies. Those who argue against this point of view seem to imply that knowing is looking and that reality is "out there," and this I think Lonergan and others successfully demolish. Marie August Neala, S.N.D., "The H. Paul Douglass Lectures for 1970: Part I. The Relation Between Religious Belief and Structural Change in Religious Orders: Developing an Effective Measuring Instrument," *Review of Religious Research*, XII, 1 (Fall 1970), 2–16, offers evidence that belief is determinative of social behavior, and that a common belief lies at the root of agreement as to what the Church should be doing.

26. Max Weber, *Sociology of Religion*, trans. Ephraim Tischoff (4th ed. Boston: Beacon Press, 1963), *passim*. Weber called this "ascetic Protestantism." *Public Opinion Quarterly*, XXVI (1962), 35–46, confirmed a causal relationship for Eugene, Oregon. Donald M. Anderson, "Ascetic Protestantism and Political Preference," *Review of Religious Research*, VII (1966), 167–71, denied any evidence of a *causal* relationship for his survey group in Illinois.

27. Talcott Parsons, "Religion in the Modern Pluralistic Society," *Review of Religious Research*, VII (1966), 125–46. Cf. Milton Rokeach, "The H. Paul Douglass Lectures for 1969: Part I. Value Systems in Religion" and "Part II. Religious Values and Social Compassion," *Review of Religious Research*, XI, 1 (Fall 1969), 3–39. Rokeach gives some grim evidence that there is a strong negative relationship between church attendance, priority to formal religion, and commitment to "salvation," "forgiveness," and social compassion. Rodney Stark, "Rokeach, Religion, and Reviewers: Keeping an Open Mind," *Review of Religious Research*, XI, 2 (Winter 1970), 151–54, states that his research, which is methodologically very different, uncovers the same results. The more "orthodox" you are in America the more likely you are to be insensitive to the plight of your fellow man.

28. Glock, *Comfort and Challenge*, p. 206.

29. *Ibid.*, pp. 205–06.

30. John Fish *et al.*, *The Edge of the Ghetto* (New York: Seabury Press, 1968), particularly pp. 109–27, 140–48. "The extent of the controversy indicates a clear lack of consensus among church members about the responsibility of their church as a corporate body in relation to the wider community," p. 157. Robert Lee and Russell Galloway, *The Schizophrenic Church* (Philadelphia: Westminster Press, 1969), particularly pp. 19–74, 114–92. "The obvious fact . . . is that worldly involvement has begun to push the church into the realm of scarce values. This has had the effect of precipitating the church into conflict situations for which it is unprepared," p. 71. "The events of that year [1966] revealed that the church has two separate and nearly unrelated personalities, and that the confrontation of the two can bring the activities of the entire group to a standstill," p. 163.

31. Hans J. Margull, "Evangelism in Ecumenical Perspectives," *The Ecumenical Review*, XVI (1964), 144.

32. Charles R. Stinnette, "The Parish, the World, and Pastoral Care," *The Lutheran Quarterly*, XIX (1967), 124.

33. *Ibid.*, p. 132.

34. Joseph M. Connolly, "The Parish—the Church's Incarnation," *Guide*, CLXXXVIII (1964), 5.

35. Gaylord B. Noyce, *The Church Is Not Expendable* (Philadelphia: Westminster Press. 1969), p. 24; C. H. Bayer, "The Rebirth of the Parish and the Minister as Politician," *Encounter*, XXX (1969), 367.

36. Hadden, *Gathering Storm*, p. 224.

37. Charles Davis in the preface to Odo Casel, *The Mystery of Christian Worship* (Westminster, Md.: Newman Press, 1962), p. xi.

38. Eric Berne, *Games People Play* (New York: Grove Press, 1964), pp. 12–15.

39. Leo Salzman, *The Obsessive Personality* (New York: Science House, 1968), pp. 55–56.

40. Bernard Cooke, "Eucharist: Source or Expression of Community?" *Worship*, XL (1966), 346; Godfrey Diekmann, "The Eucharist Makes the People of God," *Worship*, XXIX (1965), 458.

41. Richard Neuhaus, "Has the Liturgical Movement Failed?" *Una Sancta*, XXIV (1967), 54; *Worship*, XLII (1968), 54.

42. Virginia H. Hine, "Pentecostal Glossolalia: Toward a Functional Interpretation," *Journal for the Scientific Study of Religion* VIII (1969), 222–24; William Samarin, "Glossolalia as Learned Behavior," *Canadian Journal of Theology*, XV (1969), 64, says that glossolalia is not learned behavior, but a "charismatic *rite de passage*." For a sympathetic or committed treatment of the Neo-Pentecostal Movement cf. Antony A. Hoekema, *What About Tongue Speaking* (Grand Rapids: Wm. B. Eerdmans, 1966); John L. Sherrill, *They Speak in Tongues* (New York: Pyramid Books, 1964); Morton T. Kelsey, *Tongue Speaking* (New York: Doubleday & Co., 1964); and David Wilkerson, *The Cross and the Switchblade* (New York: Bernard Geis Associates, 1963) [now released as a movie]. "Scientific studies" include W. W. Wood, *Culture and Personality: Aspects of Pentecostal Holiness Religion* (New York: Humanities Press, 1963), and Frank Stagg, E. G. Huisin, and Wayne E. Oates, *Glossolalia* (Nashville: Abingdon Press, 1967).

43. Luther P. Gerlach and Virginia H. Hine, "Five Factors Crucial to the Growth and Spread of a Modern Religious Movement," *Journal for the Scientific Study of Religion*, VII (1968), 23.

44. Kilian McDonnell, "The Ideology of Pentecostal Conversion," *Journal of Ecumenical Studies*, V (1968), 105–26; Samarin, "Glossolalia," 60–64; E. Loma Kendall, "Speaking in Tongues," *Church Quarterly Review*, CLXVIII (1967), 11–19.

45. James N. Lapsley and John H. Simpson, "Speaking in Tongues: Infantile Babble or Song of Self?" *Pastoral Psychology*, XVI (1964), 16.

46. *Ibid.*, p. 17, who cite Wilkerson, *Cross and Switchblade*; Samarin, "Glossolalia," p. 62, n. 3.

47. For example, in a widely circulated tape of a talk by Kevin Ranagham, "The Charismatic Renewal in the Roman Catholic Church," the speaker holds up his previous intellectual reservations about Pietism and the Neo-Pentecostal Movement as humorous. The effect on someone who still has honest questions about these matters is to feel pressured or ridiculed, but not answered. There has also been a tendency to overrate Pauline testimony to glossolalia (as some of its opponents have perhaps been equally unfair on the other side). Little of the disciplined exegesis found, for example, in J. P. M. Sweet, "A Sign for Unbelievers: Paul's Attitude to Glossolalia," *New Testament Studies*, XIII (1967), 240–57, is evident. Cf. John L. Sherrill, *They Speak With Tongues*, pp. 73–76, particularly as relates to whether glossolalia is a sign for believers. Sweet, p. 244, says that it is not, and that prophecy is. We often get it turned around the other way.

48. McDonnell, "Ideology," p. 116.

49. *The Living Church*, XXXV (December 7, 1952), 14.

50. *Ibid.*, CLV (May 6, 1967), 16.

51. Marvin T. Judy, *The Cooperative Parish in Nonmetropolitan Areas* (Nashville: Abingdon Press, 1967), pp. 86–87.

52. William H. Whyte, Jr., *The Organization Man* (New York: Simon and Schuster, 1956), pp. 365–81.

53. Rudiger Reitz, *The Church in Experiment* (Nashville: Abingdon Press, 1969), p. 186.

54. *Ibid.*, p. 187.

55. Malcolm Boyd, ed., *The Underground Church* (New York: Sheed

and Ward, 1968), and Robert S. Lecky and H. Elliott Wright, *Can These Dry Bones Live?* (New York: Sheed and Ward, 1969).

56. Lecky and Wright, p. 184.

57. I am drawing this from the illuminating discussion of "revitalization movements" in Antony F. C. Wallace, *Religion: An Anthropological View* (New York: Random House, 1966), pp. 157–66.

## Chapter 8

1. "Revised Preliminary Report on a Study of the Salaries of Parochial Clergy," TPERPC, p. 19. *Blue Book: Part III*, para. 62, says 95% of the United Presbyterian clergy have B.D. degrees.

2. *Gallup Poll Study X: Special Report on Religion*, 1969, p. 57.

3. *National Catholic Reporter*, C, 37 (July 9, 1970), 3.

4. *Herder Correspondence*, VI, 3 (March 1969), 67.

5. *Christianity Today*, XIII, 34 (July 18, 1968), 34.

6. DDCEC, p. 8.

7. Jeffrey Hadden, "Role Conflict and the Crisis in the Churches," *Ministry Studies*, II, 2–3 (1968), 25–26, notes how secretive some churches are on this matter and how poor the reported figures can be.

8. Gerald J. Jud, Edgar W. Mills, Jr., Genevieve W. Burch, *Ex-Pastors* (Philadelphia: Pilgrim Press, 1970), p. 33.

9. *Christianity Today*, XIII, 34 (July 18, 1968), 35.

10. Cunningham, "Preacher of the Word to Physician of the Soul," p. 327.

11. H. Richard Niebuhr, *The Purpose of the Church and Its Ministry* (New York: Harper & Brothers, 1956), pp. 79–82.

12. *Ibid.*, pp. 87ff.

13. Edward H. Enberg, "A Study of Clergy Attitudes in Both Parochial and Need-Centered Ministries" (an unpublished paper, 1968), p. 16. It should be noted that this survey excluded curates, so it is probably skewed in a conservative direction.

14. "Vocational Background Training and Direction," TPERPC, p. 5.

15. *Ibid.*, p. 14.

16. Pastoral Development and Study Committee of the Fifth Province, "Questionnaire on Mental Health and Continuing Education Needs of Episcopal Priests" (a mimeographed report, 1970), p. 16 (hereafter referred to as MHCEN); "Vocational Background, Training and Direction," TPERPC, p. 16.

17. Samuel W. Blizzard, "The Minister's Dilemma," *The Christian Century*, LXXIII (1956), 508–09.

18. Enberg, "Clergy Attitudes," p. 14, shows preaching was rated third by parochial clergy and fourth by clergy in need-centered ministries. These were, of course, all Episcopalians.

19. "Role Conceptions and Relations," TPERPC, pp. 35, 38.

20. "Vocational Background, Training and Direction," TPERPC, p. 23.

21. Jud *et al.*, *Ex-Pastors*, pp. 50–51.

22. Clyde Reid, *The Empty Pulpit* (New York: Harper & Row, 1967), p. 102.

23. Hadden, "Role Conflict," pp. 22–23.

24. Enberg, "Clergy Attitudes," p. 15.

25. Mark H. Curtis, *Oxford and Cambridge in Transition* (Oxford: Clarendon Press, 1959), p. 165. Lectures in divinity were not required, however, of all degree candidates.

26. Thomas Wilson, *Parochialia or Instruction to the Clergy on the Discharge of Their Parochial Duty* (New York: T. & J. Swords, 1812).

27. Charles R. Feilding, "Education for Ministry," *Theological Education*, III (1966), 50.

28. *Blue Book: Part III*, para. 102.

29. Owen C. Thomas, "Some Issues in Theological Education," *Theological Education*, V (1968), 349.

30. James W. Bergland, "Field Education as Locus for 'Theological Reflection,'" *Theological Education*, V (1969), 343.

31. "Vocational Background, Training and Direction," TPERPC, p. 14. Areas in which the clergy said they got "just enough" included Liturgics (62%), Bible (75%), Theology (75%), Polity (72%), Canon Law (70%), and Church History (84%). Of languages, 30% said they "got too much" and 50% said "just enough." *Blue Book: Part III*, paras. 101, 103, gives a very similar picture for Presbyterian clergy. Jud *et al.*, *Ex-Pastors*, p. 66, less than a third of the UCC ex-pastors considered themselves well prepared in seminary, and almost a fourth complained that it was not practical enough.

32. E. Maynard Moore, "Theological Education for a Revolutionary Church," *Theological Education*, IV (1968), 603.

33. Feilding, "Education for Ministry," p. 136.

34. Jud *et al.*, *Ex-Pastors*, pp. 83–85.

35. "Role Conceptions and Relations," TPERPC, p. 19.

36. "Conflict and Crisis," TPERPC, p. 12.

37. "Role Conceptions and Relations," TPERPC, p. 33.

38. *Ibid.*, pp. 6, 14; 11% of the clergy complain of loneliness.

39. *Blue Book: Part III*, paras. 95–96.

40. "Salaries of the Parochial Clergy in the Episcopal Church: Phase I," TPERPC, pp. 1–2.

41. *Ibid.*, pp. 15, 17.

42. "Conflict and Crisis," TPERPC, p. 14.

43. "Report on Finances," TPERPC, p. 7. Although I shall not develop the subject to any great extent, the dependence of the priest upon the support of his wife is without question very important. This was one of the most significant points in the survey of Episcopal clergy in the upper Midwest; cf. MHCEN, p. 20.

44. Charles M. Smith, *How to Become a Bishop Without Being Religious* (New York: Doubleday & Co., 1965), p. 25.

45. "Conflict and Crisis," TPERPC, p. 14.

46. Martin Thornton, *The Rock and the River* (New York: Morehouse-Barlow, 1965), p. 145.

47. David C. Jacobson, *The Positive Use of the Minister's Role* (Philadelphia: Westminster Press, 1967).

48. Stark and Glock, *American Piety*, p. 209, make this a pivotal phrase for a conservative theology.

49. Hadden, *Gathering Storm*, pp. 40, 41, 47.

50. *Ibid.*, pp. 44–45.

51. *Ibid.*, p. 42; 88% said it is important.

52. Enberg, "Clergy Attitudes," p. 19.

53. Stark and Glock, *American Piety*, p. 63.
54. *Ibid.*, p. 210.
55. *Ibid.*, pp. 181–82.
56. *Ibid.*, pp. 223–24.
57. "Feedback," *Trans-action*, V, 9 (September 1968), 55. "Will Ethics Be the Death of Christianity" appeared in *Trans-action*, V, 7 (June 1968), 7–14.
58. Stark and Glock, *American Piety*, pp. 122, 123.
59. *Ibid.*, pp. 123, 86.
60. Thornton, *Rock and River*, p. 139.
61. Nathan M. Pusey and Charles L. Taylor, *Ministry for Tomorrow* (New York: Seabury Press, 1967), p. 51. Note that these figures do not agree with those in "Preliminary Report of the Salaries of Parochial Clergymen," TPERPC, p. 19, where it is stated that "more than 90% of the sample clergymen had at least a bachelor's degree."
62. "Vocational Background, Training and Direction," TPERPC, p. 12; cf. Pusey and Taylor, *Ministry for Tomorrow*, p. 51, for agreement.
63. *Ibid.*, pp. 71–72.
64. "Role Conceptions and Relations," TPERPC, pp. 2, 3, 6.
65. *Blue Book: Part III*, para. 64.
66. Cit. John J. Rooney, "Problem of Interpretation: a Commentary [upon Walter Kania's "Healthy Defensiveness in Theological Students"]", *Ministry Studies*, I, 4 (1967).
67. *Ibid.*, p. 23.
68. Robert J. Menges and James E. Dittes, *Psychological Studies of Clergymen: Abstracts of Research* (New York: Thomas Nelson, 1965); Robert J. Menges, "Studies of Clergymen, Abstracts of Research, Supplement I," *Ministry Studies*, I, 3 (1967).
69. Leo Waltermann, ed., *Klerus zwischen Wissenschaft und Seelsorge: zur Reform der Priesterausbildung* [Clergy between Scholarship and Pastoral Care: toward a Reform of Priestly Formation] (Essen: Verlag Herus Driewer, 1966), reports three major dangers in the German Roman Catholic seminary system: encouragement of infantile ideas that prevent maturity, failure to give tools of communication to the rest of the world, and production of guilt feelings. There is no doubt that these dangers are confined neither to Roman Catholic nor German theological schools. "The Priest's Uncertain Role," *Herder Correspondence*, VI, 3 (March 1969), 71.
70. Kenneth Keniston, *Young Radicals: Notes on Committed Youth* (New York: Harcourt, Brace and World, 1968), pp. 45–48.
71. *Blue Book: Part III*, para. 55.

## Chapter 9

1. *Blue Book: Part III*, para. 101, states that after classical languages, Presbyterian clergy consider the least valuable course they had in seminary was Christian Education (15%). Whereas the survey of Episcopal clergy did not reveal the same precise statistic, it is interesting that in stating areas of need for continuing education, only 9% indicated Christian Education. "Vocational Background, Training and Direction," TPERPC, p. 16.
2. James B. Ashbrook, "A Preface to Pastoral Research," *Ministry Studies*, III, 2 (August 1969), 5.

3. Seward Hiltner, *Preface to Pastoral Theology* (New York: Abingdon Press, 1958), pp. 15ff.

4. *Ibid.*, p. 18.

5. *Ibid.*, pp. 89, 118, 149.

6. Howard J. Clinebell, *Basic Types of Pastoral Counseling* (Nashville: Abingdon Press, 1966), p. 39.

7. Cit. Mary Bosanquet, *The Life and Death of Dietrich Bonhoeffer* (New York: Harper & Row, 1968), p. 83.

8. Edward Thornton, *Professional Education for Ministry: A History of Clinical Pastoral Education* (Nashville: Abingdon Press, 1969), gives a muddled and uncritical view of it all.

9. Thomas C. Oden, *Contemporary Theology and Psychotherapy* (Philadelphia: Westminster Press, 1967), pp. 81–91.

10. "Association for Clinical Pastoral Education: Standards" (a mimeographed paper, distributed November 1969), the page before p. 1.

11. Harrop A. Friedman, *Counseling in the United States* (Dobbs Ferry, N.Y.: Oceana Publications, 1967), p. 115.

12. Seward Hiltner, *Pastoral Counseling* (Nashville: Abingdon Press, 1949), p. 95.

13. Seward Hiltner and Lowell G. Colston, *The Context of Pastoral Counseling* (Nashville: Abingdon Press, 1961), p. 197.

13-a. Ray L. Hart, *Unfinished Man and the Imagination* (New York: Herder and Herder, 1968) pp. 89–90, makes the point that when we fail to account for a cognitive act, apprehending in the objects of consciousness the revelation of God, we tend to lapse into scepticism or fideism. This is to say that theology is built upon an epistemology in a dialectic relationship with an ontology, and an understanding of human knowledge that is far different than "just looking." My personal opinion is that within the pastoral psychology movement there is a great deal of scepticism and fideism, which I think can be attributed in part, at least, to its disregard for metaphysics and a faulty epistemology.

14. William B. Oglesby, ed., *The New Shape of Pastoral Theology* (Nashville: Abingdon Press, 1969), p. 213.

15. James Hillman, *Insearch* (New York: Charles Scribner's Sons, 1967), p. 46.

16. James B. Ashbrook, "Preface to Pastoral Research," pp. 3–5, makes a compelling plea for overcoming this problem in pastoral care. Somehow we seem to go astray, however, between the desire and the reality.

17. Thomas W. Klink, *Depth Perspectives in Pastoral Word* (Englewood Cliffs, N.J.: Prentice-Hall, 1965), pp. 33ff.

18. Thornton, *Professional Education*, pp. 234–36.

19. Theodore Wedel, "The Group Dynamics Movement and the Church," *Theology Today*, X (1954), 521–24.

20. Clyde Reid, *Groups Alive—Church Alive* (New York: Harper & Row, 1969); John L. Casteel, ed., *The Creative Role of Interpersonal Groups in the Church Today* (New York: Association Press, 1968). We need better books in this field very badly.

21. Norman Brown, *Love's Body* (New York: Random House, 1966); pp. 80ff provide some specific examples, but the whole is relevant to the point.

22. William C. Schutz, *Joy: Expanding Human Awareness* (New York: Grove Press, 1967).

23. Personal correspondence with Fr. Gooch.

24. Andrew Greeley, "Catholics and the Sensitivity Cult," *National Catholic Reporter*, VI, 26 (May 1, 1970), 10–12.

25. Richard L. Batchelder and James McHardy, *Using Sensitivity Training and the Laboratory Method* (New York: Association Press, 1968), pp. 90–91. The authors report that out of 1,200 participants, only four negative experiences have been fully identified; pp. 83–84.

26. *NTL Institute: News and Reports*, III, 4 (November 1969), 1.

27. Personal conversation with Alfred Rollins of the Executive Council of the Episcopal Church.

28. John Dittes, *The Church in the Way* (New York: Charles Scribner's Sons, 1967), pp. 136ff, 260ff.

29. Paul S. Higgins and John E. Dittes, "Change in Laymen's Expectations of the Minister's Roles," *Ministry Studies*, II, 1 (February 1968), 18–19.

30. Batchelder and Hardy, *Sensitivity Training*, p. 90; Max Birnbaum, *The Saturday Review*, Vol. LII, 46 (November 15, 1969), 82–83, 95–98.

31. Quentin T. Hand, "Personality Changes in Groups," Casteel, *Interpersonal Groups*, p. 91.

32. Edward E. Thornton, "The Lord's Supper: a New Form and Renewed Authenticity," *Pastoral Psychology*, XVIII, 173 (1967), 17.

33. Howard M. Mills, "The Urgent Need for a Truly Social Ethic," *Canadian Journal of Theology*, XV (1969), 47–49.

34. Richard Shaull, "Theology and the Transformation of Society," *Theology Today*, XXV (1968), 25.

35. *Ibid.*, p. 32.

36. Robert T. Rodes, "The Last Days of Erastianism—Focus in the American Church-State Nexus," *Harvard Theological Review*, LXII (1969), 342.

37. Howard M. Mills, "Social Ethic," 54–56.

38. Ivan Illich, "The Church, Change and Development," *Dialog*, IX (1970), 91, 92, 93.

39. There is another current model of ministry with which I have not dealt in any specific way in this book, largely because it relates more directly to specific questions of church administration and some limit must be made upon what is treated here. This model, which is based upon general systems theory, is a sophisticated effort to give meaning to the clergyman's role as "pastoral director." Systems theory is rooted in decision making theory, cybernetics, and typology. A good introduction can be found in Walter Buskley, *Sociology and Modern Systems Theory* (Englewood Cliffs, N.J.: Prentice-Hall, 1967). In this model the pastor is the "enabler" or "executive," who monitors the "input," the relationships within the system, and the maintenance of "goal." An excellent introduction to general systems theory and the ministry is to be found in Peter F. Rudge, *Ministry and Management* (New York: Barnes and Noble, 1968). Generally my criticism of the model is the same as the other three, it fails to give a clear understanding of transcendence. Despite Rudge's claims to the contrary, the causality in this model is efficient, not final, and so there is no real teleology. As far as it goes, it is an extremely helpful metaphor for parish administration and planning. See, for example, *Planning for Action: A Guide for Parish Planning Committees* (Minneapolis: [Episcopal] Diocese of Minnesota, n.d.) and a mimeographed flier from Project Test Pattern of Mount St. Alban's, Washington, D.C., "Elements and Processes of Social Systems."

## Chapter 10

1. James D. Glasse, *Profession: Minister* (Nashville: Abingdon Press, 1968), p. 38.
2. Joseph H. Fichter, *Religion as an Occupation* (Notre Dame, Ind.: University of Notre Dame Press, 1961).
3. Roderic L. Murray and Kenneth Westhues, review of *Profession: Minister*, by James D. Glasse, *Dialog*, VIII (1969), 222.
4. Hans Küng, *The Church*, trans. Ray and Rosaleen Ockenden (New York: Sheed and Ward, 1967), pp. 265–69.
5. Murray and Westhues, review of *Profession: Minister*, p. 223.
6. Edgar W. Mills, review of *Profession: Minister*, by James D. Glasse, *Journal for the Scientific Study of Religion*, VIII (1969), 180–83.
7. Fichter, *Religion as an Occupation*, p. 164.
8. Paul M. van Buren, *The Secular Meaning of the Gospel* (New York: Macmillan, 1963), pp. 123–34; Ernst Käsemann, *Jesus Means Freedom*, trans. Frank Clarke (London: SCM Press, 1969), p. 154.

## Chapter 11

1. Bonhoeffer, Dietrich, *Letters and Papers from Prison*, ed. Eberhard Bethge, trans. Reginald Fuller, Frank Clarke, et. al. (rev. ed. New York: Macmillan, 1967), p. 201.
2. The point is so obvious that it really does not need documentation. But for the sake of the sceptical, I suggest as a start Thomas Luckmann, *The Invisible Religion* (New York: Macmillan, 1967), p. 47, where he states that the evolution of society and self is essentially religious; and Myron Bloy, "Alienated Youth, the Counter Culture, and the Chaplain," *Lutheran Quarterly*, XXI (1969), 251–62, where the point is made with reference to a talk by Paul Goodman.
3. Charles A. Curran, *Counseling and Psychotherapy* (New York: Sheed and Ward, 1968), p. 74.
4. Clifford Geertz, "Religion as a Cultural System," *Reader in Comparative Religion*, ed. William A. Lessa and Evon Z. Vogt (2nd ed. New York: Harper & Row, 1965), p. 206.
5. Paul Tillich, *The Courage to Be* (New Haven: Yale University Press, 1952), p. 190.
6. Gordon D. Kaufman, "On the Meaning of 'God': Transcendence without Mythology," *Harvard Theological Review*, LIX (1966), 105–32. This idea appears prominently in the writing of Karl Jaspers.
7. Richard R. Niebuhr, *Schleiermacher on Christ and Religion* (New York: Charles Scribner's Sons, 1964), p. 185.
8. Ernst Bloch, *Das Prinzip Hoffnung* (Frankfurt am Main: Suhrkamp Verlag, 1959), p. 1520.
9. Cit. William Hamilton, *The New Essence of Christianity* (New York: Association Press, 1966), p. 66.
10. Geertz, "Religion as a Cultural System," p. 209.
11. Paul van Buren, *The Secular Meaning of the Gospel* (New York: Macmillan, 1963), p. 85.
12. Paul van Buren, *Theological Explorations* (New York: Macmillan, 1968), p. 169.

13. Langdon Gilkey, *Naming the Whirlwind: the Renewal of God Language* (Indianapolis: Bobbs-Merrill Co., 1969), p. 306.

14. I. M. Crombie, "Arising from the University Discussion," *New Essays in Philosophical Theology*, eds. A. G. N. Flew and Alastair MacIntyre (London: SCM Press, 1955), pp. 109–30.

15. Paul Tillich, *Systematic Theology* (London: Bisbet & Co., 1953), 1, 263.

16. Edward Schillebeeckx, *God the Future of Man* (New York: Sheed and Ward, 1968), p. 172.

17. Wolfhart Pannenberg, *Theology and the Kingdom of God* (Philadelphia: Westminster Press, 1969), p. 56.

18. Jürgen Moltmann, *Theology of Hope*, trans. James W. Leitch (New York: Harper & Row, 1965), p. 16.

19. Jürgen Moltmann, "Hoping and Planning," *Cross-Currents*, XVIII (1968), 309.

20. Schillebeeckx, *God the Future of Man*, p. 189.

21. Barfield, *Saving the Appearances*, p. 144.

22. *Ibid.*, p. 163 (italics his).

23. William T. Lynch, *Images of Hopes* (Baltimore: Helicon, 1965), p. 244.

24. Ray L. Hart, *The Unfinished Man and the Imagination* (New York: Herder and Herder, 1968), pp. 328–29.

25. Victor W. Turner, *The Ritual Process: Structure and Anti-Structure* (Chicago: Aldine Publishing Company, 1969), pp. 106–07, contrasts liminality with a status system after the fashion of Levi-Strauss. Transition/state, totality/partiality, homogeneity/heterogeneity, communitas/structure, equality/inequality, anonymity/systems of nomenclature, absence of property/property, absence of status/status, etc. There are twenty-six pairs in all. Needless to say, I cannot in this study spend the time to explore the many ramifications of Turner's thesis for ministry.

26. *Ibid.*, p. 128.

27. Leach, "Magical Hair."

28. Theodore Roszak, *The Making of a Counter Culture* (Garden City: Doubleday and Company, 1969), p. 267.

29. Harvey Cox, *The Feast of Fools* (Cambridge: Harvard University Press, 1969), p. 138.

30. *Ibid.*, p. 46.

31. Barfield, *Saving the Appearances*, p. 109.

32. Sam Keen, *To A Dancing God* (New York: Harper & Row, 1970), pp. 143–44.

## Chapter 12

1. Harvey Cox, *The Secular City* (New York: Macmillan, 1965), pp. 20–21.

2. Mircea Eliade, *The Sacred and the Profane*, trans. Willard R. Trask (New York: Harper and Brothers, 1961).

3. Stephen Rose, *The Grass Roots Church* (Nashville: Abingdon Press, 1966), p. 7.

4. *Ibid.*, p. 99.

5. *Ibid.*, p. 115. Those who have no fear of inclement weather do not even need the tent.

6. Cox, *Secular City*, p. 85.

7. Hans Küng, *The Church*, pp. 266–69.

8. Andrew M. Greeley, *Religion in the Year 2000* (New York: Sheed and Ward, 1969), pp. 153–54. In this chapter "church" refers to Greeley's category and "Church" to the theological category of the Body of Christ.

9. John M. Petersen, "House-Churches in Rome," *Vigiliae Christianiae*, XXIII (1969), 264–72.

10. J. G. Davies, *The Secular Use of Church Buildings* (New York: Seabury Press, 1968).

11. John H. Westerhoff, *Values for Tomorrow's Children* (Philadelphia: Pilgrim Press, 1970). Urban T. Holmes, "Quo Vadis, Christian Ed?", *The Living Church*, Vol. 162, No. 8 (February 21, 1971), pp. 12–13, discusses this issue in detail.

12. Cox, *Secular City*, pp. 40–46.

13. Peter Winterble, "Parishioners Ran St. Augustine's," newspaper of the Diocese of Washington (D.C.), May 1970, p. 10.

14. Scott Donaldson, *The Suburban Myth* (New York: Columbia University Press, 1969), pp. 111–16, 139–42.

15. Herbert Vorgrimler et al., *Commentary on the Documents of Vatican II* (New York: Herder and Herder, 1969), III, 170–71. Joseph Ratzinger in the commentary on chapter 2 of the "Dogmatic Decree Divine Revelation" notes how the Roman Catholic Church has been influenced by Barth, Ebling, Buber, etc., since Vatican I, and how revelation is now centered on the person of God. God makes known *not* the *aeterna voluntatis suae decreta* [the eternal decrees of his will] but the *sacramentum voluntatis suae* [the mystery *or* the hidden purpose of his will]. Revelation is seen as a dialogue, which is precisely the point I make here.

16. Representatives of the Anglican-Roman Catholic consultation in this country suggested in the spring of 1970 the possibility of intercommunion in "five to ten years." Basil Butler has predicted a united Anglican and Roman Catholic Church under the *primacy* (which is different than the *supremacy*) of the pope. *Living Church*, CLX, 15 (April 12, 1970), 9. A Roman Catholic bishop, Charles Helmsing, reported to the National Conference of Roman Catholic Bishops that negotiations with Lutherans and Anglicans had reached an "advanced stage." *Living Church*, CLX, 21 (May 24, 1970), 7.

17. The criticisms of J. V. Langmead Casserley are a case in point. He complains about COCU on the grounds that (1) it is unrepresentative (not a fair sampling of Christianity); (2) it is national in character (a repetition of a "pious fraud," under which we would have to include the Church of England); (3) it is bureaucratic in character; and (4) it suffers from triumphalism. *American Church News*, XXXVI, 2 (Lent 1970), 1, 4. Strange as it may seem, COCU is also attacked on the basis that it preserves Apostolic Succession at the expense of apostolicity. *American Church News*, XXXVI, 5 (Summer 1970), 10. Stephen Rose complains that as it now appears "a giant merger of what we now have will be a Kafkaesque nightmare." "Process and Power," *Christian Century*, LXXXVII, 8 (February 25, 1970), 236. Carl Howie, a disillusioned COCU executive, has said that the whole plan is bogged down in "organizational matters." *Living Church*, CLXI, 1 (July 5, 1970), 8. This sampling gives a clear indication of the small role played in the discussions by agreement or disagreement over propositional theology.

18. Rodney Stark and Charles Y. Glock, "The 'New Denominationalism,'" *Review of Religious Research*, VIII (1965), 8–15.

19. Rose, *Grass Roots*, p. 55.

20. Samuel Mueller, "The New Triple Melting Pot," an article to appear in the *Review of Religious Research* in 1971, revises Will Herberg's thesis of the three "melting pots" of Catholicism, Protestantism, and Judaism, to white Christians, Jews and humanists, and blacks. I find the most helpful point he makes is that since Vatican II it has become increasingly difficult to distinguish between some classical Protestants and Roman Catholics, as I reflect here; as well as the fact that liberal Protestants really find themselves allied with the Jewish and humanist elements in our culture. His insight concerning the distinction of the blacks is well made. My only criticism would be that he does not delineate the hard-core, fundamentalist group, which I suspect can be distinguished on the basis of endogamous marriage, distinct voting patterns, residential proximity, etc.

## Chapter 13

1. Roszak, *The Making of a Counter Culture*, p. 243.

2. Greeley, *The Church in the Year 2000*, pp. 140–42.

3. John C. Harris, "The Clergy and Their Work: Some Observations and Recommendations," *Anglican Theological Review*, LI (1969), 164.

4. Hiltner and Colston, *The Context of Pastoral Counseling*.

5. Lewis B. Whittemore, *Church and Secular Education* (New York: Seabury Press, 1960).

6. George H. Crowell, *Society Against Itself* (Philadelphia: Westminster Press, 1968).

7. Roland Allen, *Missionary Methods: St. Paul's or Ours?* (American ed. Grand Rapids: Wm. B. Eerdmans Co., 1962), pp. 81–107.

8. *Ibid.*, pp. 100–03.

9. Ned H. Cassem, "Two Healing Acts—or One?" in *Hyphenated Priests*, p. 80.

10. Charles M. Whelan, "A Brief for a Priest Lawyer" in *Hyphenated Priests*, pp. 57–59.

11. Murray and Westhues, *review of Profession: Minister*, pp. 221–24.

12. Harris, "Clergy and Their Work," p. 164.

13. Crowell, *Society Against Itself*, p. 58.

14. Harris, "Clergy and Their Work," pp. 173–74.

15. *Ibid.*, 163–64.

16. Elizabeth Gössman, in "Women As Priests?" *Apostolic Succession*, ed. Hans Küng, pp. 115–25, has written in a rather ambiguous manner, suggesting that there is no theological reason for not ordaining women, but that it is perhaps presumptuous for women to desire ordination. Mary Daly, *The Church and the Second Sex* (New York: Harper and Row, 1968), pp. 154–66, is hardly so coy. This Roman Catholic lay theologian lays it on the line and quotes Küng as saying that there are only cultural reasons for not ordaining women.

17. Raymond Tiemeyer, *The Ordination of Women* (Augsburg Publishing House, 1970), a condensation of a report authorized by the church body presidents and developed through the Lutheran Council of the U.S.A., is about the best brief survey of the questions in the issue that I know.

## Chapter 14

1. Feilding, "Education for Ministry," pp. 49, 166–72.

2. The report of the so-called "Pusey Committee" of the Episcopal Church on theological education called almost exclusively for a better educated clergy. Undoubtedly the strongly academic make-up of this committee (e.g. Pusey, Charles Taylor, Gordon Allport, and Wilbur Katz) had an influence.

3. E.g. Pusey and Taylor, *Ministry for Tomorrow*, p. 125.

4. *Ibid.*, pp. 73ff.

5. Walter D. Wagoner, *The Seminary: Protestant and Catholic* (New York: Sheed and Ward, 1966), pp. 53–54. Wagoner is a Protestant.

6. John B. Coburn, "The New Mood in Spirituality," *Spirituality for Today*, ed. Eric James (London: SCM, 1968), p. 28.

7. John Townroe, "Christian Spirituality and the Future," *ibid.*, pp. 53–54. Cf. Thomas M. Gannon and George W. Traub, *The Desert and the City* (London: Macmillan, 1969), p. 252, who in describing a contemporary spirituality refuse to be too specific, but suggests: "We are today evolving a spirituality which emphasizes the importance of the world in man's relation to God and takes as its starting point life lived in the world we know; this is spirituality which aspires to genuine personal experience and self-fulfillment in one's relation to God; it is also a spirituality that repudiates all absolute, changeless formulas and emphasizes the present historical experience of rapid change at all levels of human life."

8. "Theological Curriculum for the 1970's," *Theological Education*, IV (1968), 671–745.

9. Daniel B. Stevick, *Canon Law; a Handbook* (New York: Seabury Press, 1965), p. 173.

10. Studies in this area include Menges and Dittes, *Psychological Studies of Clergymen: Abstracts of Research*; Menges, "Studies of Clergymen: Abstracts of Research, Supplement I"; Walter J. Coville *et al.*, *Assessment of Candidates for the Religious Life* (Washington: Center for Applied Research in the Apostolate [CARA], 1968); and a rather old one, Rene Biot and Pierre Galimard, *Medical Guide to Vocations*, trans. Robert P. Odenwald (London: Burns and Oates, 1955).

11. MHCEN, p. 14.

12. *Ibid.*, pp. 14–15 (emphasis added).

13. *Ibid.*, p. 17.

14. *Ibid.*, p. 7.

15. *Ibid.*, p. 8.

16. *Theological Education*, IV (1968), 689, 716–18; although on the basis of a confidential source, I understand the AATS also quotes 12 faculty and 50 to 75 students as the absolute minimum.

17. *Episcopalian*, March 1970, p. 52.

18. *Theological Education*, IV (1968), 713; Appendix A provides a chart of such a "cluster."